Praise for *Bring Out the Best*

"MUST READING for parents who want to develop a truly loving relationship with their children."
—Robert A. Anderson, M.D.
President, American Board of Holistic Medicine
Author, *Clinician's Guide to Holistic Medicine*

"This book is elegant ... the illustrations delightful ..."
—Jean Illsley Clarke, award-winning parent educator
Author, *Time-In: When Time-Out Doesn't Work*

"After reading this book, I have developed a new level of respect for my children. In a sense I have fallen in love with them all over again."
—Ann Holabird, Marriage and Family Therapist

"Most parenting books apply to children within a limited age range. This book helps them all."
—Mary Kelso, Ph.D., California Lutheran University

"This book is great. The exercises are effective! I especially liked the sections on creating the family you want, prevention, planning and communication."
—Piero Ferrucci, Psychotherapist
Author, *What Our Children Teach Us*

"Promotes mutual respect and understanding ... The parenting method is clear and accessible, yet far reaching. The skills taught will enhance the quality of all family relationships."
—Cheryl Armon, Ed.D.
Professor of Human Development, Antioch University

"I loved the intimate tone and honesty."
—Dottie Mathews, M.Div.
Minister, Fox Valley Unitarian Universalist Fellowship

"... communicates so effectively the principles of good parenting."
—Karen Peters, MBA
Executive Director, Breastfeeding Task Force of Greater Los Angeles

"A wonderful exploration of emotionally responsible parenting. In simple language and with lots of real-world examples, Ilene Val-Essen helps us learn more about ourselves, which helps us grow closer to our children."
—Carole-Ann Scott, M.A.
Founder, Imagine Academy Public Ch

D0290906

All children yearn to bring out their best—
to grow and fulfill their highest potential—
to develop and express their finest qualities.

Once we acknowledge that truth,
we see our children with new eyes.
We realize that negative behavior
is actually a cry for help:
"Help me find a more effective way
to meet my needs."

Half the job of being a good parent
is to look for and support
the best within each child.
The other half is
finding the best within ourselves.

Bring Out the

B E S T

in Your *Child* and Your *Self*

Creating a Family Based on Mutual Respect

ILENE VAL-ESSEN, Ph.D.

Bring Out the Best in Your Child and Your Self: Creating a Family Based on Mutual Respect by Ilene Val-Essen, Ph.D.

ISBN: 978-0-9675371-1-5
Library of Congress Control Number: 2009913150

Printed and bound in the United States of America

10 9 8 7 6 5 4 3 2 1

Published by Quality Parenting
4909 Saint Louis Court
Culver City, CA 90230-4317
www.qualityparenting.com

Cover art and design by Dotti Albertine, www.dotdesign.net
Cover Photo by Getty Images
Author photo by Ed Schuman
Interior design and typesetting by Jill Ronsley, www.suneditwrite.com

To
Ed Schuman,
the loving and skillful midwife
for "our baby."

Contents

Acknowledgments

On our first date I told Ed Schuman, who is now my husband, that I wanted to write a book. He has helped me realize this dream with every inch of his heart, mind and soul. He has taught me a new appreciation for the meaning of loyalty, talent and commitment.

I want to thank my son, Derek Scott Derman. My love for him motivated me to be the best parent I could be and inspired me to devote my life to helping parents bring out the best. Now Derek and his lovely wife, Brette Genzel Derman, have given me the gift of being Grammy to their two sons: Gavin and Cayden. I also want to thank my stepdaughter, Celine, and my husband's oldest son, Steve, and his partner, John, and his youngest son, Greg, for enriching our lives and deepening my understanding of the ongoing role of parent.

My affection goes to the many dedicated *Quality Parenting* instructors who have inspired me with their talent and devotion to the material. Special thanks to Sue Bryan, the first certified and very talented *Quality Parenting* instructor, Tamara Effron, who has stood by me through thick and thin, and Eveline Lange, who has spread the program widely in Holland. And deep appreciation to the many translators: Victoria Barcelona, who translated the material into Spanish; Hiroko Hongo, the Japanese translator; Nillan Bergman, the Swedish translator; and Anne von Gaster, the Dutch translator.

To the loving and caring parents, who gave their best and shared their very real stories.

Thanks to the early readers, Dani Adams, Marco de Heer, Mary Gill, Katherine Gillespie, Penny Gillette, Gitte Hartjesveld, Dorothy Mathews, Margot Parker, Carole-Ann Scott, Hanneke van Hasselt-Mooy and Cindy Winkenwerder, who helped me see the book through the eyes of parents. And to the professionals, Suzanne Goldstein, Dorothea McArthur, Ph.D., June Payne and Zhixin Su, Ph.D., who contributed their varied and valuable expertise. Special thanks to colleagues in the psychosynthesis community: Judith Broadus, Ph.D., Vincent Dummer, Ph.D., Dorothy Firman, Ph.D., Cherie Martin Franklin, Ph.D., Sharon Mandt, Mary Kelso, Ph.D. and to Douglas Russell, who introduced me to psychosynthesis.

Many thanks to my teachers, particularly Drs. Robert Gerard, Tom Gordon, Thomas Yeomans, Janette Rainwater, Edith Stauffer, Thomas Lickona, Thomas Armstrong and Jean Illsley Clarke, M.A. And to my mentors: Drs. Hugh Redmond, Terri O'Fallon and Roger Dafter.

Thanks to loving and dear friends for their support and trust in this project: Andrea Tarabek, Martha Carpenter, Elke Heitmeyer, Virginia Meyn, Sally Daynes, Cheryl Armon, Maia Zohara, Miriam Martineau, Linda Post, Esther Sobel, Jessica Sutton, Heidi Rorick-Evans, Stephen Wolcott and Steve Venables.

Special thanks to artist, Gary Collins, for his brilliant talent in capturing the illustrated characters so poignantly. Thanks to Ray Harris for his artistic support. And thanks to the parents who shared their subpersonality drawings.

The Author's Journey

I MADE A PROMISE to myself, that first moment when I felt a new life stirring inside my body. Overwhelmed by feelings of awe and love, I promised that I would become the very best parent I could be. I would do everything I could to understand my son, to support him and meet his needs, so that he could become a strong and confident adult.

Then came reality. Derek was a joy and I loved him immensely, but he was a real child: he fussed and whined at times; often he tested my patience. In frustrating moments I would find myself wondering, "Why is it so difficult? Do I have what it takes to be a good mother? How can I learn to be a better parent?"

As it turned out, those questions set in motion a journey that became the greatest adventure of my life. It initiated an intellectual and spiritual search that led me to become a parent educator, a psychotherapist, earn a Ph.D. and create a program for parents in the US, Europe and Asia.

Yet it all began in those first years, with the sense that reality didn't match my dream. I knew that somehow I could be a better mother.

How Can I Be a Better Parent?

The warmth and closeness I felt with my son was precious. But when he became a toddler exploring everything in sight, I realized I didn't have a clue about how to discipline effectively. On the worst days, when I felt weary and frustrated, I'd sometimes "lose it" and yell at little Derek.

Later I felt so ashamed. It was humiliating to remember that promise I'd made to be the best parent I could be. "I won't ever do that again," I would tell myself.

For the next few days, I'd have the patience of a saint. And then I'd lose my cool once again.

What should I do? Certainly, not take a parenting class. "No one is going to tell me how to raise my child." The truth is, I felt far too vulnerable about my parenting to expose myself in front of others. How sad it is that so many parents feel that way. Yet, the opposite is true: taking a parenting class is an act of courage and love—a gift for the whole family.

In the end I found a perfect way to save face: I would train to become a parenting instructor. "Just for the extra income, of course." The skills I learned soon made a real difference in my family. And from the very first class I taught, I learned as much from the parents as they learned from me.

An Unsolved Mystery

I'll never forget the father whose teenage son was acting out and even had a brush with the law. This dad tried hard, but he just didn't *get* the skills; he lagged far behind the rest, who were becoming skilled and confident.

Yet over the weeks, something else was happening. Instead of describing his son as "stubborn and defiant," he began to talk about him as a boy in pain, needing guidance, consistency and support. Instead of blaming his son, he became more involved, listening patiently and encouraging him to grow beyond this difficult time. Gradually his son became more cooperative and responsible. Their relationship improved dramatically.

But why? As a young, new teacher, I had no framework or words to describe what had happened. I knew we had witnessed something profound—even more powerful than the valuable skills we were learning. I felt humbled, yet excited. Still I had no idea how to replicate it.

I promised myself I'd do whatever was needed to understand exactly how that dad had changed, and why it had such a powerful effect on his son. I knew there was something valuable to learn for my own family and for the parents I taught.

Why Do Parents "Lose It"?

Teaching was deeply satisfying; we supported and cared for each other. We laughed at our own mistakes and celebrated stories of success with spontaneous applause. Sometimes we were so touched that our eyes would begin to tear.

Yet, even these caring and capable parents would "lose it" at times. Children or teens would be difficult or rebellious, or parents would feel tired and frustrated. Sooner or later, under stress, Mom or Dad would go out of control and "blow up," just as I had done. Others would just give up in those moments, and let the children roll over them.

What was happening? Why were these competent, caring parents resorting to behaviors they'd grown beyond weeks before? Just when it mattered most, they seemed to ignore all the skills they'd learned. And sooner or later, it happened to us all!

Why do *all* parents lose it at times?

Searching for Clues

So now I had *two* unsolved mysteries:

- What *is* the change that's even more powerful than skills?
- How can we *hold onto* our skills, even when the pressure is on?

I searched every source I could find, but never found answers that were truly satisfying. And so I kept looking.

Parent education had become my passion; I wanted to learn everything I could to become more effective in helping families. I studied to become a psychotherapist. Soon, serendipity provided a remarkable gift: I discovered *psychosynthesis*. This growth-oriented approach to psychology and education helps people develop their strengths; it embraces Western science, while including insights from Eastern cultures.

To appreciate the value of this discovery, I'll put it in context. Our understanding of human nature has evolved significantly in recent decades; we've seen at least four major perspectives in psychology. Under Freud's influence "good" parents were *authoritarian:* "Do as I say, it's for your own good." Then came *behaviorism*, which suggested that we should "train" children through reward and punishment. The third development in perspective came with *humanism*: "When we treat children with respect, they learn to respect themselves and others."

And we continue to learn. At the forefront today is another expansion in our understanding—an approach called *transpersonal* psychology. It builds on the contributions of the past, especially humanism, but also expands our awareness to help us express the best of human qualities. Psychosynthesis is part of that fourth advance.

Recognizing the power of these ideas, I enrolled in a Ph.D. program to further my studies. What I found was a valuable new way of understanding human nature. At long last, I found meaningful answers to my questions.

A New Understanding

The "mystery" of why some parents were so effective, even without skills, was becoming clear. These parents had changed their *attitudes:* the way they viewed their children—how they interpreted their behavior. They realized that when children or teens act out, they're having a hard time; they don't like their behavior any more than we do. These parents recognized that difficult behavior is a child's cry for help: "Help me to grow beyond this." That new perspective allowed them to be patient and supportive, yet firm. And their children responded!

Those parents who were mastering skills were gaining the same awareness: effective listening and communication inevitably altered their attitudes.

As I helped families learn from those insights, other discoveries and realizations rippled out like waves in a pond. In time we had an answer to the second mystery: why all parents lose it at times. Under stress, emotion literally takes over. At those moments, the primitive, "survival" part of our brains overpowers our ability to reason; our bodies prepare to fight or run.

What psychosynthesis revealed is that we can learn to deal with stress more effectively, and gain the ability to think before we act. We can learn to slow down before it's too late; we can *choose* how we react. Even when the pressure is on, we can learn to remain calm and centered more consistently.

When families I worked with responded to these ideas, remarkable and rewarding changes occurred.

Practical Help for Parents

Excited by what I was learning, I wanted to organize these insights and principles and put them into practical form, so that they could be shared more widely. I created a program called *Quality Parenting*. Everything in it was put to the test in my own expanded family (by now, I was also a step mom). Then the parents and instructors in our classes tested it in their families.

In diverse communities and cultural settings, parents in our program have learned to create an environment that brings out the best—a family based on mutual respect. That's what you'll learn in this book.

Throughout these years I've seen so many beautiful changes—real transformations—in families that make a commitment to growth. I invite you to share the insights, knowledge and support these pages can offer, as you follow your own path of learning and growth.

Surely no journey in life can be more rewarding, or more worthwhile.

Ilene Val-Essen, Ph.D.

CHAPTER 1

To Bring Out the Best

Treat a person where they are and they will remain at that level.
Treat a person where you expect them to be and they will rise
to that level.

—Johann Wolfgang von Goethe

PARENTS KNOW THEIR CHILDREN and teens are good at heart.
Despite all the problems, we've felt their goodness and know it's real;
they can be incredibly loving, kind, cooperative and responsible. Why
do those endearing qualities seem to evaporate at times? Why do we find
ourselves nagging, threatening and bickering—even "losing it" and blowing up? How can we make the limited time we have with our children
more consistently nurturing for everyone?

In other words:

How can we create a family
that brings out the best in everyone?

That's what this book is about. Whether you're married, single,
divorced or a stepparent, the chapters that follow will help you to solve
many problems. You'll learn how to create a family based on mutual
respect—one that nurtures and encourages the best—a family that

supports children and teens to develop their highest potential and grow
into capable, caring adults.

A Unique Insight

What distinguishes this approach from others—and opens a new
world of possibilities—is that it allows you to see your children and teens
with new eyes, to look beneath the surface and discover a deeper truth:
*Within each child there is an innate drive—indeed, a yearning—to grow
and mature, to become capable and responsible, to fulfill his or her highest
potential.*

Despite all the resistance, testing and negative behavior, a core part of
every child or teen wants to grow and bring out the best. Yet children can't
do it alone; they need and want our help. They want us to be steadfast—
to expect and insist on the best from them. We're on the same team.

That insight gives us a whole new way of seeing our children and
teens—and a better understanding of how to work with them.

When our patience and wisdom are tested, that knowledge can give
us the strength and courage to remain calm and firm, to set limits and
hold boundaries—yet consistently model mutual respect.

A Different Kind of Book

Rather than "managing" children (as if they were our employees) or
"modifying behavior" (as if training animals) this book is about encouraging growth. It also guides and supports us to grow as parents, along
with our children. It sheds light on the reasons we lose it at times and go
out of control, and provides step-by-step guidance to help us be at our
best more often.

Rather than offering ready-made advice for situations such as bedtime or homework, this book will provide you with sound *principles* that
you can apply in your own personal style: building healthy relationships,
creating an atmosphere of mutual respect, encouraging the best within
your children and yourself. You'll learn to use those principles to resolve
conflict, to solve problems and often to prevent them before they occur.
You'll acquire a wealth of useful skills, all of them valuable in meeting the
challenge of raising a family in the twenty-first century.

What Will I Learn?

So—how can this book help you as a parent? Let me count the ways:

1. *You'll learn to create an environment that brings out the best in your children and teens.* That's the foundation of it all. Every child has rich and unique potential. Our job as parents is to provide an environment that nurtures the best within each child and encourages it to flourish. You'll learn how to create that environment in practical, down-to-earth ways.

2. *You'll learn how to be the parent you want to be.* If you "blow up" at times, get frustrated, feel stressed and lose it, yelling or "being mean"—or if you just give up and give in—welcome to the crowd. Most parents have that experience more often than you'd guess, and later feel ashamed or guilty. You can learn to be calm and at your best much more often—and that will create a fundamental change, benefiting you and the whole family.

3. *You'll learn how to convert resistance into cooperation.* Resistance is inevitable, yet it often evaporates when parents are skillful. You'll learn to be prepared for resistance, to not take it personally and to respond in ways that encourage cooperation.

4. *You'll become more effective in setting limits.* Too many parents give up and become nonassertive; children and teens need appropriate boundaries in order to grow, to feel safe and cared for. You'll learn when it's wise to say no (and when it isn't) and gain the courage and skill to set limits—as you remain calm and firm and model mutual respect.

5. *You'll understand your child's negative behavior and develop better ways to handle it.* Seeing beneath the surface, gaining a new understanding of what's going on with your child or teen, provides new and surprising insight. You'll have a whole different view of your children—and how to work with them effectively.

6. *You'll learn to resolve and prevent problems.* "Impossible" problems can be resolved when you learn sound principles and a practical, step-by-step process. You'll gain skills to help you communicate your needs and listen to your children's needs in ways that encourage cooperation. You'll learn how the skill of planning can prevent many problems before they happen.

7. *You'll learn how to create the family you'd like to have.* Most of us overlook the possibility that we can sit down, think about the kind of family we'd really like to have—and take practical steps to achieve that goal. You'll learn how to create a practical vision of the family you'd like, and then use your skills, day by day, to move ever closer toward that ideal.

8. *You'll learn skills that can improve all relationships.* As you become more adept in using conflict resolution and communication skills, you'll find yourself using them in all your relationships.

9. *You'll have an opportunity to grow as a person.* To be the parents we'd like to be—to help our children grow—requires us to grow too. Any close relationship that is truly alive requires everyone involved to stretch and change. This program supports you to take an honest look at how you respond to frustration and stress—and learn more effective ways to handle it. The more capable you become, the more confidence and self-esteem you gain. You'll learn how to take better care of your needs as well as your children's. You'll find yourself growing in a variety of ways.

10. *You'll discover the best within yourself.* And that makes all the difference in a family.

The principles in this book are based on *Quality Parenting*, a program that is unique because it enables children and parents to grow and bring out the best. Thousands of parents have been influenced by the *Quality Parenting* programs in the U.S. and abroad; included among these are single parents, stepparents and divorced parents.

Useful Concepts for Parenting

As you move through the chapters ahead, you'll acquire many skills. You'll become more aware of the immense power of attitudes and how they can help you to be more effective. And you'll also gain some valuable concepts for parenting. The first is a way of viewing human nature; it can help you understand your children's behavior—and your own.

Three Levels of Self

> My daughter is an angel at times: so sweet, good-natured and helpful. But other times—look out! She can be demanding, rude, self-centered, unwilling to listen ... Why does she get like that?

One moment our children and teens can be cooperative, mature and responsible—and the next ... well, we all know what that's like. Why does a good-hearted child or teen become so difficult? For that matter, why do we, as parents, exhibit the patience of a saint sometimes—and other times totally lose it? If we can gain some insight into what's driving difficult behavior, we'll be in a better position to influence it.

Three levels of self is a way of viewing behavior that parents in our classes find especially valuable. It is adapted from psychosynthesis, a school of psychology developed by the Italian psychiatrist, Dr. Roberto Assagioli. This concept recognizes that as we move through the day, encountering a variety of situations, distinct aspects of our personalities become active. Depending on what's happening, different "parts" of us come out:

- lower self
- centered self
- higher self

The *lower self* is on stage when a child or teen is whining, acting out or being destructive—or when a parent blows up or gives up and caves in. When a child or adult is calm and composed, the *centered self* is in charge; the thoughtful, reasoning part of the brain is active. There is also a *higher self,* the part of your child that is creative, loving and wise—and the part of you that yearns to become the best parent you can be. The higher self is associated with qualities we admire, such as courage and compassion.

We can use this way of looking at behavior in very practical ways, as we'll see in a moment. But let's continue with the concept: there are three levels, and we move back and forth among them, sometimes several times a day. When we're calm and composed, the centered self is in control; we feel relaxed and can think clearly. But when a child or adult feels stressed or overwhelmed, alarm bells go off in the nervous system. The body tenses as if survival were at stake. Emotions take over; we can slip into a crisis mode controlled by instinct. Reason disappears; we act impulsively and behavior can be ineffective or destructive. The lower self is on stage.

The lower self is often an *automatic response to stress*. Physiologically, when we feel threatened, our more primitive "emotional brain" takes charge as if our survival were at stake, sending signals to attack or run. Our impetuous, unthinking behavior is a response to what feels like a "crisis." If we look at our children and ourselves in that light, it transforms our way of seeing.

Normally, we might respond to a child who is acting out by thinking, "She's being defiant and selfish," or "He needs to be taught a lesson in no uncertain terms." Then we might say something critical or even punish the child. But our response will be quite different if we recognize that the child is stressed and unhappy. To be sure, we will make it clear that the behavior is inappropriate. But seeing this perspective, we can take a very different approach, and do so much more than criticize or punish. We can work with the child, first helping him to become calm (shift to the centered self), then assisting him to learn more effective ways of coping with stress and meeting his needs.

In the same way, we can view ourselves with new insight. When we feel upset and "lose our cool," we can understand it as an automatic, unthinking response to stress; attempting to cope, we've slipped to the lower self. Instead of feeling guilty or ashamed and resolving "never to do that again" (which seldom lasts for long), we can learn how to step back and cool off—and move to a calmer, more level-headed state of mind: the centered self.

A primary goal of this program is to give you the awareness and ability to shift, when appropriate, from lower self to centered self. That removes a central obstacle to effective parenting; it allows you to spend an increasing amount of your time being more centered, open and effective—so you can help your children do the same. (Working with the higher self in parent and child is the subject of the book that follows this one. For most situations, the centered self is what we need.)

Three Levels of Self
We all shift back and forth

The Lower Self

Children whine or ignore us completely, criticize or become sarcastic. They hit, curse, yell or act as if they cannot see or hear.

Parents yell, threaten, criticize, over supervise or otherwise express aggressive attitudes. Or they withdraw, give up and give in, and become passive, letting the children take charge.

Parents describe children's behavior as: out of control, irritating, demanding, hurtful, unpleasant, frustrating, frightening, overwhelming.

Children experience us as angry, mean, unkind or unfair.

The Centered Self

Children are reasonable, responsible, cooperative, independent, considerate and loving. They do their homework without being told, get ready for school on time, do their chores, talk kindly to their siblings, enjoy entertaining themselves, share openly with us and feel good about themselves.

Parents acting from the centered self are patient, express their needs clearly, listen with interest, care and concern. They are relaxed, clear-minded, flexible, realistic and capable.

Parents describe children's behavior as: thoughtful, open, content, even, confident, competent and grounded.

Children experience us as calm, patient, caring, reasonable, loving.

The Higher Self

Children are generous, sensitive, humorous, giving, courageous, persistent, loyal, ethical, conscientious and highly creative.

Parents are compassionate and have a deep sense of trust; they act wisely and love without conditions. They're in touch with their finest qualities.

Parents describe children's behavior with humility: "These qualities seem to come from deep within the child; we are enriched by their gifts."

Children experience us as wise, compassionate, joyful, "special."

Becoming Centered

So it's been a rough day. Your child or teen has tested you to the limit —stretched your thinning patience beyond infinity. You're definitely about to lose it, big time. You're either going to blow up or give up, lie down and become a doormat. Now what? Is there anything you can do to head off the impending eruption? Never fear; the cavalry rides to the rescue.

When behavior is at its worst—when your child's lower self is running the show (and your own is threatening to burst on stage), there is a place to turn for help: the *Three-Step Process*. It gives you a way to let go of stress, to step back and become calm. And then it can help you to become centered. Becoming centered is the crucial skill for parenting; when we're "off center"—stressed, upset, overwhelmed or angry—we're certainly not at our best, and likely to bring out unfortunate responses in those around us. We can't help a child or teen become calm and centered until we're there ourselves.

When you don't like the way things are going, these three steps offer a practical, systematic way to make a change. Each one will be explored at length in later chapters.

With practice, this process can help you to remain calm and centered more often, so you can avoid the storms or sail through them more smoothly. Eventually, making this shift becomes second nature; something you do informally and spontaneously. It can help you to be more effective, patient and skillful—to become the parent you want to be.

The Three-Step Process is the framework; everything you'll learn in this book fits within these three steps. Whatever problem you're facing, these steps give you a place to turn, a process to rely on. Thousands of parents have shown us how useful they can be.

Three Steps to Becoming Centered

Step One: *Recognize the Lower Self*

The first step will give you a useful, new way of understanding why things go wrong; it will give you insight into the thoughts and feelings that trigger your child's negative behavior, as well as your own. It's fully explained in Chapter Three.

Step Two: *Cross the Bridge to the Centered Self*

The second step consists of two potent exercises that will help you to become calm when the going gets rough—to make the crucial shift from lower self to centered self—and help your children do the same. You'll find a full explanation in Chapter Four.

Step Three: *Express the Centered Self*

In Step 3 you'll learn to use the skills and adopt the attitudes that can help you create a family based on mutual respect—an environment that brings out the best (Chapters Five through Fourteen).

The Five Relationship Issues

Parents deserve a road map. Too often we feel a bit lost. Dealing with conflict can be bewildering and confusing. "What went wrong? Is there a better way to handle it?" This third and final concept for parenting allows us to clear away the confusion.

Imagine that you're at the supermarket, approaching the dreaded cereal shelf:

> *"I told you before, that kind has too much sugar." "But I want that kind," my daughter insisted. "I know, but it's not good for you." Soon I was entangled in a verbal tug-of-war, wondering what the other shoppers thought of me and how I could possibly get out of this.*

Or ...

> *My teenager was late coming home—again—and within*
> *minutes, we were spinning in a whirlpool of excuses, nagging,*
> *blaming and defending.*

Is there a way out?

All the problems we face with our children and teens can be grouped into five core themes. These are the underlying issues in every relationship. If we can identify which theme we're dealing with, we can gain some clarity—and find a way toward resolution. The five relationship issues and the questions they address are outlined on the next page.

The Five Relationship Issues

AUTHORITY: *Who knows what's best?*
Who is the expert?
Whose information is accurate?
Who is most informed?

NEEDS: *Whose needs will be met?*
Do I meet my child's needs or my own?
(This theme may involve how we spend our time,
money and energy.)

PERCEPTION: *Whose point of view is right?*
Whose view of reality do we accept?
Whose thoughts and feelings do we believe and trust?

CONTROL: *Who should decide?*
Who's in charge?
Who makes the final decision?

EXPECTATIONS: *How do we deal with expectations?*
How do we respond when our expectations are met—
and when they aren't?
How do we behave when our children place expectations on us?

To see how these issues work, consider the examples at the beginning of this section. On the surface, these conflicts are about cereal and
curfew. But just under the surface, both are about the fundamental issue
of Control. Conflicts about control address the question *Who should
decide?* That's the *real* core of the problem. And once you know the
underlying issue, you're more able to find an effective way to approach it.
It's like having a road map: if you can see where you are—and where you
want to go—you can find the best road to take.

In Chapter Seven, you'll find a Help Chart illustrated with humorous characters; there you can discover which relationship issue

you're dealing with—and then find an effective way to approach that issue. What makes all the difference is the mindset or thinking you bring to the problem. For example, if that conflict is about the issue of Needs, the chart will suggest an approach that is likely to encourage cooperation and bring out the best—a mindset that models respect for the child's needs and for yours. You'll find no set solutions; your own style and judgment are best. For each issue, the chart will show you the kind of thinking that expresses mutual respect. In other words, it helps you avoid the attitudes of the lower self (which can creep in when we don't realize it) and adopt the more effective mindset of the centered self. Over time, if you model mutual respect consistently, you'll discover something wonderful: your children and teens will begin to do the same.

The next chapter reveals the importance of parents' attitudes and expectations, and the profound effect they have on our families. The pages ahead offer a journey of discovery and personal growth, for your children and for you. Beginning something new requires courage and faith; hold onto them both. Nothing is more rewarding than learning to bring out the best—in your children and yourself.

CHAPTER 2

A New Way of Seeing

In my life I have found that if you expect the best of someone,
they will tend to prove you right.

—Nelson Mandela

LET'S GO RIGHT TO the bottom line: *What are your goals as a parent?* Take a moment to think about what you really want.

Ask a group of parents that question, as I often have, and you'll hear phrases like the following:

I want to raise children who are ...
- good human beings
- able to fulfill their highest potential
- responsible
- independent
- successful and happy
- compassionate and kind

I want a family that is caring and supportive.

Most of us share similar goals. How do we reach them? Everything we know about parenting can be boiled down to one fundamental challenge:

How can I *create an environment*, which brings out the best in my children and teens?

A parent's role is like that of a person who plants a garden. Gardeners don't *make* the seeds grow; they provide soil, sun and water—an environment that supports the seeds to realize their full potential. Our job as parents is to create the best possible environment—one that encourages our children to flourish.

What Environment Brings Out the Best?

What environment do children need? What nurtures and encourages them to develop their best qualities and potential? The clearest way to discover the answer is to look at what happens in real families. Consider these two stories, told by a mother in one of our parenting classes:

> *Our five-year-old, Tammy, had been looking forward to seeing her favorite video all afternoon. But her friend next door brought out her new doll and they got caught up in playing until dinner. Tammy then insisted, "Since I didn't see my video this afternoon, I'm going to see it after dinner." But she knew the family rule quite well: no videos in the evening.*
>
> *I made a point of being gentle as I reminded her of the rule, but she pleaded and whined for a long time; I didn't give in—and finally she just snapped. She started calling me stupid—and then kicking me. I was frazzled myself after an exhausting day and I had two other kids to feed and get ready for bed. "She's really being selfish," I said to myself. "She knows the rule; she just wants to defy me." "Hey, who do you think you are?" I yelled, grabbing hold of her arms. "Ouch!" "Stop acting like a brat every time you don't get your own way!" The whole time I kept thinking, "What have I done; I've created a monster." Out loud I said, "Get into your room and stay there! No TV and no bedtime story for you tonight!"*
>
> *I felt ashamed of my reaction, but I was worn out and frustrated. For a long time, Tammy kept yelling the meanest things she could think of from her room. It took some time before*

our relationship returned to normal. I think we all came away feeling worse about ourselves.

This well-meaning parent responded to a difficult situation in a way that allowed the worst in everyone to prevail. No one grew from the incident. Yet, a few months later, when a similar situation arose, the result was surprisingly different:

Tammy had been asking for ice cream all week. She knows the rule by heart: ice cream for dessert on Fridays only. We made that agreement months ago when her doctor told us she was hypoglycemic and needed to limit her sugar intake. Tammy accepted my explanations pretty well until Thursday night, when she came in tired and tense and once again asked for ice cream. "Do you remember when you're going to be able to have ice cream?" I asked. "Yes, on Friday." "Do you know what day it is today?" "It's almost Friday." "That's right," I said. "You want ice cream today, but you'll have to wait until it's actually Friday—and that will be tomorrow."

Tammy went ballistic; that's the only way to describe what happened next. She screamed, jumped up and down and kicked the chair. She pulled a book off the shelf and threw it. Suddenly I thought, "This couldn't be just about ice cream; she's really frazzled." Part of me was observing the scene, looking beyond her immediate behavior; that helped me to stay calm. I folded her in my arms and carried her into her room. Once again, she shouted for a while.

When she quieted down, I said, "Tammy, you know that destroying things isn't okay. And it's not like you. Do you know what's going on? Maybe I can help." Her anger flared up again and I thought about leaving her room. But I sensed that it could be useful to talk; I decided to be patient and wait. "Would you like me to read to you for a while before we talk?" "No, this book is stupid." She started grinding her heels into it. Calmly, I said, "No, not library books. Not any book for that matter," and took the book away. All of a sudden, I could feel her change.

Something sort of relaxed or collapsed in her; she climbed into my arms and I was holding my six-year-old like a baby. She was just sobbing ... weeping. Afterwards, it was almost funny: she became so loving! She stroked my arm and then gave me a foot massage!

Quietly, I said, "You know everyone gets angry at times; that's just natural. But it's not okay to hit or call names or hurt anyone. "She buried her head—and when I persisted, she murmured, "I know, but I was really mad; you wouldn't give me what I wanted! I don't like being different than other kids." Finally, I understood and acknowledged her pain, "It's hard to have restrictions; especially when other kids don't have them." She nodded and continued to rub my foot. "Tomorrow," I said, "during our special time, we can talk more. How about a hug for now? Then I'll fix dinner."

What made the difference? In the first incident, Mom acted as she did based on certain *beliefs* about her child. In the heat of the moment, these negative thoughts ran through her mind:

I've told her this a million times. She knows the rule. Why doesn't she behave? She's just being selfish and trying to defy me.

As her stress increased, Mom reverted to some discouraging beliefs:

My daughter is:
- *stubborn*
- *spoiled*
- *becoming a brat*

In the second incident, when a similar blow-up occurred, the same mother had a different understanding—a different picture of her child. A very different set of thoughts ran through her mind:

This child is exhausted or terribly unhappy; she doesn't like this behavior any more than I do. This is probably about something more than ice cream. How can I help my daughter find a better way to meet her needs?

Mom now held a very different set of *beliefs* about her child:

My child wants to do the best she can. When she acts in ways that are difficult and trying, she …

- *doesn't feel good about her behavior.*
- *has a legitimate need that isn't being met.*
- *doesn't know how to meet that need in a better way.*

This behavior is a cry for help.

Holding that view created a very different result. Instead of losing control herself, Mom remained calm. That alone made a crucial difference. It wasn't a "fake" calm. It came from looking beneath the immediate behavior, realizing that her daughter had lost control. That it wasn't really about the ice cream; underneath this tantrum was something else. In her immature way, her daughter was saying something like, "I'm overly-tired," or "I don't know a better way to deal with my frustration right now."

Above all, Mom had faith that her daughter didn't enjoy behaving this way; a core part of her wanted to do better—to mature and learn more positive ways to meet her needs.

When her daughter finally calmed down, Mom was truly interested in hearing her feelings. Yet she never bent the rules; she had set clear boundaries and held them consistently. She believed that, at heart, her daughter wanted help in growing toward her best.

Look again at the set of beliefs this mother held (box, above); that *is* the psychological environment children need.

The way we interpret our children's behavior determines how we react. What we believe about our children—what we expect of them—makes all the difference. Our beliefs are a crucial part of the child's psychological world.

What Children Need

Children and teens need parents who do what a great coach does for his athletes:

- cares about them
- recognizes their best potential
- encourages and teaches them how to reach for that potential
- sets clear guidelines and holds to them consistently
- seeks to understand their unique attributes
- has faith in them; expects that they will realize their full potential

This is the environment that nurtures and encourages children: one that provides love and acceptance, recognizes and nurtures their highest potential, holds firm and consistent limits and supports them to bring out their best.

How Can We Meet Those Needs?

Everything in this book is designed to help you create a family environment that brings out the best. The core of that environment—the bedrock foundation—is created when parents recognize this fundamental truth:

Principle One

*Children have an innate drive to express their best selves—
to develop their highest potential.*

Like all living things, children have a natural impetus to grow and mature and develop their best potential fully. The key word is *innate* drive; it's built-in, part of being human. We all have that inner desire—a yearning to find and express our best selves—to become all that we can be.

Do we fall short? Of course! And children certainly do. Parents often misunderstand at first and think this principle is naive or idealistic. On the contrary, we all know that children and teens can be selfish, mean, destructive and even cruel. But those are the behaviors of unhappy children and teens. They don't like themselves when they behave that way, any more than we like ourselves when we behave destructively. It's usually a sign that we're hurting in some way.

When children act out or behave in negative ways, they're sending us the same message: "I'm hurting. I don't know a better way to meet my needs right now."

Principle one gives us a new way to understand our role as parents: when we look beneath the surface, we see that our job is not to impose appropriate behavior; we're actually working *with* that core part of the child that yearns to mature and bring out the best.

> *After a string of rough days at school, six-year-old Jason sat at the kitchen table, absorbed in his drawing. I'd been worried about his behavior, thinking about what I would do. When he finished, I asked, "Would you like to tell me about the picture?" Pointing to different parts of the drawing, Jason said, "It's a picture of 'happy me.' He has a mouth that doesn't curse, hands that don't hit and legs that don't kick!"*
>
> *I thought to myself, "Wow! He really wants to be able to control himself."*

If we fail to acknowledge that drive, we're missing something essential. Our job is to be like Michelangelo: to look at a block of raw marble and visualize within it the beautiful sculpture waiting to be revealed. An analogy can be helpful: Imagine that you're holding an acorn in your hand; can you command or persuade it to grow into a magnificent oak tree? You don't have to, of course. It has an innate impetus to manifest its fullest and best potential. All you need to provide is a nurturing environment.

Human beings have a built-in drive to grow not only physically, but to develop all of their unique potential—mental, social and spiritual. We carry, at the core, a longing to develop the "highest" human qualities: those we respect most in others, such as courage, wisdom and compassion. Children want to be accepted and respected; they want to become cooperative, contributing members of the family.

We all have a deep need to see ourselves as good people. Even people whose behavior is malicious—people like violent criminals—want to see themselves as good people. The renowned criminologist, Dr. Stanton Samenow, has studied the thinking of criminals for decades. "Virtually every criminal thinks of himself as 'a good person,'" he says. "A murderer may help an old lady across the street; one thief passed bad checks and donated the money to the Red Cross." Even people who lead destructive lives have a desire to see themselves as good—to earn their own respect. Despite their utter failure to live it out, the yearning is there.

The fact that we often fall short—that children and adults can easily slip into unproductive behavior—doesn't mean we don't have that innate drive! It isn't easy to become a good human being; we need all the help we can get. And that leads us to ...

Principle Two

Children depend on us to help them.

Like all of us, children want to respect themselves: to feel good about their behavior. But they're not always capable of that; they need and want our help. By definition, children are immature—works in progress— still learning how to handle their feelings, develop strength of will and self-control. In some areas, they haven't yet learned how to handle life's challenges in constructive ways. And so it's important to recognize that children can't do it alone.

That's a central part of our role as parents: to help our children and teens mature—learn to meet their needs—in constructive ways.

> *Six-year-old Davis asked what I was reading. I explained, "I'm reading a book to help me be a good mommy." He blurted out, "Sometimes you're a bad mommy." Surprised and stunned, I asked, "What do you mean?" Davis said, "Sometimes you tell me no and I don't like that. I want you to read a book that teaches you to do what I want!" I acknowledged him, "You would be happier if I'd say yes to you more often." I added, "I love making you happy, but my job also is to protect you, to keep you healthy and help you to learn things. So sometimes I have to say no." Then I gave him a hug. Soon he relaxed and his mood changed. "Okay," he said, and ran off to play.*

Next day Davis didn't want to turn off the TV. I reminded him, "It would be great fun for you if I would never say no. But if I did that, you wouldn't have time to go to preschool and meet all your friends and learn your letters." He seemed lost in thought. Suddenly he ran over and hugged me tight.

Children can't do it alone. They need us to recognize their yearning and help them fulfill it. We need to act with faith, to hold age-appropriate expectations, to remain calm and steadfast as we help them to mature and bring out the best. They need an environment that invites healthy growth; you can create that environment by adopting effective beliefs and expectations.

Creating a Nurturing Environment

We can help our children to bring out their best by acting as a facilitator: providing an environment that invites the child to grow and learn effective behavior. We help by:

- remaining calm
- setting clear, firm boundaries and holding to them consistently
- modeling respect and insisting on receiving it
- recognizing that, at heart, the child or teen wants to grow and learn more positive ways
- holding high expectations consistent with the child's age and maturity level
- looking beyond the immediate behavior to underlying needs

Looking for the underlying need is a key. Often, what children or teens seem to be upset about—the ice cream or the curfew—is least important: that's only the surface. The unmet need may be to learn better ways to deal with frustration, to feel more accepted, to have more independence and so on.

Even when children and teens protest and resist our help (which they often do)—even when their behavior is destructive—children desperately want us to help them do better. They test us and hope that we win.

How do we know that? Watch their behavior, as I have, during thirty-five years as a parent educator and family therapist. Observe a child or teen that is allowed to continue behavior that's inappropriate, unkind or destructive. Notice what happens over time. Does the child or teen seem happy? Not likely! Then watch what happens when parents show their faith in the child's ability to do better, by calmly setting limits and remaining firm. You'll see some resistance and testing, but a short while later you're likely to see the child or teen become serene—and even affectionate! If we have the courage to see it through, children virtually thank us for helping them grow and express their best potential.

Is it true for teens? Anyone who works with adolescents knows that when parents fail to set limits, teens feel unloved. "I feel like they don't care about me." Despite all the rebellion and stormy protests, teens also need and want our help. Here's a typical example, told by a father:

> For several weeks, our son, Damon, had been consumed with preparing for a talent show—at the expense of everything else; nothing was getting done. I reminded him several times, with no visible results. Finally I took action: "You've neglected your schoolwork and broken family agreements. I've reminded you often, but it's clear you're not meeting your responsibilities. I can't let you be in the talent show." I wasn't surprised at Damon's anger and disappointment. But I wasn't prepared for what happened a short time later: he warmed up to me considerably, acting more friendly and cooperative than he had in a long while. When I finally got up the nerve to ask him why, he just shrugged. Then he said, "I don't know; I guess it feels like you became a dad again."

We know that teens are learning to be independent; but don't be fooled by all the protests. We still have a role: they still need and want our help.

Seeing Children with New Eyes

What a difference it makes if we keep these fundamental principles in mind. Without them, we might view a child or teen that's acting out and be tempted to think, "She just wants to get my attention," or "He's a brat right now." Viewing the same behavior with the principles in mind, we see a very different reality: unhappy children who don't like their behavior any more than we do.

Now we recognize the message they're sending: "I don't know a better way to handle this right now." We identify their misbehavior as a cry for help: "Help me find a more effective way to meet my legitimate needs!"

The principles not only allow us to understand our children with increased empathy—they also increase our resolve to be firm: to help them find more constructive ways to solve problems and strengthen self-discipline. After all, they want us to help them grow and become their best.

When parents use the principles as a lens—a way to view and understand their children—family relationships are transformed in positive ways. "Transformed" is a pretty strong word, but that's what actually happens; parents in our classes experience fundamental changes in their families.

If you recognize your children's yearning to grow,
You'll understand them better,
You'll treat them differently,
And, over time, your children
And your relationships with them will transform.

The remainder of this book will provide you with resources, skills and support to make that transformation possible.

Our Role as Parents

The principles give us a different way to understand our children; they also suggest a different set of beliefs about our role as parents. The beliefs we hold affect our outlook in fundamental ways. That idea is beautifully illustrated in an Asian folktale called *The Three Stonecutters:*

A traveler from another land comes upon a stonecutter, hard at work. "What are you doing?" "I'm wasting my life, sweating in the hot sun day after day, pounding big rocks into little ones." A few yards down the road, the traveler sees a second stonecutter. "What are you doing?" His eyes reveal that he is tired but proud. "I'm supporting my wife and children." A short distance away, the traveler sees a third stonecutter working on the same project. "What are you doing?" His face is radiant: "I'm building a temple for God."

Each man worked at the same task, but understood it in a different way. If we believe that our role as parents requires us to impose discipline on children who are basically unruly—in other words, to work against the tide—we're likely to grow weary in the long run and our confidence may suffer. We may give up more easily and expect less than what we want, or become frustrated and angry.

But if we see our role as supporting children to do what they really want to do—grow and actualize the best within them—we view the relationship quite differently; we'll be more courageous and more persistent. We're on the same team; we share the same goals. When we hold that perspective, we expect and work toward the best.

The principles express a set of beliefs and expectations—an attitude toward children. And, as we'll see, nothing is more crucial than attitudes.

Your Attitude: Nothing Matters More

Attitudes make the difference between a family that works and one that doesn't. That's how potent they are. If that statement surprises you, you're not alone. When I first began teaching parents, classes were all about skills, such as communication and conflict resolution. Experience showed that skills were certainly helpful; but I was surprised to observe that parents who had trouble learning skills were able to be quite successful. Skilled or not, it was the parents with effective attitudes whose families truly blossomed.

What are attitudes? They are the *beliefs* and *feelings* we bring to a situation. The optimist and the pessimist are two familiar examples. Attitudes color our perceptions—our view of reality—and affect our behavior. Attitudes can discourage or encourage cooperation. They inevitably affect our children's self-esteem. To a large degree, our attitudes are the environment in which our children spend their formative years.

What attitudes help parents to be effective? Throughout this book, you'll become aware of specific attitudes that encourage growth and positive reactions—and others that don't. Perhaps for the first time, you'll have the opportunity to identify some of the attitudes you hold and discover whether they produce the results you want.

One of the core attitudes we'll explore in depth is *respect*—for our children and for ourselves (beginning with Chapter Five). However, if there is one key attitude that underlies and supports all the others, it is the attitude expressed in the two principles. Principle one reminds us that children yearn to develop the best within them. It creates an attitude that expects and encourages the best. Principle two tells us that children depend on us to help them mature and become their best. It reminds us that at the core, despite testing and resistance, children want our help. It creates the attitude that we're working with our children—that we're on the same team.

Why Are Attitudes So Powerful?

What we believe creates very real effects. There is a classic study in psychology (by Rosenthal and Jacobson): teachers were told that certain students had exceptional potential. By the end of the semester, every one of the chosen students had performed beyond normal expectations—though their names had actually been selected at random! Their abilities were no greater than those of the other students. What the teacher believed about those youngsters somehow translated into better performance.

Did she work harder to bring out their potential? Did she show more faith in them? Did her belief encourage them to work harder? Probably all of those were true, plus a lot more. What we know for sure is this: the teachers' beliefs and expectations had a profound effect. That experiment has been repeated by other researchers with similar results.

Even as adults, we're influenced by what others think of us. When our spouse sees positive or negative qualities in us, we tend to see ourselves in a similar way.

*What we believe about people affects how we treat them.
And how we treat them influences who they become.*

Remember George Bernard Shaw's "Pygmalion," the play that became "My Fair Lady?" Liza says,

> *The difference between a lady and a flower girl is ... how she's treated. I shall always be a flower girl to Professor Higgins, because he always treats me as a flower girl. But I know I can be a lady to you because you always treat me as a lady.*

What people believe about each other has potent and tangible effects.

Your Beliefs May Come True

What parents believe about their children has the most profound impact of all. At the beginning of a child's life, we're powerful giants who comprise the whole universe. A child's first image of himself grows out of the way that universe treats him. He learns from us that "I'm special," "I'm talented," or later, in some families he may learn that, "I'm stubborn and lazy." All the way into the teen years, parents remain an influential "mirror" reflecting back a picture of "who I am." What parents believe about a child strongly influences the child's picture of himself. And children and teens tend to act out that self-image. And so parents' beliefs often become a *self-fulfilling prophecy*. What you believe about your children will tend to become true.

It's tempting to think that our beliefs are private; that our kids don't know what we think about them. The truth is, our attitudes are never a secret. Children have sensitive antennae; they detect our beliefs and feelings about them readily. Our words reveal our attitudes. But research shows that our *nonverbal* communication has an even more powerful impact on others; facial expression, body language, touch and tone of voice all reveal what we think and feel.

Attitudes show, and they make a crucial difference. So what can we do? We can become more aware of the attitudes we hold (a process we'll begin in the next chapter); gaining awareness is a big step. Then we can decide whether those attitudes serve us well, or whether we want to trade them in for more effective ones.

What If I Don't Believe It?

The principles express a view of human nature that has proven valuable for me and a great many other parents. But what if that view doesn't match your own experience? What can you do if it feels uncomfortable to adopt this view?

Many parents have asked that question. Here's what has proven effective: during the time you're reading this book, simply act *as if* the principles are true. Interpret the behavior of your child or teen as the actions of someone who would like to bring out the best. Despite resistance and protests, imagine your child wants your help, needs you to recognize that yearning and expects you to insist on the best. Then your own experience will tell you whether it makes a difference.

A good way to begin is to use the exercise called, *Acting As If.* We invite parents in our classes to try this exercise for one week. Those who are most skeptical often find it surprising. Later, when you're equipped with the many skills you'll acquire throughout this book, you'll be able to carry it out far more consistently. But for now, it can give you an eye-opening glimpse of what is possible.

Exercise: Acting As If

During the next week, keep an eye out for the positive qualities in your child; assume, just for now, that there is a part that yearns to mature and bring out the best.

When behavior is negative, see if you can remain calm; look beneath the surface content and assume that your child is trying to meet some legitimate need—in the only way he or she knows at the moment. Ask yourself if the child's real message is something like, "I'm just too frustrated or stressed out right now," or "I just don't have the maturity to handle this."

Despite all the protests, assume your child wants your help—wants you to remain calm and steadfast and help him or her to learn more appropriate ways to meet that need. Try it for a full week. Be generous with yourself; expect to slip; pat yourself on the back when you move toward your goal or manage to succeed even once. Keep notes on what happens.

Holding onto the attitudes in the exercise can be a challenge. The very next chapter provides one of the central keys; it will help you to look beneath the surface and understand the roots of your child's difficult behavior. Equally important, it will help you to discover why *parents* lose it at times and go out of control. That awareness is crucial; it can give you new insights about your child and yourself—and allow you to learn how to remain centered and calm more often.

As we end this chapter, I will offer you one more exercise. This one is easier; it's called *Catch Your Child Doing Something Right*. It's fun to do and can be quite an eye-opener. Please keep in mind that it does not embody a full expression of the principles; they are about much more than recognizing what your children do that pleases you. Yet the exercise is remarkably useful; the results are often impressive.

Exercise: Catch Your Child Doing Something Right

During the next week, observe your child or teen and identify as many specific, positive behaviors as possible.

Every time you find one, let your child know that you appreciate that behavior. Express your feelings *sincerely*.

For example, "I appreciate that you brush your teeth without being told," or "Thanks for helping your sister with her math homework while I was making dinner."

Notice whether your appreciations have an effect. What sort of week does the family have?

STEP ONE

Recognize the Lower Self

CHAPTER 3

The Awful Secret

Whatever we want our children to be, we should become ourselves.

—Carl Gustav Jung

I KNOW A SECRET about you. Sometimes you blow up or scream at your children. You lose it so badly at times that you wouldn't want anyone to see your behavior. Or you become a doormat and let the children have their way. Later you feel angry or ashamed. Yet time after time, it happens again. How do I know this about you? Because it's true of every parent I've ever met. Welcome to the club! Come in and take off your shoes; we're all charter members.

A father we'll call Tom reluctantly made the following "confession" in class; he was feeling so defeated and ashamed that he wouldn't look any of us in the eye.

> *I just screamed bloody murder at the kids again. I couldn't help it. Here I am on the phone, trying to hear the directions for tonight's meeting and they're making machine-gun noises at the top of their lungs and roughhousing all over the room. Three times I said, "Boys, I can't hear," and they kept right on, like I didn't exist. I felt so frustrated!*

When I got off the phone, I really let them have it. "You don't think about anyone but yourselves. What's wrong with you! Go to your rooms and don't come out for an hour." Later, after I cooled down, I felt like I'd been a monster, screaming as if they'd committed a crime. Every time this happens I tell myself I'll never do it again—but then I always do.

Does that father's experience sound familiar? Or have you ever felt a little like Alice, the mother who told us this story?

I'm really upset; this morning my daughter's first grade teacher calls. She tells me Dana won't do anything without special help; she clings to the teacher and is less mature than the other children. It's obvious that Dana's bright, but she acts as if she's been babied. That's what makes me feel so awful. It's true. And it's my fault!

I don't want to baby her, but ... Take this morning, for example: We're late getting ready for school and Dana dallies around forever and complains it's too hard to put on her socks. We're getting later all the time ... and I end up dressing her! I tell her she has to dress herself, but it just doesn't work. That happens with a lot of things: I cut her meat, fix her hair ... I promise myself I'll stop, but I never do. I hate when Dana complains. But I can't tolerate the thought of being late. Now I see that I'm not only spoiling her—I've set her up for trouble in school!

Strangely, it seems universal to parenting that, at times, we find ourselves behaving in ways that surprise and disappoint us:

Why did I lose my cool and threaten David that he couldn't be in the Little League game when he forgot to feed the cat?

I don't know why I just stand there and act like a mute when my teenage daughter tells me to be quiet in front of her friends.

How could I go around yelling and slamming doors? I used to feel so ashamed when my mother went on her rampages.

Why do I grab him by the ear when I hated—absolutely hated—when my father did the same thing to me?

At moments like this—when we're anything but calm—we develop a kind of blind spot. Our emotions prevent us from seeing the deeper truth:

- Even when their behavior is at it's worst, our children actually want to bring out their best (principle one).
- They depend on us to help them do that (principle two).

Yet we're not able to provide that help until we see *ourselves* more clearly.

Why Does It Happen?

Why do we lose it so badly at times, and fall so short of being the parents we'd like to be? One reason is stress. When we feel pressured and tense, we can behave in ways that disappoint us. We might scream at our children, be bossy, sarcastic or make threats. In other words, we become aggressive.

Some of us simply give up under stress or cave in and let our children do whatever they want. In other words, we become passive or nonassertive. But why? Why do we react to stress in those ways?

Old Patterns Persist

Our first experiences with stress come in childhood. Something frightens us, or is unpleasant or painful, and somehow we have to cope. Some children cope by attacking; they "fight" with their anger, fists or words. Others cope through "flight"; their solution is to avoid the situation or become passive. They isolate themselves, disappear into TV, books, fantasy—and often block access to their feelings.

Without realizing it, we tend to carry those same coping styles into adulthood. When we feel stressed and don't see a better way out, we revert to old patterns. The adult, rational part of us disappears. Emotion takes over; we switch to "automatic." It's as if a different part of us comes on stage.

Meet the Lower Self

The part of us that goes out of control is sometimes called the "lower self" (remember the three levels described in Chapter One: lower self, centered self, higher self). The lower self is like a child within us who hasn't learned a better way to cope. It's immature and primitive, yet essential for our survival.

We can actually locate the "lower self" physiologically by examining briefly the three distinct parts of the brain. The oldest and most basic part, at the bottom of the stem, controls "autonomic" functions like breathing and heartbeat. The most evolved part, at the top, handles reasoning and rational thinking. In between is the limbic system, which some people think of as the "emotional brain." When we feel threatened, this part springs into action (as it does in a wild animal) striking out or running away *before the reasoning part of the brain even knows it's happening!* That's a useful function for survival. If a lion suddenly threatens you, there is no time to reason through your options; action is needed *now.* The "emotional brain" takes charge and acts.

And that *is* the lower self. It can take over when we feel we're threatened, whether the threat is physical or emotional. When it springs into action, we have raw, intense feelings and limited ability to reason; we have no access to skills. Needless to say, in family relationships, our lower selves are less than effective; their behavior often makes matters worse.

None of us is immune; everyone has a lower self. In fact, we each have *several* lower-self characters that can show up under stress. These so-called "subpersonalities" try, in their own clumsy ways, to meet our needs. Our goal as parents is to learn from these characters and minimize the trouble they cause.

What Situations Bring Out Our Worst?

We noted earlier that our subpersonalities show up when we feel *stressed.* Often, it happens when we also feel *helpless.* That is, we feel under pressure and can't find a good way to handle it. Parents say they feel stressed—and helpless—in situations like these:

> *I'm in a crowded supermarket checkout line and my child is screaming endlessly, "I want candy!"*

I'm halfway through a sentence when my teenager says, "Could you make it short? You've said that a million times!"

No matter what I say or do my five-year-old finds some excuse to hit his younger sister.

My in-laws are over for dinner. I remind my son to say please, and he stalks out, shouting, "I hate you!"

If you look for the underlying cause—what makes parents feel pressured—the answer is often *fear:*

- fear that our *authority* will be threatened
- fear that our *needs* won't be met
- fear that our *perception* will be denied
- fear of losing *control*
- fear that our *expectations* won't be met

Whenever we experience fear—especially if we also feel helpless—an alarm within us can go off and scream, "Crisis!" In response, a subpersonality rides to the rescue and takes over; its sole purpose is to reduce our anxiety. The situation that triggers the subpersonality might not look serious to an outsider, but internally it feels like our emotional survival is threatened. The scared child within us will do anything it can to ease our panic and fear. Unfortunately, that immature part of us has no effective skills; it doesn't know what to do, except to become aggressive or passive. The amygdala or "emotional brain" springs into action, attempting to protect us. It acts in a mechanical fashion, like a robot. We're on "automatic" and we don't even know it.

A Legitimate Need

Parents often feel shame or guilt when they slip into lower-self behavior. While it's true that this behavior is ineffective and can be harmful, it helps to see it in context. If we look beneath everything else—the feelings of fear, helplessness and stress—we discover the true root of our behavior: a legitimate need. It might be the need for peace and order or the need to feel in control or simply the need to take care of practical matters. There's nothing "bad" about having a legitimate need; we just have to find a more effective way to meet it.

In the process of being good parents, we often put aside our own needs for a while; yet if we go too far in that direction, we pay a price—and so do our children. If we neglect our own needs too often, including needs for solitude, adult company, recreation and stimulation, resentment and pressure can build up. Then, any bit of stress can cause a blowup; the lower self is off and running. Good parents are happy, fulfilled people, who make sure their own needs are met too. That requires a delicate balancing act for most of us. The skills of assertion and planning, explored in later chapters, are helpful tools for achieving a healthy balance.

Sometimes we not only *put aside* our own needs, we lose track of them altogether. At such times, the presence of the lower self can actually serve a valuable purpose. Just as a fever warns us that our body needs attention, so the behavior of the lower self can serve as a *valuable signal,* alerting us—telling us we have a legitimate need that isn't being met.

Working Effectively with Our Subpersonalities

When the lower self shows up—when we lose it, go out of control or turn our backs and become passive—what can we do about it? Chapter Four provides practical steps to help us relax, become calm and then make the shift to a more composed and capable state of mind: the centered self. But we can't take any of those steps unless we recognize when a subpersonality has come on stage. Odd as it seems, at the moment when a subpersonality takes over, *we don't know it's happening*—we have no clue that we've "lost it" and slipped into the lower self. We feel totally justified in our behavior, giving ourselves "reasons" for what we're doing, saying to ourselves: "He's asking for it," or "She's being impossible; what else can I do?" We're completely unaware that we're in the lower self. It's only later—after we calm down and look back on what happened—that we feel badly about our behavior.

So if we're not aware it's happening—how can we take action to fix it?

The key is *recognition*. If we want to improve our parenting—and our self-esteem—we need to become aware of a subpersonality *at the time it's acting out*. The only way we can do that is to become thoroughly acquainted with it, to learn how we think, feel and act at those times. Then we can recognize what's happening *before* we go off track—find a way to change course. Getting to know our own subpersonalities is an essential first step on the path to change. That's why Step One of the Three-Step Process is called, *Recognize the Lower Self.*

But how many of us want to look at parts of ourselves that act out? Very few! Naturally, we tend to resist looking at our least attractive behavior. So before we take a look at our lower selves, let's consider the resistance we're likely to meet.

The Courage to Look Within

It's true that we don't *like* to dwell on our behavior when it's embarrassing or unpleasant. But the only way to grow beyond that kind of behavior is to take an honest look in the mirror. That takes some courage; it can be one of the most difficult things we ever do. But this is where the road separates. If you want to become the best parent you can be—and bring out the best in your children—a little effort and discomfort are essential.

It helps to remember that you're not alone. Every parent is in the same boat; we all slip to the lower self at times. The benefits you'll reap are more than worth it, I promise you. By taking this step, you'll do much more than learn useful skills—you'll place yourself in a process of personal growth that can make all the difference for you and your children or teens. Please come along; it's a fascinating journey.

Begin with Recognition

Parents in our classes begin to recognize their subpersonalities by making a simple drawing. I urge you to make one as well. It's an essential part of the process of growth. Don't worry if you can't draw; it doesn't matter. All you need are a few supplies: a piece of paper, a box of crayons, colored pencils or chalks. Color adds meaning, so I encourage you not to settle for a pencil or pen.

Draw Your Subpersonality

To begin, ask yourself:

- *Who or what is that part of me that most interferes with a positive relationship with my child?*
- *Who is my subpersonality?*

Draw a picture of the image that comes to mind, whether a character or an object. The quality of artwork is irrelevant; stick figures are fine. Drawings are often humorous exaggerations.

If you feel stuck when you begin to draw, simply allow yourself to reach out to the different colors in front of you and choose a few. Then give yourself permission to accept whatever you draw. I have never found a drawing that wasn't valuable.

After you've drawn the picture, write down answers to the following questions:

- *How does it look and act?*
- *How does it feel?*
- *How does it think?*
- *What does it need?*

When you finish drawing, give this character a name. It's fun and often helpful to use alliteration; for example, one of my subpersonalities is called, Frenzied Franny.

Monster Man was the name Tom gave his subpersonality. (Remember the father on the phone who went out of control?) As he showed his picture to the parents in class he told us, "This is the part of me that yells and screams at the kids; he looks like a raging monster." Asked to explain the picture, he points to the red lines in the neck, jaws and forehead. "These are the parts of my body that are tight as a rope when I feel tense."

Monster Man

In response to the question, "How does it act?" Tom said, "He screams and curses at the kids, 'Stop acting like damned idiots and do what you're supposed to do!'" When he answers the second question, "How does it feel?" he discovers rage. Looking sheepish and embarrassed, Tom admits, "I really hate them then. I feel at my wits' end, totally frustrated."

To the third question, "How does it think?" Tom answers, "I usually think, 'They're really asking for it; they're being selfish and unreasonable.'"

These answers to the first three questions will help Tom to recognize when his subpersonality has come on stage—or is about to. He can be on the lookout for tension in his neck, lips and jaws, where he drew the red lines. He can watch for times when he feels rage at the kids, or when he screams at them. He can be aware of his thinking, knowing that when he tells himself, "They deserve this!" he's probably in a subpersonality. The more intimately Tom comes to know Monster Man, the quicker he'll be able to sense when that character is around. When he's able to recognize that it's on-stage or "in the wings"—Tom will have a *choice:* he'll be able to choose a more effective approach. *And that's a key to being a more effective parent.* Awareness allows you to make a different choice; it allows you to change and grow.

Am I a "Bad" Person?

Tom barely looks at us as he shows his drawing and answers the questions. "I feel like I'm a terrible parent," he mumbles. The other parents quickly reassure him that he is not alone. As each one shows his or her drawing, it becomes clear that all of us (and that certainly includes me) have had plenty of experience with lower-self behavior.

I remind the group that subpersonalities are not evil or bad; they are simply the children within each of us, lacking skills but trying desperately to meet our legitimate needs.

That's where the fourth question comes in: "What does it need?" "That's a hard one," Tom says at first. "But after a while I realized that I need respect. I need the boys to listen to me. And I need a place where I can talk on the phone without interruption."

Remember, underneath all subpersonality behaviors are legitimate needs—and often we're not fully aware of them. When we become aware of these unmet needs, we open new possibilities: we can find more effective ways to meet them. In the weeks that followed, Tom began to use the skills of assertion and planning to meet his needs *before* they got out of hand.

My Subpersonality: Frenzied Franny

I first identified my own subpersonality when my son and stepdaughter were quite young, and guilty of little more than a messy room. Here's how I answered the questions about Frenzied Franny:

How she looks and acts:

> *She has a very stiff body. Her eyes are bloodshot from constant crying; her face is wrinkled, frozen into a permanent expression of pain. Her hair coils out as she screams at her startled kids.*

Frenzied Franny

How she feels:

> *Anxious, frustrated, alone and isolated. She feels inadequate in her role as mother and fears she's doing an injustice to her children. She feels profoundly guilty when she yells, but cannot stop herself.*

How she thinks:

> *She wonders if she's crazy. Or spoiled. She thinks no one else seems to have such a hard time accepting the role of mother. The constant mess drives her nuts.*

What she needs:

> *She yearns for order. She needs adult stimulation and to be challenged intellectually.*

Making the drawing and answering the questions revealed many clues. Now I could be on the lookout when my body began to tighten up. When I felt like screaming, I could say to myself, "Uh, oh. Time to slow down; I need to take a breather and cool off." Most importantly, I became more aware of my need for adult companionship and stimulation. It wasn't easy to manage, but I created more time to be with friends and made sure I did something for myself every day.

Later, as I began to keep a journal, I discovered other insights. Knowing that subpersonalities begin in childhood, I thought about my own early years. As a child, I experienced a painful lack of love and attention. I thought I wouldn't hurt as much if I told myself I didn't need anything anyway. Then I realized that as a young mom I continued to act as if I had no personal needs. I did whatever my son wanted, pretending that my own needs weren't important, denying they even existed. And then those unmet needs caught up with me (as they do for everyone). Out of nowhere I would suddenly explode; all of my frustration would blast out at little Derek. The drawings and journal sharpened my awareness so that I could make some crucial changes.

Going a Little Deeper

After studying their pictures for a while, parents often decide that there's something they want to add. I encourage you to do this too. It's also valuable to keep some notes in a journal. For example:

Expand your answers to the basic subpersonality questions:

- *How does it look and act?*
- *How does it feel?*
- *How does it think?*
- *What does it need?*

Ask yourself these additional questions:

- *What kinds of situations bring out your subpersonality behavior?*
- *What people? Why?*
- *Are there other unmet needs?*

Knowing more about your subpersonality has practical value. A week after starting a journal, Tom felt encouraged about what he was discovering: "I go ballistic when I'm hungry. My fuse is really short then. And it's especially hard for me when I first come home from work. I need time to catch my breath and relax before the family descends on me. I don't have a complete solution yet, but at least I know why it happens. And now I'm aware of needs that have to be met."

So *That's* Where It Came From

As you take a closer look at your lower self, you may also discover clues to how it began. Here's a confession a young mother made:

> *When my older daughter torments the younger one, I want to wring her neck. Now I realize the source of my feelings: as a child I was bullied by my older sister. I still remember how painful that was. No wonder I go bananas.*

When Tom (Monster Man) began to write a brief journal, he too discovered a connection to his own childhood:

> *One scene always sticks in my mind: my father towers over me, warning, "If you ever do that again, you'll be very sorry; believe me, you'll never forget it." To a frightened child that translated as some nameless, terrible thing will happen to you!*
>
> *I had no idea what I had done wrong. And that made me really scared; anything I did could be dangerous. I know I made a decision then: don't draw attention, stay out of sight, keep quiet. I became a very good boy. I didn't make noise or ask for anything. It worked, in a way. I was praised for being good and I never got into trouble. But in the process I closed down my feelings—I didn't express joy or show anger. I haven't fully overcome that tendency yet.*

Tom brightened as he shared this insight:

> *I think I'm beginning to understand Monster Man. When I'm around my boys, I'm often closed down; I don't know what*

I'm feeling and I don't say much. I act easy-going and let them do what they want. Then they do one more thing that gets to me, and Bang! I explode. All the built-up tension from holding my feelings in—not only that day, but from the past—roars out at them. I never saw the connection before.

Seeing himself a little more clearly will open a new door for Tom. He will have more compassion for himself and be able to make more effective choices. You'll gain the same benefits as you learn more about your own subpersonality.

Donna Do-It-All

Here's how a mother named Alice described her drawing and what she learned from it:

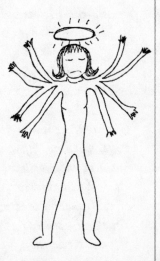

Donna does everything she's supposed to; that's why I drew so many hands and gave her a halo. In her own mind, she's an angel.

I had an alcoholic mom and lots of brothers and sisters; I took care of them all as if I were an adult. There was no one else to hold the family together. I'd pay any price to stop the screaming and keep the peace.

And Donna Do-It-All continues to carry the world on her shoulders. Whatever Sarah wants, I do im- mediately. My daughter doesn't lift a finger.

Donna Do-It-All

The more you know about your subpersonality— the more able you are to recognize when that character is taking charge—the more power you have to choose a different option.

Meet Your Spouse's Lower Self

Another opportunity opens when mom and dad learn to know their lower selves: the potential to strengthen their relationship. When we argue or disagree about how to parent, we're obviously not at our best. Parents often discover that the root of relationship problems lie in their own early years. One mom told this story:

Dumb Dora

> *When my husband expressed concerns about how I was dealing with the kids, I'd accuse him, saying, "You think I'm dumb." Feeling hurt, he'd insist, "That's not what I think. I respect your mind; I think you're very bright." It took years to realize why I was so hypersensitive: as a kid, my mother often told me I was dumb.*

Later that mother drew a picture she named Dumb Dora. The more she learned to recognize that insecure part of herself, the more able she was to hear her husband's comments objectively.

By the time we marry and create our own families, we all harbor lower-self characters. Inevitably, they create problems in a marriage. Now we have an opportunity to see what's happening and find ways to create more harmonious relationships.

Your Child's Lower Self

Our children respond no differently than we did when we grew up. When they have strong needs they cannot meet, when they try to cope with frustration and anxiety (and life offers plenty of both), they too develop subpersonalities. The behavior that follows at those times is the *best solution the child can find* at that moment. It may be ineffective or even destructive, yet beneath it there is always a legitimate need.

One obvious example can happen when a new baby is born. Imagine how that feels to the first child. In their best-selling book, *Siblings Without*

Rivalry, the authors, Faber and Mazlish, use this analogy: Picture your spouse putting an arm around you one day and saying, "Honey, I love you <u>so</u> much that I've decided to have another wife (husband) in the family." That's how the first child often feels: "Hey! What about me?" The older child might regress and act like a baby again. When that doesn't work, he or she might be mean to the new baby. Both are attempts to cope with the anxiety of losing attention and love: ineffective ways to meet legitimate needs.

You know your child's lower-self behavior; perhaps you've seen it all too often. It can test your patience like nothing else. But the next time you see it, remember that somewhere beneath those exasperating antics there is a legitimate need. That subpersonality thrashes around doing all the wrong things because it doesn't know a better way to meet the need.

That's where our job comes in. If we want to assist our children to mature and realize their best potential, we must recognize their lower selves when they appear—and look beneath the surface to understand *why* they appear. The better we know those subpersonalities, the more quickly we can recognize them and help our children find more effective ways to meet their needs.

Parents in my classes learn about their children's subpersonalities in the same way they learn about their own: through a drawing and four questions. You will be rewarded if you take the time to do this exercise; it can form the basis for a transformation in your relationship with your child.

My Child's Lower Self

Before you begin:

You'll need paper and crayons or colored pencils or chalks. Remember, drawing skill is not relevant.

If you have more than one child, do a drawing for each one.

Instructions:

Draw a picture to answer this question:

Who or what is that part of my child that most interferes with a positive relationship with me?

Draw a picture of the image that comes to mind, whether a character or an object.

After completing the drawing, write answers to these four questions:

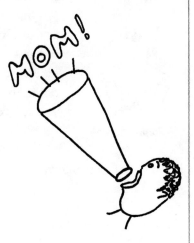

- *How does it look and act?*
- *How does it feel?*
- *How does it think?*
- *What does it need?*

Complete the exercise by giving the character a name. I called Derek's subpersonality, Demanding Derek.

Demanding Derek

What Parents Learn

Parents in class make some fascinating discoveries when they share drawings of their children's subpersonalities. A father who named his own subpersonality Old Yeller joked before he began drawing, "I'll just use this drawing of my own subpersonality and rename it Young Yeller."

Old Yeller / Young Yeller

The other parents laughed with him, but he had revealed a valuable insight: the child's subpersonality is often a mirror image of the parent's. Often, but not always.

Linda, the mother of a teenager, gained a different insight: "My daughter's subpersonality, Raging Robin, has folded arms and narrowed eyes, as if she were a vessel containing venom. Her face radiates rage; she believes I favor her brothers. She strikes at me with sarcasm, saying, 'You're supposed to be the mother of this family; why don't you act like a grown-up?'"

Raging Robin

When Linda looked back at the drawing of her own subpersonality, she began to understand: "Looney Linda was frazzled and out of control. No wonder my daughter says, 'Grow up.' Now I see that she's scared and confused. I think she's really saying, 'I need you to be there for me, someone steady and calm I can count on.'"

Looney Linda

One parent's comment touched me at the core because she intuitively discovered what subpersonalities are all about: unmet needs. She named the drawing of her daughter's subpersonality, The Devil's Daughter. She was quite upset when she shared it; the name had just come to her, without thinking. The whole picture was drawn in bright red. The child's subpersonality had horns and long nails—used to scratch her brother—and

The Devil's Daughter

an "X" where her heart should be. But her mother was most taken by the sad eyes. In a voice filled with feeling she told us, "This child hits her brother and says she hates me. But I see now that she also seems very lonely and in need of love. I feel sad for her. How can I help?"

A Cry for Help

Drawing your child's subpersonality can give you a new way of seeing your child's aggressive or passive behavior. It allows you to look beneath the surface and discover the truth we noted in Chapter Two: a child's most difficult behavior is a cry for help.

Children *don't want to* behave in these ineffective ways, any more than we want them to. They want to be free of painful anxiety, to feel good about their behavior. When they act in inappropriate or negative ways, they are, in effect, sending us a message. That message says, "Help me to deal with my stress; help me learn a better way to meet my legitimate need!"

How can we help? By remaining calm and having faith in the child. Despite their protests, our children and teens want us to remain steadfast, to gently and lovingly *insist* that they take a step toward maturity and learn more effective ways. Often that means setting limits—*not* accepting negative behavior. And it means teaching new skills: more effective ways to cope. Children lack experience as well as maturity. They need us to help them learn how to meet their needs in positive ways—with siblings and family, with friends and at school. Once again, the skills you'll find in the following chapters will help you to guide them in all these ways.

The Next Step

Learning to know those troublemakers—your most difficult subpersonality and your child's—is an ongoing process. The tools introduced in this chapter will help you to recognize those culprits quickly. In the next chapter, you'll learn what to do when you spot them. You'll learn how to take step two: a systematic way to slow down, relax and become calm, and then make the shift to your centered self. And there you'll discover—quite literally—a whole new world of possibilities.

STEP
TWO

---

*Cross the Bridge to the
Centered Self*

CHAPTER 4

Exit the Lower Self

*Human beings, by changing the inner attitudes of their minds,
can change the outer aspects of their lives.*

—William James

Y OU'VE SWORN IT WOULD never happen again. And then you find
yourself screaming at the kids one more time. Or giving up, caving in
and letting the children do what they want—again. How frustrating that
feels! Having read the last chapter, you're aware that your lower self may
be on stage. But what can you *do* about it?

Take heart. We all know how that feels: something like the golfer
who watches his ball soar, only to splash into a water trap and sink to the
bottom—one more time. This chapter will show you how to take that
old duffer (lower self) out of the game and put in a far more effective
player: your centered self. It will give you the tools to accomplish the *most
important task in parenting:* to limit lower-self behavior—for yourself,
first of all—and then for your children.

You already know why that matters so much: only when we're calm
and centered are we able to see the truth: our children really do want and
need us to help them become their best. Only when we're centered do we
have the *ability* to help.

In the next few pages, you'll learn two simple, yet profound exercises that will allow you to slow down and relax, and then "cross the bridge" *from your lower self to your centered self.* You'll gain the ability to be more consistently in touch with the part of you that is more centered, mature and skilled. Together, these two exercises make up step two of the Three-Step Process.

The first exercise helps us to relax—and gain more control over our emotions. Practiced daily, it gradually reduces tension and enables us to remain calm, so that over time, we are less and less likely to lose it. The second exercise is also practiced daily, after the first; it helps us remember that we have choices. It strengthens our ability to choose how we think, feel and act.

I think of these exercises as a "magical key" to parenting; they've made a crucial difference for parents throughout the world. Many feel they are the most valuable part of the *Quality Parenting* program. Why? Because they free us from the impulsive, unthinking behavior of the lower self—the real troublemaker in the parent-child relationship. They give us greater access to a more effective part of ourselves: the calmer, wiser centered self. Each time we practice the exercises and move across that bridge, we strengthen our ability to cross it again—to leave the subpersonality behind and act from center.

And that opens a world of possibilities: you discover that you can shift to a new state of consciousness, where you're more able to think clearly and use communication skills. You're better equipped to help your child or teen become centered, and to model mutual respect consistently. In other words, you're more able to become the parent you want to be.

The Relaxation Exercise

This exercise combines two well-proven relaxation techniques, confirmed by numerous research studies and used successfully by athletes, people in stress-reduction programs and pain management clinics. Both techniques—focusing on your breath and visualization—create measurable changes in the human body.

Here's how the exercise works: many of us experience tension in the gut or "solar plexus" area. We use expressions like, "My stomach is in knots" or "butterflies in my stomach." This exercise uses relaxation and the power of imagination to transform that energy. Breathing deeply, we visualize moving the energy up an imaginary elevator, and transforming its quality. The human mind is extremely sensitive to suggestion, especially in visual form. That attribute can help us create practical and useful results.

The Relaxation Exercise

Preparation:
Find a comfortable sitting position: legs crossed or placed evenly on the floor. Spine erect, eyes closed.

Step 1: *Inhale slowly as you raise tension up an imaginary elevator.*

As you breathe in, visualize lifting tension from your solar plexus in an imaginary elevator, located just behind your body, parallel with your spinal cord. Raise this energy up so that it can be transformed by the loving heart—and then by the wise head.

Step 2: *Retain the breath as the energies of love and wisdom blend.*

Imagine the energies from the heart and head fusing, filling the head with the energy of loving wisdom.

Step 3: *Exhale the relaxed energy into the room.*

Allow the energy of loving wisdom to radiate out through the space between the eyebrows, filling the room with calm and tranquility.

Step 4: *Affirm that you changed tension into the relaxed energy of loving wisdom, creating peace and calm.*

Affirm what you did: you raised tension-filled energy from the solar plexus, lifting it in an imaginary elevator—first to the loving heart and then into the wise head. Through this action you created the relaxed energy of loving wisdom. You then radiated that energy from the area between the eyebrows, filling the room with peace and calm.

The exercise is complete when it is repeated three times.

Time Required:
28 seconds per cycle x 3 cycles = 84 seconds total

Once you're familiar with the exercise, feel free to shorten or simplify it (it takes longer to *describe* the exercise than to *do* it). Don't worry about counting or being precise; find a way to develop a natural rhythm that feels comfortable.

Some benefits of the exercise:

- relaxes your body and mind
- helps you to remain calm and gain more control over your emotions
- helps transform a negative frame of mind into a positive one
- reminds you that you have the ability to alter your moods

Calmer Every Day

Just as regular physical training builds strength, so this exercise builds psychological strength. The more you practice, the more you strengthen your ability to handle stress. Daily practice helps you deepen your sense of inner peace and harmony. Then, when confronted with stress, you're more able to stay calm and centered.

The analogy I like to use is to imagine yourself as the water inside a teakettle. If you begin the day with a temperature of 200 degrees Fahrenheit—hot and ready to boil—it doesn't take much for the whistle to blow. *Practicing the exercise daily lowers your initial water temperature.* Imagine beginning the day with the water cool. You could handle a lot more stress without reaching the boiling point. You'd be more able to deal with the chaos of daily life while remaining calm.

A cool frame of mind is always a gift to the family. It's especially useful when the kids are having a rough day or living through a difficult stage. Whether you're living with a teenager or a tenacious two-year-old, a strong and steady sense of inner calm will stand you in good stead.

Some parents find special meaning in the relaxation exercise because it has its roots in the Eastern traditions and works with the chakra system. Its power, similar to yoga and meditation practices, increases over time. However, if you have your own practice, continue to use it. Or create a ritual that has meaning for you; some parents use favorite psalms or verses. What matters is that you find a way that works for you and that you practice it daily.

Any time you feel under pressure and ready to "boil over," you can repeat the relaxation exercise. In addition to daily practice, use it as an "emergency" stopgap whenever you feel yourself tightening up, getting ready to boil over. It takes just a few moments and makes a real difference. Follow it up with the bridge exercise.

The Bridge Exercise

So far, we've set the stage. The relaxation exercise has helped us to become calm and adopt a positive frame of mind. That prepares us for the next step: to gain perspective—to see our options more clearly.

We've all had the experience of "blowing up" or being out of control and not realizing it at the time. Then, at some point, we recognize what's happening and say to ourselves, "Uh-oh; I'm over the edge." It's as if *one* part of us is acting out while *another* part is able to watch it happen. The bridge exercise helps us gain this all-important "dual awareness": we're able to watch ourselves go out of control—to recognize that a subpersonality has come on stage. We realize what we're doing *and* realize that we have a choice—we can handle the situation in a more calm and caring way.

I encourage you to make both the relaxation and the bridge exercises a part of your daily routine. Over time, they open the door to a new state of consciousness—a new world of relating.

Centered Self

The Bridge Exercise

Purpose: To recognize that you are more than the lower self—and that you have the choice to identify with the centered self.

Preparation: The *Relaxation Exercise.*

Directions: Remain in a comfortable sitting position with legs crossed or evenly placed on the floor. Be sure your spine is upright, eyes closed. Recall the drawing of your subpersonality and your description of it. Use that information to practice this exercise silently.

Step 1: Describe the *physical appearance* and *actions* of the subpersonality.

Affirm to yourself:
I am more than the appearance and actions of the subpersonality.
I am the centered self.
I choose how I act.

Step 2: Describe the *feelings* of the subpersonality.

Affirm to yourself:
I am more than the feelings of the subpersonality.
I am the centered self.
I choose how I feel.

Step 3: Describe the *thoughts* of the subpersonality.

Affirm to yourself:
I am more than the thoughts of the subpersonality.
I am the centered self.
I choose how I think.

Step 4: Reassert *who you are* and the *choices* you have.

I am the centered self.
I choose how I act, feel and think.

The Bridge is an adaptation of the "Disidentification Exercise" found in Roberto Assagioli's book, *Psychosynthesis*.

How Parents Use the Exercises

Discovering that you have a choice makes a profound difference. Here's a sample of the creative choices parents have made after practicing the exercises for a while:

I've got a new routine now. When Sarcastic Sam starts to say cutting things to the kids, I've learned to just stop; then I say, "Whoa!" out loud. The girls laugh—and sometimes even I do. That helps. Then I can slow down, take a breath and talk in a reasonable way.

Sarcastic Sam

Bossy Betty

More and more, I can sense when I'm about ready to blow up. But I can't change on the spot. I tell the kids I have to go to the bathroom; that's where I cool down. It's just a beginning, but it's better than becoming Bossy Betty.

Whenever I hear myself say, "Let me tell you something, young man!" I know Preachy Paul is about to give a lecture. Without that clue, I don't recognize that I'm about to go off track—holding an attitude that only makes things worse. But I'm starting to catch myself more often.

Preachy Paul

You might think it's strange, but when I start to feel frazzled, I walk around the house or the supermarket saying to myself, "I have a choice, I have a choice ..."

When my own son and stepdaughter were growing up, I practiced the exercises every day. But they had a special purpose when I faced an emotional "emergency." Here's how they helped me on a day when I needed support in a hurry:

My heart nearly stopped when the voice on the phone said, "This is officer Johnson; I'm with your son." Fifteen-year-old Derek was truant, apprehended in a donut shop across from the school. My fear turned to anger. On the phone, Derek said, "The school rules are stupid; all I did was skip class to study for a test." Driving to meet him, I was furious. Part of me knew this could become an opportunity for Derek to learn and grow, but I feared I would blow my top and encourage resistance. To prepare myself to face him, I practiced the relaxation exercise; it took less than two minutes. At the end of that time I was still upset—but more clear-headed and able to lead the frank and open discussion Derek and I needed.

Other parents find their own unique ways to use the exercises:

My five-year-old and I use the hand signal from sports to ask for a "time out." We call it when the other is getting too upset. The one who's "losing it" then takes a few minutes alone to do what he calls 'Loving heart.' I simplified the exercise and explained that at five he has a 'wise head' that will help him as soon as he calms down. It really works! It helps us both cool off.

Late last night I was exhausted and Serena was screaming, afraid to let me remove a splinter. I couldn't face what might have been an hour of shrieking. I leaned my head against the door and did the exercise—and gained the patience to help her calm down.

Eddie dripped chocolate on our new car upholstery—after I asked him twice not to eat in the car. I was in a sour mood and so was he; I got furious, ended up shouting and he started crying. I pulled over to the curb and said I was going to take a few minutes to rest. Walking behind the car, I took some deep breaths and did the two exercises. After I opened the car door, Eddie said in a wavering voice, "Mmm-Mom, were you doing that cooling off thing?" When I answered yes, he said, "Oh, thank goodness."

When and Where to Do the Exercises

The earlier in the day, the better

First thing in the morning is ideal. The exercises can help you remain relaxed and alert to the choices available to you throughout the day. If morning doesn't work for you, choose a time when you can give the exercises your full attention.

At the same time each day

We gain a sense of order from repeated ritual. Choose a set time, such as 7 a.m., or a regular place in your schedule, such as after breakfast.

In a comfortable and quiet place

Select a pleasant room where you can have privacy. Some people prop up a pillow in bed; others prefer a chair or sofa. It's important to keep your back erect to help you stay alert and focused.

I've practiced the exercises in my parked car, in a public rest room and a darkened hotel conference room when nothing better was available. You can always find a time and place if you're committed; it's the daily practice that counts.

Helping Children with *Their* Subpersonalities

One of the great challenges in parenting is being with a child who is acting in negative or destructive ways (as if you didn't know). It's tempting to think, "She's turning into a brat," or, "Maybe it's my fault for not being a better parent." Those thoughts are likely to lead to negative results. A more effective way to begin is to recognize that you're watching your child's lower self. Just as we can slip into the lower self under stress, so can our children. Like us, they develop their own subpersonalities.

However ineffective or destructive their behavior, they're *attempting* to cope—to meet legitimate needs. Our job is to help them become centered; only then can we have a reasonable conversation and turn a problem into an opportunity for learning and growth. But how can we help a child or teen to make that shift—to become more centered?

Some parents teach their children to do simple versions of the relaxation and bridge exercises. They find that it works well; we'll describe their experiences shortly. But some children are too young to practice these exercises; older children and teens may not be willing. In those situations, we can make a useful contribution by doing the bridge exercise on *behalf* of our children.

What good does that do? It helps us to be alert—to *recognize* when a child's subpersonality is in action—and to remember that such behavior is really *a cry for help.* It helps us to keep perspective: to remember our children are much *more* than their lower selves. Then we have a choice; we don't have to respond to their subpersonalities by slipping into our own. When *we're* able to stay calm, we can help *them* to become more centered.

Practice the Bridge
On Behalf of Your Child or Teen

Purpose: To create a vivid image in your mind of your child's subpersonality—so that you can recognize it easily and respond effectively.

Preparation: The *Relaxation Exercise.*

Directions:

1. Recall the drawing you made of your child's subpersonality (Chapter Three).
2. Review the answers to the questions:

   - *How does it look and act?*
   - *How does it feel?*
   - *How does it think?*
   - *What does it need?*

3. Think of times when you've seen that subpersonality in action.
4. Resolve to be alert to it the next time it appears.
5. Be aware that you can help your child to make a more effective choice.

Here's how one father used the bridge exercise with his daughter:

> *I was about ready to blow a fuse when Cary screamed,*
> *"You're so mean!" I was right on the edge, ready to lose*
> *it—when I suddenly realized, "Wait a minute; what I'm*
> *seeing is her lower self." For the first time in years, I didn't*
> *react. Instead, I asked Cary gently, "Would you like to sit next*
> *to me on the couch and tell me why you think I'm mean?"*

This was the father who had named his subpersonality, Old Yeller
and his daughter's, Young Yeller.

> *For several weeks I've been alternating the bridge exercise:*
> *doing it for myself one day and for my daughter the next.*
> *By now, both subpersonalities were clearly etched in my*
> *mind—and that enabled me suddenly to see the destructive*
> *game we had been playing: one limited part of my daughter*
> *bringing out one limited part of me. Finally I could see her as*
> *a child trying to cope who hadn't found a better way to meet*
> *her needs. Her upsetting behavior really was a cry for help.*

The bridge exercise had paved the way.

> *A few minutes later Cary revealed what was really going on*
> *for her: "I'm mad that you won't let me be with Mommy" (who*
> *was visiting Grandma in a hospital in another city). Soon she*
> *climbed on my lap and said, "I really miss her."*

This father and daughter were then able to share their loneliness and
grow closer, instead of hurting and misunderstanding each other.

Children's subpersonalities take many forms: they can wheedle or
whine and say, "Please! I promise I'll be good ..." and we're tempted to
collapse. Other times we hear, "You're mean! That's not fair!"—and our
buttons can easily be pressed. Or they become seductive when they want
something they shouldn't have, snuggling close to say how much they
love us. And all too often we give in when we should be setting limits.

Doing the bridge exercise for ourselves—and on behalf of our
children—keeps *their* subpersonalities in our minds as well as our own.

It helps us remember that our child or teen is much more than a whiner, a pleading seducer or an angry voice. It reminds us that, like adults, *children have a choice:* they can move to a more centered place, especially when we're calm and able to help.

When Children Do the Bridge Exercise

Children are quite capable of doing the bridge themselves. Those who are willing often enjoy it and benefit. Parents sometimes invite their children to make a subpersonality drawing and then teach them a simple version of the bridge exercise. Of course it's not wise to try it when the child is upset; wait until you're both calm, perhaps a few hours or a day after an incident.

Here are some of their stories:

> *Jamie followed me everywhere, whining and pulling at my skirt. "Just one more program ... Come on Mommy ... Just one more ..." At five years old, he knew the rule very well; he'd already seen three programs, his TV limit for the day. But he whined on and on, raising the pitch and the volume. I said calmly, "If you need to be more upset you can do that, but I'd like you to be in the backyard or your room. I'm not going to change the rule or talk about it any more right now."*
>
> *Fifteen minutes later he walked out of his room and said calmly, "I'm going out to play." His mood was entirely different. "I can watch TV tomorrow." I just stood there wondering, "How did that happen?"*
>
> *A few days later I asked if he'd like to draw a picture of how he felt when he was angry. In red crayon he drew a picture of himself with a big frown. After looking at it, I said, "You know, we have different parts of us. They come out at different times. What name would you give the boy in this picture?" He said, "That's Angry Jamie; he screams and jumps on the bed and says he has the meanest mommy in the world. He hollers, 'I never get to do what I want!'"*

Angry Jamie

I asked if he'd like to draw a picture of how he feels when he's happy. In bright orange (his favorite color), and with great gusto, he drew a boy with a broad smile. He said, "This is Happy Jamie."

Happy Jamie

We put the pictures away for a couple of days. Then I took them out and said, "I'm curious. The other day you went from Angry Jamie to Happy Jamie. How did you do that?" "I kicked the bed hard. Very hard. I said some bad things. Then I took very deep breaths (he sees me do that). I just sat on the bed for a long time. Then I felt better." I said, "I see that you can decide; you can be Angry Jamie or Happy Jamie." "I know I can decide," he said. Then, with a lot of emphasis, he declared, "When I have no more TV time left, I can still see my programs the next day. Anyway, I like Happy Jamie better than being mad." Suddenly he jumped up. "Can we put the pictures up on the wall in my room?"

A father told this story about himself and his nine-year-old daughter:

Emily is often sweet, but she teases her younger brother in a mean-spirited way, goading him until a fight breaks out. On a day when we had some pleasant time alone, I told her what I've been learning in parenting class. I showed her my picture of Sarcastic Sam, the part of me that makes angry jokes instead of asking for what I want. I asked if she'd like to make a picture like mine. She wasn't sure what to do, so I explained, "Well, what I drew was the part of me that isn't so nice to people—a part I'm not so proud of."

Sarcastic Sam

Emily's picture showed a fierce eagle, diving down to attack. I asked her the questions in the exercise: "How does it look and act?" "Mean and angry; its beak is open, screaming. It attacks baby eagles and other things." "How does it feel?" "Mad. Very mad. It wants to destroy, but inside it doesn't really want to hurt. It feels out of control." "How does it think?" "It's very proud. It thinks, 'I'm a powerful eagle; I don't want to look weak. All I can do is attack. If I try to comfort those baby eagles, I will feel very weak.'"

Destructive Eagle

It seemed clear that she felt quite uncomfortable about her behavior—"out of control"—yet she could see no other choice. I sensed that she was just then discovering some of her feelings about it. I told her about the bridge exercise and asked if she'd like me to help her do it; I simplified the words as I led her through it. She sat quietly with her eyes closed.

When we talked later on, Emily said she liked doing the drawing and the "relaxing part." She seemed surprised by the feelings she discovered. "Would you want to use it in the future?" "Yes, but I want to do it myself; when I feel mad. Maybe when I fight with Jeremy and storm off. I could come back later and talk with him." I think the exercise opened a door for Emily.

As a family therapist, I can tell you that it's amazing how quickly children can modify behavior when they become aware of a better choice. Their ability to grow and change far outpaces adults.

An Addition to the Bridge Exercise

There is an additional step that many parents find useful: to visualize in detail the way they would *like* things to go during the day, to see themselves acting from the centered self. This exercise is especially useful when you anticipate a stressful situation. Professional athletes use this technique, envisioning themselves in the game, relaxed and making the perfect moves. Practice makes perfect, even in imagination; mental preparation helps to make it happen.

The exercise is called *Staying Centered.*

Staying Centered
A Visualization

Purpose: To strengthen your ability to remain centered
To prepare for stressful situations

Directions: Silently repeat the final words of the
Bridge Exercise:

I am the centered self.
I choose how I act.
I choose how I feel.
I choose how I think.

Centered Self

As you repeat each sentence, focus on a specific situation that concerns you. Or envision activities that will take place that day. In your mind's eye, see yourself in each activity, watching it unfold exactly as you would *like it* to happen. With each statement, decide how you'd like to act, feel and think.

The more detail you give the scene, the better: see the setting, hear the conversations, experience your actions, etc.

The goal is to create a "dress rehearsal" in your mind. You're the director; replay each scene as often as necessary, until it happens just the way you'd like.

A final tip: the mind responds best when we give it suggestions in positive form. For example, instead of saying your body will not be tense, say, "My body will be relaxed."

How Parents Use the Exercise

One mother used the staying centered exercise when she faced a trying day:

> *My stomach was already in knots. I had too little time to prepare for a crucial meeting; it was going to be one of those days. And then the school nurse called me at work: "Timmy has a sore throat; he needs to be picked up." Of all the days in the year, this was it. How could I be patient at home all day with a restless six-year-old, really meet his needs—when I felt stressed and uptight about letting everyone down?*
>
> *"I don't know if that exercise will help," I thought, "but I need something." When I repeated the last line, "I am the centered self," I allowed myself to let go—a little—and feel more relaxed and capable. Then I went back and spent a few moments with each line separately:*

I choose how I act.

> *I realized, "I want to help Timmy feel comfortable and I want to respect my own needs as well." It took a long while before I could envision anything that worked. Finally I could imagine setting up several activities at bedside for Timmy, spending some time playing with him, but reserving some time for my work. I imagined talking with him, discussing his needs and mine, and creating a plan together.*

I choose how I feel.

> *I told myself, "I feel thankful that I can be with Timmy while he's sick. I want him to know that and I'll be sure to tell him. And I'm also glad that I won't forget my own needs or feel resentful. It will feel good to make it work for both of us."*

I choose how I think.

> *I reminded myself, "I'll be a better mother to Timmy if I respect my own needs as well. I'll have more to give and more*

*room to take him in." I visualized feeling good about our day.
Then I affirmed, "To be a good parent to Timmy, I must also
be good to myself."*

*Doing the exercise made me feel more in control; it shifted
my attitude, and it helped me feel more loving. I could adjust
and make the best of it for both of us.*

Another mother used the exercise to open her heart to her older
daughter:

*I feel loving and open to my younger daughter—but Carina,
the older one, gets to me! I hate to admit it, but Melinda is my
favorite. That's awful, I know, but Carina complains and rolls
her eyes at almost everything I do. I feel so frustrated! I'm not
proud of that, but it's true. I decided to use this exercise to help
me visualize a different way of responding to her.*

I choose how I act.

*I told myself, "I will not raise my voice at her. When I have
a request, I will speak calmly and quietly. I will talk directly to
her, not yelling from another room. I also will notice her nice
qualities. She's always singing; I'll let her know I enjoy her high
spirits. She's also a sharp dresser; I'll notice and acknowledge
her creativity."*

I choose how I feel.

*I assured myself, "I feel thankful that I have two daughters.
Carina deserves to be loved and accepted. I will enjoy her and
consciously open my heart each time I see her."*

I choose how I think.

*I reminded myself, "I was so happy when she was born. We
had such joyful times when she was younger. I loved reading
to her and planting flowers in the garden together. She was so
alive and curious. I know we can improve our relationship and*

that it's important for me to take the first step. I imagine she hurts, just as I do. I will trust that as I become more loving, she will return that feeling in time."

Practicing the exercise made me feel like a better person. It gave me a direction and lifted my spirits. That was a whole lot better than resenting her. I know it's a good start; I feel lighter just knowing that I'm taking positive steps.

A father used the exercise to envision less conflict between his children:

They fight over anything—like who gets to pour milk in their cereal first. After a while it can drive you nuts! I try to tune it out, which my wife hates. Or I threaten them: "Keep it up and nobody gets milk." That works—for about three minutes. I was an only child; I don't know how to handle this sibling rivalry stuff!

My wife made me take this class. She spent a whole day with her sister and mom recently and I was alone with the kids. Let's put it this way: Things have to change! And I'm willing to start with me.

I choose how I act.

I told myself, "I'll pay more attention to the kids in the morning. I'll talk with them at breakfast, instead of reading the paper. I'll show more interest in their world, or ask them about school and their friends. I'll engage them in conversation and imagine that will be much more satisfying than their usual fights. I'll try to help them listen to each other, by saying things like, "Stacie hasn't finished yet; I want to hear what she has to say. I'll be happy to listen to you, Jimmy, after she's finished."

I choose how I feel.

I realized, "I'll feel good about getting to know my kids better; they're changing every day. And I feel good about becoming more active as a dad. I always wanted my father to be interested in me."

I choose how I think.

> *I assured myself, "I can help our family treat each other with more kindness. My kids really do love each other. I see them playing and laughing together all the time. They just have some bad habits they slip into. I can help them form new habits and find more respectful ways to relate."*
>
> *Practicing the exercise helped me feel constructive and powerful. I like taking positive action. I realize now that my behavior—tuning out or barking at them—was really no better than theirs.*

A young mother used the exercise to feel less stressed around her critical mother-in-law:

> *She's driving me nuts! My mother-in-law was always a challenge, but now that she's a grandmother, she really gets to me. I'm still nursing the baby and she worries that he's not getting enough nutrition. The doctor says he's thriving! Where does she get these ideas? Anyway, the facts have nothing to do with her feelings. I really want to change something so that she won't get under my skin like that.*

I choose how I act.

> *I told myself, "I don't need to have my mouth sealed when I'm around her. I can say calmly, with confidence, 'The doctor says Jeffrey's doing great. I feel sad and uneasy when you worry. We have so much to celebrate; let's enjoy this miracle of life.'"*

I choose how I feel.

> *I assured myself, "If my mother-in-law doesn't change her behavior, I know I'll feel better just by speaking up. I've always*

clammed up around authority figures; I feel proud that I'm willing to be respectful, and yet tell my truth. I also feel great that my husband fully supports my nursing. That's what I want to focus on: the joy of being with Jeffrey and having his dad's support."

I choose how I think.

I reminded myself, "My mother-in-law knows very little about the health benefits of nursing. I've offered her articles to read, but she always changes the subject. I accept that providing research is not a good approach. I'll just pay attention to the bottom line: grandma's concern shows that she cares."

Just thinking it through has helped me feel calmer and so grateful for my husband and son!

What Works for You?

Parents find their own ways to use the staying centered exercise. One father said, "I use the visualization to smooth out my rough spots." Like many others, he uses it to strengthen qualities such as patience, courage and love.

The comments below might suggest still other ways you can adapt this exercise for your own needs:

I choose how I act.

I will move throughout the day with my body at ease; I will relax my shoulders, jaw and brow. I deserve to live in a body that feels good. I will pace myself, so I have enough time to feel calm. If I detect any tension in my body, I will take time to relax it, stretching or breathing deeply.

I choose how I feel.

I will feel patient and loving. I will appreciate that my teenage son often thinks in a different way than I do. I will be

open and interested in what he has to say and respect myself as
well. I will feel good about being receptive.

I choose how I think.

> *I will trust that I can handle my talk with Samantha today*
> *with confidence and ease. I will think on my feet and will know*
> *what to say. I will stay focused on the concerns that I have.*

Be free and creative in the ways you use this exercise. You really *can*
choose how you act, feel and think!

It's Not about Perfection

Even when you practice the exercises faithfully, there will be times
when you'll slip—when you "wake up" after a while and discover that
your lower self is on stage, acting out. But the exercises in this chapter
will help you *shorten* the time a subpersonality is in charge. And, with
regular practice, you can eventually catch yourself *before* it happens. Use
the knowledge you gained about your subpersonality in step one to be on
the lookout: watch for the actions, feelings and thoughts that tell you the
lower self is creating trouble.

Where We Are—Where We're Going

You now have the tools to recognize your child's subpersonality
and your own—and to remain aware that you can both learn to make
different choices. The tools, in this chapter and the one preceding, are:
Step One—Recognize the Lower Self and Step Two—Cross the Bridge
to the Centered Self. These two steps can help you accomplish the most
important task in parenting: to remain centered more often.

You now have a way to transform that culprit who lowers your self-
esteem and your child's. Eventually, you'll be able to recognize when your
lower self is in the wings—when you're feeling stressed and about to slip
into a subpersonality. Then you'll be able to stop it before it happens.

Regular practice of the exercises will lay the foundation. Even as you absorb these ideas, you're taking the first steps toward becoming the parent you want to be. You're opening the door to a new consciousness—a new way of relating that encourages mutual respect.

In the next few chapters we'll explore valuable skills and attitudes available to us when we're centered. These skills and attitudes enable us to be more effective and confident as we create a family environment that brings out the best.

STEP
THREE

Express the Centered Self

CHAPTER 5

The Golden Rule:

Mutual Respect

*My mother taught me that people should be judged by
the respect they have for themselves and others.
Her words helped me do the hard things I had to do later in life.*

—Rosa Parks

NOW THAT YOU'RE LEARNING how to give your subpersonality less time on stage, you'll be able to spend more time feeling composed and in control. You'll be able to deal more effectively with stress, instead of responding by becoming aggressive or nonassertive. You'll have less reason to feel guilt or shame. In other words, you can spend more time in touch with your centered self.

And that's an exciting prospect. When we stay centered even under stress, our emotions no longer control us. Instead of reacting impulsively, we have the ability to remain calm and *think clearly*—and to use skills and adopt attitudes that build positive family relationships. We're more able to see clearly and discover that—even when behavior is challenging—our children really *do* yearn to grow and bring out their best.

Being in touch with the calmer, more capable part of ourselves is hardly a new experience, of course. We all move back and forth— sometimes within the same hour—among the three aspects of ourselves: lower self, centered self and higher self. Our goal is to spend less time at the bottom end, so we can have more time and ability to nurture and enjoy the family.

In the Three-Step Process, we've arrived at Step Three: Express the Centered Self. In the chapters ahead, you'll learn a variety of skills you can use when centered; each one will help you to create a family based on mutual respect. But before we explore those skills, there is something more fundamental we need to address. As noted in Chapter Two, it's the key ingredient for effective parenting.

What Matters More Than Skills?

Valuable as they are, skills alone are not sufficient. Parents who raise happy, secure and responsible children share something even more crucial: they hold *effective attitudes.* They believe in their children and have high, yet realistic expectations of them. If there is one thing I've learned during thirty-five years of working with parents, it is the power of attitudes. *Even when they have few skills,* parents who hold effective attitudes are more likely to have positive relationships with their children and far greater influence.

So what's an effective attitude?

The best way to get a feel for attitudes is to be on the receiving end. Imagine yourself in the adult situation below. How does the other person's attitude make you feel?

> *You're getting dressed in the evening, putting on an outfit you especially like. Your spouse walks into the bedroom and insists, "Don't wear that; it looks awful!"*

How does that approach make you feel about yourself? About your spouse?

More often than we realize, we talk to children that way. With the best of intentions—and without being conscious of it—we approach children and teens with an attitude that implies, "I don't need to show you respect."

Have you ever heard other parents or yourself say things like:

> *If you don't hurry up, I'm leaving without you.*

Don't act like you're helpless.

You're so bossy with your friends—no wonder they don't want to play with you at recess.

Why can't you get better grades, like your brother does?

Even if we *intend* to be helpful, approaching children that way leaves them feeling inadequate or resentful, just as the spouse felt in our example. What's more, these attitudes are ineffective; sooner or later, they fail to get the results we want.

Without realizing it, we learn these ways of approaching children during our own early years, and from the cultural attitudes that surrounds us. Then—despite our love and good intentions—we convey a message that says, "You don't deserve respect." In a child's mind, that message can easily translate to, "I'm not worthwhile; I'm not lovable."

How often have you heard other parents—or yourself—talk to children in an angry tone like this?

Dana, you're late for school again. Can't you ever be on time? Get a move on! You're as slow as molasses!

Imagine yourself as Dana. How does that make you feel?

Or imagine yourself as little Nick, lost in a daydream at the table after dinner, when your dad says in a critical voice:

Is your head in the clouds again? Why aren't the dishes in the sink? You're dreaming as usual; get in there and put the dishes away!

How does that feel? You'll probably clear the dishes, but *what does it do for your self-esteem?* How will you feel about *Dad?*

Parents have to set limits and help children be responsible, of course; that's not in question. It's the underlying attitude that makes all the difference. If our attitude says, "I can talk to you any way I want; I'm the parent," we create a very different atmosphere than if our attitude says, "I will treat you with respect even as I tell you I'm unhappy with what you're doing." Only the latter creates an atmosphere that encourages cooperation, supports self-esteem and brings out the child's best.

The Attitude of Mutual Respect

Every one of us, children and adults, wants to feel loved and valued. That can only happen when we *consistently treat each other with respect.* When we treat children in ways we would not want to be treated ourselves, the result is that they don't feel good about themselves—nor do they feel good about us. And they certainly don't feel like cooperating. We create an environment opposite to our desires: one that inhibits children from developing a sense of self-worth, responsibility and independence.

When we fail to treat *ourselves* with respect, we diminish our sense of self-worth and provide a negative model for our children. As mentioned previously, sometimes we even become afraid of our kids and give in to their every desire, at the cost of our own needs. We fail to set limits; we become nonassertive.

Either way, the underlying message is, "One of us doesn't deserve respect."

By contrast, the essence of the centered self is to hold an attitude of equality. That attitude reflects the understanding that "We treat each other with <u>equal</u> respect." Our age and experience are not equal, but we *can* see each other as equally worthy of respect.

What *Is* an Attitude?

You can think of an attitude as a picture you hold in your mind. If you have an image of yourself and your child or teen as two human beings, *equally* deserving of respect at all times, that's the attitude of equality. The simplest way to think of it is to remember the golden rule:

> *Treat your children as you would want to be treated.*
> *Teach your children to treat you the same way.*

It seems so basic—and it is. This is the foundation for creating an environment that brings out the best.

A child's first notion of self—"What sort of person am I?"—comes from the powerful mirror we provide as parents. Self-image develops from early experiences: "How am I treated?" "How am I touched and spoken to?" Whatever children experience, the message is internalized: "I must deserve to be treated that way."

Children sense our attitudes in all of our behavior: tone of voice, facial expressions, body language and touch, not just our words. What we say to them is important, but our subtle behaviors are even more powerful. Children have sensitive antennae: they know how we feel about them.

Children and teens are equally tuned in to the way we feel about ourselves. If we have doubts, children sense our uncertainty. If we feel confident, they sense that too. Researchers tell us that more than ninety percent of communication is nonverbal. Children, even more than adults, readily read these cues.

Another reason attitudes matter is that children learn how to treat others by watching us. The most powerful influence we have on our children is the behavior we model all through their formative years. *Nothing has a greater effect on them.* And the best model we can present is that of a person who consistently treats others as he or she would like to be treated.

When you talk with your children, listen for the attitude behind your words. If a friend or your spouse expressed that same attitude with *you,* would it be okay? That's the acid test.

When your boss notices you're late for work, would you prefer sarcasm:

> *I hope you had a good sleep!*

... or an open mind?

> *Is everything okay? You're thirty minutes late; we were concerned.*

When there's a difference of opinion, would you want to hear a negative judgment:

> *Why must you be so obstinate?*

... or a factual request?

I'm not sure I understand. Would you clarify your point of view?

Would you want to hear an order:

Go get the mail!

... or a request?

Would you pick up the mail, please?

Though it sounds simple, holding the attitude of equality *consistently* is not easy. But holding that attitude—following the golden rule—plants a powerful seed that blossoms to create rich rewards:

- We provide compelling, positive models for our children.
- Our children feel valued and respected .
- We communicate our needs clearly, without hidden negative messages.
- We help our children—and ourselves—to build self-esteem.
- We encourage children to remain centered rather than slip into lower-self behavior.
- We create an atmosphere that encourages children to become responsible and kind.

Examples of Mutual Respect

To get a quick feel for practicing mutual respect in everyday situations, let's look at ways to transform the negative examples we looked at earlier in this chapter.

Remember the mother who said,

Dana, you're late for school again. Can't you ever be on time? Get a move on! You're as slow as molasses!

If Mom were talking from her centered self, expressing the attitude of mutual respect, she might have said something like:

Dana, you haven't come down to breakfast yet and we're supposed to leave in ten minutes. I'm worried we're going to be late.

Mom's sense of urgency is the same, but her attitude is very different. She has no negative assumptions about her daughter; instead, she gives her a chance to say what's going on.

Remember Nick's dad, who said,

Is your head in the clouds again? Why aren't the dishes in the sink? You're dreaming as usual; get in there and put the dishes away!

If he were centered and holding the attitude of equality, Dad might have told his son:

I see the dishes are still on the table, Nick.

Nick might simply reply that he forgot, and put them away. But what if he protests? "I'm busy right now; I'll do them later." In that case Dad could remind him:

Remember the family agreements? We all agreed to clean the table right after dinner.

We're not talking about being a goody-goody; you don't have to be a saint. Nor does it mean becoming permissive, not in the least. It's simply a matter of *attitude*, of treating your children with genuine respect at *all* times—exactly as you'd like to be treated.

Holding onto Respect

You already practice mutual respect, I'm sure. The goal is to hold that attitude consistently. Let it become so much a part of you that you express it without thinking—even when everything goes wrong: when you're frustrated, under stress and you've absolutely had it.

To help parents in our *Quality Parenting* classes absorb the essence of mutual respect, I've created five characters that personify this attitude. Each character shows us how we can model mutual respect in a different area of potential conflict. (Remember in Chapter One we saw that every problem between parent and child reflects one of five core relationship issues.)

Together, these "centered-self" characters shed light on one of the great mysteries of parenting: how to deal with conflict respectfully.

The following pages describe the five characters and the mindset each brings to a key relationship issue. You'll discover how each character thinks, and you'll gain a more tangible feel for that point of view.

As you'll see, all five characters reflect the attitude of mutual respect. When you learn to hold that mindset consistently, you will create an atmosphere that encourages cooperation. And you'll provide a model that has a powerful influence on your children. At the heart of each character the essence remains the same: *treat others as you would like to be treated.*

Taking Stock

Let's pause for a moment and appreciate once more how far you've come. You've taken a giant step forward by learning to know your lower self, respecting the needs it reveals and practicing ways to remain centered more often.

Now, when you're calm and centered, you have an opportunity to see your children with new eyes, viewing them through the lens of mutual respect. Holding the attitude of mutual respect consistently allows you to model it daily and create an environment that brings out the best.

We want this attitude to permeate our thinking and become second nature. To help us in that process, we're about to meet the five "centered-self characters." Each addresses one of the five relationship issues; each gives us a clear model of the mindset of mutual respect. They're summarized in a chart on page 93.

Just before we begin that process, it would be wise to take one last look at the *attitudes* we'd like to shed. Unfortunately, we find them all around us, every day. While we might not hear these exact *words,* too often we recognize this mindset:

Because I said so!
It doesn't matter how you feel.
I'm not going to listen to you.
You couldn't be hungry; you just ate!
I don't believe you.
I'm the parent; I'll make the decisions.
I know what's true and what's best; you don't.

Hearing these attitudes all around us affects our thinking, *even when we don't realize it.* They can seem like the "normal" way to treat children. And, of course, many of us were raised in ways that we would not consider ideal today. Those attitudes inevitably become "second nature"—our "natural" way of relating to children.

In another era the same attitudes might well have been a step forward; each generation does the best it can. But too often they relied on power—and power inevitably leads to resentment and resistance; it teaches children that relationship is about domination.

If you want to make use of the best knowledge and wisdom of *our* generation and teach your children that relationship is about giving and receiving respect, then be on the lookout for *attitudes based on fear and control.* Tune your radar to detect them, especially in yourself. Inevitably, we all carry some of that thinking at times; the trick is to notice how we approach a situation and choose another way.

Will I Be a Pushover?

Some parents fear that treating children with respect means being permissive or becoming a doormat. The truth is quite the opposite: giving children respect provides a model of a healthy relationship; children mimic what they see. And, as you know by now, it's mutual: *we teach them to respect us in return.*

To gain a deeper feel for this mindset, let's take a closer look at the thinking of our guides, the five centered-self characters. As you study their approach, allow this attitude to permeate your thinking:

Children and parents are equally deserving of respect.

Mutual respect is the foundation for effective parenting.

Centered-Self Characters

ISSUE	CHARACTER
Authority *Who knows what's best?*	**LISTENER** *We respect each other's knowledge.*
Needs *Whose needs will be met?*	**HUMANIST** *We respect each other's needs.*
Perception *Whose point of view is right?*	**OBSERVER** *We respect each other's thoughts, feelings and perceptions.*
Control *Who should decide?*	**PRAGMATIST** *We respect each other's desire for autonomy.*
Expectations *How do we deal with expectations?*	**REALIST** *We respect each other's expectations and create family agreements.*

The Centered-Self Characters: A Closer Look

The Listener

We respect each other's knowledge.

Sadly, many of us don't really dialogue with our children. We talk *at* them.

If there is one skill that lays the foundation for respect, it's the skill of genuine listening. It's at the heart of creating an environment of mutual respect. Later, you'll learn the *skills* of listening; in this section you'll learn the attitude—the thinking behind it.

Each centered-self character listens with interest and respect. The Listener, dedicated to help us with the issue of Authority, plays a unique role. When the question arises, *Who knows what's best?* this character recognizes that we must make a major shift: we must acknowledge that parents are not the only ones with relevant information. The Listener affirms, *We respect each other's knowledge.*

Obviously, we're far more experienced and mature. But children have their own unique and separate lives. They experience their own bodies and reactions; we don't. While they share our homes, they also live in their own worlds. The older they are, the more time they spend in environments that we know little about. It's important to remember that children have a great deal of knowledge about themselves and their worlds—knowledge that we do well to respect.

In many areas, our children are the experts. Consider this story about my son:

> *It's summer and it's hot. I dress two-year-old Derek in short-sleeve shirts. To my great surprise, he complains bitterly, "I want my turtlenecks!" Everyone I talk with agrees, "He's odd!"*

Yet Derek remains consistent over the years. In the winter he wants short sleeves, in the summer, his turtlenecks. Surely Derek knew something about his body (or at least his preferences) that defied us all!

Obviously, we must use our knowledge to protect children from unsafe choices. But children know what they like and dislike, what is comfortable *for them* and what is not. They know how the world looks through their eyes—what *they* experience with friends and siblings and teachers, at school and at home. Their subjective worlds are filled with information that they know and we don't. Through skillful listening we can learn about and respect that world—an essential step if we hope to establish genuine communication.

And listening does something else: it opens our children so that we can teach them to listen to what *we* know. When children feel genuinely heard, they're more willing to take in *our* information and knowledge.

"I want some popcorn!" Tommy shouts. It's five o'clock and I plan to serve dinner at six. So I explain, "We'll have dinner in an hour; I don't want you to spoil your appetite." With complete certainty, Tommy replies, "There's no way the popcorn will spoil my appetite; I'm starving."

As the Listener, Mom is aware that Tommy is talking about *his* tummy, and *his* hunger. She realizes, "I wouldn't want anyone to tell me how *my* body feels." And so she listens to Tommy with respect and acknowledges what he says.

You're saying there's no need to worry.

Of course it's also our job to teach our child what *we* know. We want *our* knowledge respected, too. So Mom explains,

Tommy, I do have concerns. When you've had snacks so close to dinner, you've poked at your food and eaten very little. So I'm figuring the snacks must have spoiled your appetite. They certainly affect mine.

Listeners are not competing with their children. It's not about one-upmanship, trying to prove one's superior knowledge. Rather, the goal is to listen to your children and to teach them to listen to you—to model respect and expect it in return.

Respect changes the dynamics. Since you're not questioning your child's authority or denying your own, there's no need for a lower-self reaction. Tommy is free to think creatively.

> *I'm really in the mood for popcorn. Can I have just a handful?*

Mom then agrees readily, "Sure, help yourself." What might have deteriorated into a fight or tense feelings was amiably resolved.

The attitude of the Listener is a two-way street. Here's another example:

> *"Mom, I don't want to take voice lessons anymore!" Eight-year-old April had her mind made up. I wanted to blurt out, "This doesn't make any sense; you love to sing!" Instead, I said to myself, "Take it easy; try to relax." Then I acknowledged April: "Sounds like you want to stop taking lessons right now." "Yes. I hate my teacher; she's too strict."*
>
> *Now I had a clearer picture. "I'm wondering if the answer is to stop the lessons or to think about finding a new teacher— someone you might enjoy a lot more." April said nothing for a moment, but she seemed relieved. "Yeah, we could think about that. I just want to feel good when I sing."*

When we struggle with conflicts regarding knowledge, our willingness to listen proves essential. The Listener's symbol, the "receptive ear," represents the commitment to hear what others have to say.

Summing Up: the Listener

Listeners have a genuine interest in learning what their children know. They understand that children and teens have a great deal of knowledge about themselves and their worlds. Parents show respect for that knowledge by listening and acknowledging what their children share.

The Humanist

We respect each other's needs.

All week I'd been exhausted, desperate for sleep. If we didn't go home right away, I knew I'd have to be up all night to finish preparing for work. But Jamie was having such a great time in the park. He was finally playing well with the other kids. "Pleeease can we stay?" he begged. I felt so torn.

We've all been in situations that made us wonder if we should meet our children's needs—or our own. When we face the issue of Needs, we can find guidance in the character I call the Humanist. When the question arises, *Whose needs will be met?* the Humanist reminds us that our goal is to respect our children's needs and our own. The symbol for the Humanist is a handshake between parent and child. It portrays an agreement: *We respect each other's needs.*

The Humanist helps us clear up a common confusion. As parents, we know that sacrifice is required; but it's easy to go too far, ignoring our own needs so that we end up running on empty. Too often, parents confess they've agreed to a child's request only to regret it later.

Samantha begged for a sleepover. I had long-standing plans for that night with friends, but I thought, "I shouldn't deprive her of a fun time with her cousins." So I gave in. I stayed home—and ended up feeling resentful.

Oliver wanted to invite twenty-four kids to his birthday party. I knew that a group that large would get hyper and our condo was far too small. I'd be a wreck. Still, I'd feel like an ogre saying, no.

We've all done it: buying children things they want beyond the family budget, or becoming a perpetual chauffeur. Trying to meet our children's needs, we can neglect our own and end up feeling drained.

What our children need most is our genuine love and interest, our presence and aliveness. We can't give them that when we're depleted. Of course, we *do* sacrifice at times, that's a given. But we have to meet our own needs often enough to remain vibrant. Children need happy parents.

We have a responsibility to teach our children that adults, too, have needs. We want our children's respect as we attempt to meet our needs or their help if we request it. If we ignore this job, our children may become self-absorbed and insensitive to those around them. If we allow their wants to come before our needs, we help them to erect a monument of self-importance.

A mother of a teen told this story:

> *"Mom!" Sara shouted, "I'm gonna be late for the party!!! We have to leave right now!"*
>
> *She just turned fourteen and her emotions are so strong! In the past I would have put my needs aside, no matter what. But this time I said calmly, "I know you're eager to leave right now, but I have to go to the bathroom and can't wait. I'm sure you can understand; we'll leave in a few minutes." I know it's a small thing, but finally I'm respecting my needs as well as hers.*

Is It a Need—Or a Want?

We need to be careful, however; sometimes we use the word "need" when in fact our request is merely a want. For example, "I need you to get me the newspaper," is probably just a want. It's fine to make a request or ask for a favor, but it's no more than that. If you're capable of getting it yourself, it doesn't qualify as a need.

Sometimes we feel we do so much for our children that we have a right to order them around. Children feel the difference. Think about your own reaction. If someone said to you, "I need you to get me the newspaper," how would you feel?

In the same way, when our *child* makes a request, it's useful to distinguish between needs and wants.

Buy me some of those.
Why can't I have more?
But I really want it!
Pleeease—just a little bit more.

Children want *lots* of things—especially these days. It's our job to sort out their *wants* from their *needs*. There's no obligation to meet their wants.

Indulgence often creates an endless cycle: the more we give, the more children want. The more they have, the less appreciative they seem to be. And that can make us feel resentful, even as we spoil them.

The Humanist reminds us to listen with respect to children's desires, but fulfill them only when appropriate.

Needs are essentials, like food, safety and love. Children and adults require them in order to be healthy physically, emotionally and mentally. You're probably familiar with the *hierarchy of needs* described by the renowned psychologist, Abraham Maslow (see illustration below and the chart on the next page). The needs at the lower levels of his pyramid are fundamental: we can't survive well without them. Only when those are fulfilled can we focus on the higher level needs. Over a lifetime, all levels of needs must be met if we're going to realize our highest potential.

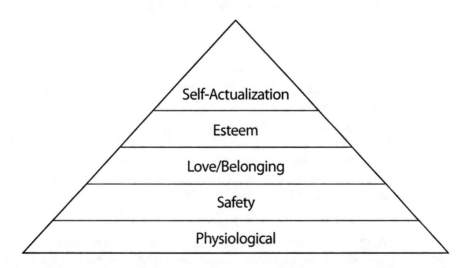

Human Needs

Physiological Needs

These are the basics: air, food, water, sleep, etc. Any time they're not met, discomfort motivates us to satisfy them as soon as possible. Once these needs are met, we're free to focus elsewhere. Babies model this cycle quite visibly.

Safety Needs

Humans have a strong need to feel safe. In all areas of our lives we try to establish a secure, stable and consistent environment. Home, family and school are the obvious key areas for our children. If they experience a chaotic, dysfunctional world, this heightened stress can negatively affect the very development of their brains! Until the need for psychological safety is satisfied, children cannot move on to meet higher needs.

Love and Belonging Needs

Once the first two needs are met, we experience a need for love and belonging. The experience of love is powerful: it enhances our physical, emotional and mental well-being. Belonging—feeling accepted by others—plays a major role in shaping our sense of self. A child's experience with peers can help to meet or to frustrate that need.

Esteem Needs

When parents and others value and respect us, we learn to value and respect ourselves. Parents help to build esteem when they spend time with their children and genuinely enjoy and value them. Recognition from siblings, relatives and peers helps to meet these needs as well.

We also acquire self-esteem by gaining competency: we learn to master tasks and then experience our own success. Parents and teachers who hold high, yet realistic expectations encourage children to achieve their best.

Self-Actualization

When all other needs are met, we experience the need to become all that we can be—to fulfill our highest potential. The best way to help children reach that place is by creating an environment of mutual respect. When their fundamental needs are satisfied, children will seek to realize their fullest potential.

Human beings are driven by needs. Much of our energy is spent trying to satisfy them. At any given moment, recognizing our own needs and those of our children is valuable; it helps us understand our behavior and find ways to model mutual respect.

Children focus on different needs at different stages. While an infant may be more involved with physical needs, a teen might be concerned with the need for the esteem of others. Each child tries to meet those needs in different ways. One might fulfill the need for esteem by having many friends, another might try by excelling in sports or perfecting artwork. Our job is to observe our children with interest and empathy—and discover what they need at each stage.

As we saw in Chapter Three, even the most difficult behavior is driven by unmet needs. The child's coping style may be ineffective or even destructive; yet, at the root of lower-self behavior is always an attempt to meet a legitimate need.

> *It happens right in front of me. Jake sticks out his foot when his baby brother walks by. At first, I want to send him to his room. Then I remember, "Okay; maybe he has a legitimate need." Becoming a bit calmer, I say, "Jake, sometimes I see you treat your brother so tenderly, but now I see you trying to trip him. I'm guessing that you're mad and there's probably a good reason for it. Am I right?" Jake explains, "He messed up my Lego tank; I worked so hard to build it just right!" I empathize, "That really upset you; I can understand that. But, you know, hurting your brother is not an okay way to solve the problem." Jake agrees, "I know. I should talk to him. And I'm thinking about putting my tank on the top shelf so he can't reach it"*

Summing Up: the Humanist

The Humanist helps us to be alert to our children's needs—and to our own. Sometimes that means listening and watching for needs that may not be obvious at first. It also means distinguishing needs from wants. First and foremost, it means teaching our children that we respect each other's needs, and do our best to help each other meet them.

The Observer

We respect each other's thoughts, feelings and perceptions.

> *Derek was seventeen; he was considering college choices. I offered enthusiastic advice: "A small school would be ideal. You'll get to know all the students and you'll get individual attention from the professors." Derek did his best to be patient with me. Then he explained, "Mom, that type of school would be perfect for you. You like small groups. I want a good school too, but I want a big one, with more facilities, great teams and leagues where I can play sports!"*

Derek showed me that he and I were approaching this decision from very different perspectives. That's the starting point for real communication: the recognition that there is more than one way of responding to an experience. Unless we can recognize the other person's world, we have little hope for understanding each other.

When the issue is Perception—*Whose point of view is right?*—the Observer offers simple wisdom: *We respect each other's thoughts, feelings and perceptions.* By imagining ourselves in the other person's shoes, identifying with their world, we open the door to communication and understanding. As we'll soon discover, that enables us to know our children at a deeper level.

How It's Done

If we truly want to hear and appreciate another person's experience, the first step is to put aside our bias and preconceived notions. The symbol for the Observer illustrates this process: we *empty our minds*—temporarily—to make room for another person's view.

How do I empty my mind? It's not something we're used to doing. Without even realizing it, we bring our personal views and agendas to most situations; it's the "natural" thing to do. It takes some effort to put our views aside, for the moment, and be completely open to hearing another perspective.

That's all it takes: our conscious intent. As we prepare to talk with our child or teen, we can tell ourselves, "I will put aside my judgments and preconceived ideas about my child or this situation. I will make my mind a blank slate. I will be available and open to my child, as if meeting him or her for the first time."

> *Twelve-year-old Cynthia was discouraged and upset, "My science project still looks lame and I've worked on it for weeks." My first impulse was to reassure her. Instead, I showed respect by acknowledging her feelings: "You're very disappointed; you put in a lot of effort and you don't think it shows." Having heard and acknowledged Cynthia's perception, I switched back to my own. "If it's okay with you, I'd like to tell you what I see." Once she agreed, I said, "The information in the report and the colorful graphics seem impressive to me."*

> *"All I need is ten minutes to study for my spelling test," Kevin says confidently. "I'll play now and study just before I go to bed." I had doubts about Kevin's estimate, but didn't want to impose my view. Instead I acknowledged my son's evaluation respectfully. "You're saying ten minutes should be ample time to prepare for your test—so it will be fine to continue playing." Kevin nodded his head. Having heard his thoughts, I decided to share my own. "I'm thinking about last time. Remember? You started studying just before you went to bed, and it took longer than you expected. Then you grumbled at me when I insisted that you go to bed on time." Kevin looked sheepish. Moments later he said, "Okay, I'll study now, but I'm going to have extra time to play before I have to turn off the lights."*

When parent and child both feel that their point of view is understood and respected, the stage is set for a truly productive discussion.

Again, the skills you'll need are in later chapters; what matters now is the mindset.

Who Is This Child—Really?

> *I express my frustration and anger, "You tell me you're doing your homework and I hear you on the phone with your girlfriend. I want to believe you care about raising your grades, but now I feel let down." Fifteen-year-old Sandra yells, "Why don't you ever believe me?" I tell myself to slow down; I take a deep breath to become calm. Sandra continues, "I was on the phone with Kathleen. She's a math wiz; I asked her to help and she explained how to make sense out of algebra." I'm embarrassed. "You're right; I jumped to conclusions without listening. I'm really sorry."*

When we empty our heads, we're able to discover who our children really are—revising the picture or fantasy we hold of them.

This mom learned a lot about her daughter just by listening with an open mind:

> *I've always admired my older daughter's ease with people; Bethany seems at home with everyone. But as I listened while my kids were chatting after Thanksgiving dinner, I was astounded. Saro, the younger one, confessed, "Bethany, sometimes I envy you; you can talk to anyone and I can't do that. When Grandma asks me about school or anything, I just sit there like a lump." Bethany's response shocked us both. "Don't be fooled. Sure, I can talk, but half the time I feel like I'm putting on an act—like it's not the real me. And that feels awful."*

Becoming a blank slate at times—putting aside our judgments and opening our minds—allows us to move beyond our habitual way of seeing. It helps us to understand our children as they evolve and change, day by day.

The Observer reminds us that all children are unique, deserving respect for their own thoughts, feelings and points of view.

But that's only half the story.

It Goes Both Ways

> *Eight-year-old Jesse is quite proud of his independence these days. "You're not my boss!" he said, turning away from me. I wanted him to do his eye exercises. An hour later, when I was calm, I said, "I only asked if you remembered to do the exercises by yourself. I felt hurt when you yelled at me and disappeared. I just want your eyes to get stronger, as I know you do." He softened a little; I knew he understood. Soon after, we were able to talk respectfully.*

Children and teens need to understand our point of view, of course. The Observer reminds us that it's our job to teach our children that we, too, want our feelings, thoughts and perceptions respected.

Summing Up: the Observer

We all see the world through different eyes. The Observer helps us to respect those differences—and to teach our children to do the same. What makes that possible is a mindset free of judgments or expectations: a "blank slate" that allows us to truly see and hear our children.

The Pragmatist

We respect each other's desire for autonomy.

Imagine that your spouse, partner or friend tells you where you are allowed to go and where you can't go. Also, what you can eat, what friends you can see and what time to go to bed. How would you feel?

Children live much of the time in this restricted world. Can you sense how powerless they must feel? Everyone else is bigger, older and more imposing. Someone else decides what they can do today—and nearly everything else in their lives. (No wonder children are fans of powerful super-heroes.) If there's something they *can* control, like what to wear or what to eat for breakfast, they often guard that power jealously. They have strong feelings about it. If an adult tries to take away that power, well—there's a recipe for conflict.

Who should decide? Clearly, parents have to make decisions much of the time. Still, when the issue is about Control, the Pragmatist offers sound advice: *We respect each other's desire for autonomy.* As the symbol suggests, parents and children want to steer their own lives as much as possible. Since we want our children to become capable and independent, we give them opportunities to make real decisions as often as practical.

By the age of eighteen, we want our children to be capable of making the minor and major decisions that determine the course of their lives. Obviously, we can't expect them to learn that skill suddenly, on their eighteenth birthday. We need to give them opportunities that are age-appropriate throughout their lives.

Whenever possible, Pragmatists support their children's independence. When toddlers want to exert their mastery by feeding themselves, we provide foods they can manage easily. When children or teens make suggestions for how to spend their time or money, we listen with an open mind and support their ideas whenever practical.

Sure, we can go to the park; that would be fun.

Yes, we can see if there's a dance class for you; let's see what kind of classes there are and when they meet.

For younger children, we can offer choices:

Do you want to wear your blue sweater or your green one?

As children get older, we can seek their input whenever possible:

These are the summer camps we've explored. Let's discuss them so we can think about which one sounds most appealing?
(vs. *Here's the camp you're going to.*)

Let's talk about what clothes you'd like before we go shopping; then we'll think about where to go.
(vs. *Here's what I bought.*)

Let's talk about some after-school activities and see what you'd like best.
(vs. *I signed you up for soccer; I thought you'd like it.*)

In a family I know, everyone takes turns deciding what "fun activity" they'll do on the weekend. They have a rotating chart, so it's clear whose turn it is. On Sunday afternoons, everyone agrees to participate in the activity that person chooses.

A system like that may or may not appeal to you, but it does have certain advantages: it gives each family member a voice. Each person's tastes and preferences make an imprint on family life. When diversity is respected, a wider and richer range of opportunities becomes available to all.

When children feel respected, when they're given choice in their lives, their feelings of being powerless diminish; they see themselves as capable rather than as victims. They're less likely to be angry and rebellious when they're older. (If that doesn't motivate you, nothing will!)

When my son was in middle school, he expressed that idea in a way that made me laugh—once I recovered from the shock:

I feel really out of it, Mom. All the kids bad-mouth their parents; they're on their case all the time. But you're always so reasonable. I don't have a reason to rebel!

Think of a child who has felt controlled all of her life. When she approaches the teen years, with more time away from parental supervision, she may release her anger and "get back" at Mom and Dad by rebelling and becoming manipulative. Of course teens rebel for all sorts of reasons, but the rebellion is less likely to be extreme when the teen has felt respected and empowered.

This is one of the ways we can be sensitive to our children: recognizing their desire to have some power—to help steer their own lives. And when we're sensitive to our children, they become more sensitive to us.

Who Decides?

Of course there are decisions we make in our children's interests, whether they agree or not. But more often than we think, it's possible to give them a real voice in deciding. Even if a decision turns out badly, the child has an opportunity to learn by experiencing the consequences. With each decision, children become more capable, more able to make wise choices.

Parents often hesitate to trust their children: "Finish your homework as soon as you come home. Then you can play." The Pragmatist reminds us that children thrive on autonomy and trust. Sometimes children know themselves better than we know them. Finishing work before playing might be best for some children; others might do better by unwinding after school and doing homework a little later.

Trusting children means being open, listening with genuine interest to understand their point of view—and then giving them real opportunities to make choices and succeed. If they come through, everyone wins. Help them to make that happen.

If children betray our trust, that's another matter. Then we continue our dialogue, expressing our concern, and listening with genuine curiosity to discover what went wrong. Ideally, we can create another plan together.

Of course we can't always agree with our children's choices. When we say no, we show respect by providing a clear explanation for our objections.

Here's how a dad answered his daughter's request to sleep at her friend's house on Friday night:

> *I know you'd like to sleep at Lisa's, but I can't let you go when her parents aren't available to supervise; it wouldn't be safe.*

Dad listened with respect and acknowledged his daughter's request. When he couldn't agree, he explained the reason for his refusal.

The Benefits

When children have more opportunities to make decisions, they benefit in many ways. They spend less time in the lower self: they're less needy and demanding. They learn how to make wise choices, feel more capable and more independent. And hopefully, they'll have less reason to rebel in extreme ways.

We Like Steering Too

As in all issues of respect, it's a two-way street; adults *also* want to steer their own lives. The Pragmatist reminds us to teach our children to respect *our* choices.

> *Mom explains to seven-year-old Robyn, "I'm going to take a dance class on Wednesday nights. I don't like being away when you're home, but dancing means a lot to me. I need the exercise and the recreation. I'm excited; I heard the teacher is great."*

Children and teens need to know that we have lives in addition to our roles as parents. Sometimes our activities will take time away, yet it's important that we pursue our interests so that we feel whole and fulfilled. Then we're more likely to bring our best selves to parenting.

When we ignore our own interests and goals—whether social, creative or simply recreational—we're likely to feel deprived and resentful. Inevitably, that will affect the way we treat our children.

Children need happy parents. And they need positive models.

When I made the decision to earn a Ph.D., I feared that I was taking something away from Derek. While it did take a great deal of time, we often did our homework together. We talked about the dream I was pursuing—and about his dreams. Now, in hindsight, I've discovered what a powerful influence it had on him. Derek saw my tenacity, hard work and devotion to achieving my dream. He saw me as a strong woman; he had never seen that side before. As a young adult, he told me that it influenced the course of his own life.

Just as we support our children, they can put aside their priorities at times to support us. If Mom is going to school, they can help by doing more chores. Parents and older children can help each other with school projects.

It's all a matter of finding the right balance, of course, depending on the child's age. But try to integrate some of your world into the family—rather than centering everything on the child, then doing your work late at night or at the crack of dawn.

When we help children to tune in to someone else's priorities, they become less self-centered. Children need that experience, to gain empathy (one of the most beautiful and important qualities) and to mature into caring people.

Make an effort to share with your children more of who you are. Bring those things you love into your home whenever appropriate. Don't keep your world a secret; tell and show them what you do when you're not with them. The way you live your life models your values. Help your children understand you as a whole person. The more they know you, the more their experience is enriched. They gain a more expansive picture of the choices that exist for them.

Summing Up: the Pragmatist

Pragmatists recognize how important it is for children to have some control over their lives. They give them opportunities to make decisions and encourage their suggestions whenever appropriate. Pragmatists also want to direct their own lives. As fulfilled parents, they bring positive energy to the family and serve as powerful models. By empowering their children and themselves, they create an environment that supports both independence and cooperation.

The Realist

We respect each other's expectations and create family agreements.

What do we expect of our children?
What do we expect of ourselves?
What do our children expect of us?
What do our children expect of themselves?

Though we may not be aware of it, we hold many expectations of our children and of ourselves. And what we expect has a powerful effect on our thoughts, feelings and behavior.

When our expectations are not met, we're likely to feel disappointed. And when our children's expectations of themselves or others are not met, they also feel let down. To help us deal with those difficult times, we can find a model in the Realist, the centered-self character for the issue of Expectations. The Realist affirms, *We respect each other's expectations and create family agreements.*

For example, parents often hold expectations like these:

Children and teens will ...
  • tell the truth
  • do their homework
  • say "please" and "thank you"
  • brush their teeth

These expectations reveal our values, guide our behavior and help us organize our lives. On the other hand, children's expectations often reveal their needs and wants.

Children may expect that we will ...
- follow through on promises
- love them
- buy them clothes and toys
- spend time with them

We all have expectations of ourselves. Some relate to our role in the family, others may not.

Children may expect themselves to ...
- make friends
- do well in sports
- get good grades
- take care of their pets

We may expect ourselves to ...
- earn an adequate income for the family
- stay in shape
- be well liked
- save money for the future

Were You Pleased? Or Disappointed?

When we meet our own expectations, we feel pleased, of course. The parent who gets a promotion or the child who hits a double feels proud.

The challenge comes when our expectations—or our children's—are *not* met. Dad groans,

> *Three weeks in a row I've had to miss our golf game! When will I see my friends? I need a break!*

Nick complains,

> *Bummer! I studied so hard—and only got a C on the test!*

When we feel frustrated, unable to meet our own expectations—or we hear our children's frustration—it's easy to slip to the lower self: we may blame ourselves, others or life itself.

Nick's father rose above this when he heard his son's complaint and modeled respect:

> *You worked hard, Nick, and you expected to do much better.*

The Realist reminds us to treat ourselves kindly, as Nick's dad treated him, and acknowledge our disappointment. It's not a "poor me" mindset; it's simply respect for our feelings at the moment. We can tell ourselves, "It's frustrating to look forward to something and not have it happen." That kind of self-talk shows respect. It also can help us to calm down, freeing up energy to create a better plan for tomorrow.

Meeting My Expectations—and Yours

> *Coming home from work was becoming unpleasant. Getting dinner ready often took too long and we all became cranky; evenings were filled with tension. Finally, my daughter and I brainstormed and created an agreement: I'd prepare a meal beforehand, and she would heat it up. Then we'd be able to eat much earlier. Before work, I put a note on the fridge, with the details Sophia needed. When I walked in the door at 5:30, the tempting aroma and my daughter's proud grin warmed my heart.*

When we meet expectations, we feel we can count on each other. Trust is built—and that's the very essence of family.

But it's hard to meet expectations when they're not clear—when we don't really know what they are. It's surprising how often that happens.

What Does Your Child Expect?

> *Three-year-old Eddie was delighted with his new pair of children's scissors; he loved learning to use them. One day when he was alone in the dining room, he carefully trimmed about two inches all the way around the bottom of his Mom's best tablecloth. He expected to be praised for cutting straight.*

Imagine his surprise and shock when he discovered that Mom did not approve!

Even older children may have expectations quite different from ours:

> *Carina's sixth birthday is a week away—seven long days to wait for the party. Some presents arrive in the mail; Carina is thrilled and excited. After dinner Carina announces, "It's time, I'm going to open my presents!" I'm astonished. "Where did she get such an idea?"*

> *Eleven-year-old Jason and I agreed to meet at the bus stop. When he didn't show up, I panicked; I even called the police. After we found each other and calmed down, I discovered that Jason expected me to meet him at the bus stop near school. I expected him to take the bus and I'd pick him up near home. I was amazed that our expectations were so different!*

Children and teens often think quite differently than we do; the result can be distressing. Still we want to model respect. Being curious—putting judgment aside—helps us stay calm as we attempt to discover the world in which they live.

In the story above, Carina reasoned that birthday time was all about *her*. "If they're *my* presents, why can't I open them?" The exact day meant nothing to her; she'd get more presents then, anyway.

In the story about the school bus, it turned out that there was a video store by the bus stop near school. When Mom said "bus stop," Jason thought about the store, imagined the fun it would be to look around and assumed that had been their agreement.

But I Thought You Meant ...

We can't meet expectations if we don't know what they are. If we want to build a family based on trust, expectations must be clear and explicit. The more we spell them out in detail, the more likely we are to succeed.

- Mom had assumed that Eddie knew it was wrong to cut the tablecloth. If she had told him where it was appropriate for him to use his scissors, his upset and hers could have been avoided.
- If Jason and his mom had been more explicit, naming streets and estimating the meeting time, it's likely the misunderstanding would not have occurred.
- Sophia's success in having dinner ready can be credited, in part, to the clarity of the expectations and the concrete reminders that supported her accomplishment.

Family Agreements

A wonderful way to encourage success and to clarify everyone's expectations is to create a family agreement. Has the family experienced problems around bedtime or chores? Do you fear problems may surface in other areas? To solve existing problems and to prevent new ones, it's helpful to arrange a family meeting. It's an opportunity for everyone to talk openly about their expectations, work out differences and ultimately to make agreements. Once made, the family agreements should be *written down*. Be specific and thorough for the best results—and for future reference.

Here's an actual agreement that spells out the "ground rules" or guiding principles for the family. It's a clear statement of this family's values.

How Our Family Works

- In family discussions, all ideas will be listened to with respect and without interruption. Each person has something valuable to offer.
- We use respectful language (no name-calling or cursing).
- When there is a conflict, all family members have the right to take breaks from a discussion, as long as they state a specific time when they will return to work on resolving the conflict.
- Before using or borrowing someone else's things, we always ask. The owner has the right to say no.
- Privacy is respected. We knock on a family member's door and wait for permission before we enter.
- We value time together as a family. We have agreed that Sundays from 5 pm–9 pm is reserved for family time. The answering machine is on and cell phones are turned off. Part of this time we hold our family meeting and plan for the week ahead.
- Each of us has family chores. The Chore Chart spells out the details—who does what, and when it must be done. Trades can be made only if both parties agree. Two people can work as a team if both agree.
- Our family will volunteer for a minimum of 2 hours of community service work each month. Each member agrees to contribute money to charity monthly, the amount to be discussed in the family meeting.
- We have agreed to support each other's activities and interests. Every effort is made by all family members to attend each other's sports events, recitals, etc.
- We agree that each family member will have no more than one "sugary" treat per day.
- Children are allowed one hour of TV on a school day, after chores and homework are complete. Under the same conditions, two hours of TV are allowed on non-school days.
- Computer can be used for homework. Computer games can be played only on the weekends, limited to two hours per day.
- Parents must approve the use of all Internet sites. Emails and IM's (instant messages) are acceptable from known friends only.
- Family car and other transportation needs are requested at the family meeting.

Another way to use a family agreement is to address a specific problem. In the example below, the parents and children wanted to create a better bedtime routine: less yelling and a full half hour for story time. To help everyone relax and stay on track, they decided to write down their goals:

Bedtime Goals

1. Guinea pigs fed, watered and covered.
2. Toys from living room put into baskets or on a shelf in bedroom.
3. Pajamas on.
4. Clothes for next school day picked out.
5. Teeth brushed, hands and faces washed.
6. Use toilet.
7. Books picked out.
8. Nee and Baubu are put in children's beds.
9. Story time for half an hour.
10. Family hugs.

You can create a family agreement in any form that suits you. The key to success is to design it with the full participation of everyone (who's old enough) in the family.

Do we really need to write it down? Parents are often reluctant to talk through and write a formal agreement. It does take time and patience to insure that everyone's ideas are truly respected. Yet the rewards are more than worth the effort. It's amazing what can happen when everyone's "picture" of the family is in sync—when agreement is reached and expectations are clear.

So When Shall We Write It?

It's never too early to begin developing a family agreement. I know a couple that during their engagement period started thinking in some detail about their ideal family! That doesn't happen often, but it probably should. During pregnancy is another great time, when a myriad of new decisions need to be made.

What's that you're saying? Your children are older and you still don't have a family agreement? Relax, you're in the majority. You can always create one when you feel the need.

Whenever you get ideas, write them down! There's nothing like a written "contract" to clarify your ideas and watch them mature over time. A family agreement will *always* be a work in progress, to be modified as children grow, parents learn and life presents new challenges.

The skills and exercises throughout this book will help you to clarify your thoughts and engage your children in this democratic process— so that ultimately you can create a family agreement based on mutual respect. Ideally, it can be a lifelong project, changing and evolving as the family matures.

Summing Up: the Realist

The Realist reminds us that parents and children have expectations of themselves and of each other. Expectations serve a useful purpose, providing goals and guidelines.

We feel good about family members and ourselves when expectations are met. But even when we're disappointed, parents and children deserve to be treated with respect. We increase the likelihood that expectations will be met when we make them explicit; the more detail, the better the odds. When problems have occurred, family agreements can spell out new guidelines to help insure that changes will be made. Written agreements are also useful for clarifying and expressing the family's core values.

Five Characters, One Attitude

All through our years as parents, we'll face these questions again and again:

> *Who knows what's best?*
> *Whose needs will be met?*
> *Whose point of view is right?*

Who should decide?
How do we deal with expectations?

The way we answer these questions significantly affects the quality of our family life. Each addresses one of the five core relationship issues. The more we're able to identify with the centered-self characters, the more consistently we can model mutual respect.

In Chapter Seven, these characters and their thinking will be available in the form of a Help Chart. When you face a problem, the chart will help you find a respectful and effective way to approach that issue. In later chapters you'll also learn skills; they'll help you prevent and resolve problems.

In a Nutshell: Mutual Respect

In this chapter we've seen a glimpse of the potential we have when we're centered more often: we have the ability to be objective, to listen openly without judging and to express our own needs clearly. We're at the beginning of our exploration of Step Three: Express the Centered Self.

With ever-greater frequency, we can treat our children and teens as we would want to be treated. And as we give our children respect, we can teach them to give it in return.

When we're consistent in modeling mutual respect—even when our children and teens test us severely—we create an atmosphere that invites them to respect themselves, others and us. Self-esteem grows, for them and for us.

That word "consistent" is the key. Holding onto mutual respect in the rough and tumble of daily life can be difficult. In the next two chapters, we'll look more closely at how and why most of us slip—and what we can do to be more effective more often. Later chapters will explore specific skills: assertion, listening, planning and problem solving. They'll provide the tools to help you build the relationships you want: an environment that brings out the best in everyone, a family truly based on mutual respect.

CHAPTER 6

Losing Respect:

Ineffective Communication

*If there is anything we wish to change in the child,
we should first examine it and see whether it is not something
that could better be changed in ourselves.*

—Eleanor Roosevelt

A FEW YEARS AGO there was a popular T-shirt with these words printed boldly across the chest: *Because I'm the parent. That's why!* Something about that felt satisfying: it expressed the frustration of dealing with kids who resist us. And it was meant as a joke. Or was it?

Deep down, most of us in this culture hold the belief that when there's a difference in point of view, children should take direction from parents. Period. When children or teens challenge us, listening or negotiating might feel as if we're coddling—being overly submissive. We have those feelings because there's an old paradigm in our culture that tells us, in effect, "Parents should take charge." What that really says is, "Control kids through power." But power creates fear, resentment and, ultimately, rebellion. Mutual respect is far more effective: it encourages cooperation, self-esteem and responsibility.

Of course children *do* need our guidance and direction. When a three-year-old bolts into traffic, our immediate response is not to sit down and have a discussion. We will take charge, not out of anger, but for the child's safety.

But most of the time we don't need to throw our weight around and give orders. We sometimes feel as if our only choice is to exercise full power—or give up and let the children be in charge—as if there were nothing in between. There *is* another option, of course: we can speak to our children's higher nature by relating to them with mutual respect. In the long run, it makes our job much easier. But until we build that habit, it's a challenge to practice it consistently.

When Respect Slips Away

Why should it be difficult to act with mutual respect? After all, we practice it every day with friends, co-workers and, hopefully quite often, with our children. It's easy, right? Wrong! After working with parents for thirty-five years, I can tell you that expressing mutual respect consistently is one of the most difficult challenges parents face.

It *is* easy to respect our children when we're in a good mood and there's not much at stake. But think of situations like these:

- You ask a child to take care of an overdue chore and he says, "No. I'm busy now."
- Your child asks, "Can I sleep over at Pat's tonight?" You explain, "No, Grandma's coming." Your child replies, "I don't care; I'd rather be with my friend."
- You make a request: "I need you to set the table now." Your child retorts, "I'm not your slave!"

Whoa! Why should we respect children when they're not respecting us? Why not use our power? After all, we're the adults.

Power Has Consequences

We're older, and we have more experience than our children or teens. Why not exercise our power, rather than taking the time to listen to their feelings, concerns and points of view—especially when they're being unreasonable or rude?

The problem with using power is that it creates some highly undesirable consequences. It may achieve our goal in the short run, but it often leaves children feeling resentful. Sooner or later they respond by withdrawing from us or becoming rebellious. If they comply because of fear, that fear will diminish as they grow older and more powerful themselves. Then look out: you've sown the seeds for trouble. Resentful of power, children may cope by developing difficult behaviors, especially as they enter adolescence.

And what are we modeling for children when we relate to them by wielding our power? They're certainly not learning to treat themselves or others with respect. Sooner or later they're likely to emulate us, and learn to relate by dominating others. These are hardly lessons we want to teach.

So what can we do, when children or teens don't show respect for *us*?

We can be quite clear about why that's not okay, how it feels and what we want. The skills of assertion and reflection (Chapters Eight through Ten) enable us to do that effectively—even as we express mutual respect. We can stand up for our needs and feelings *and* model respect for theirs (that's why it's called mutual, of course). We can learn how to hold onto respect even when it's difficult. But that calls for a major change in thinking.

Why Respect Gets Lost

It happens when children resist us. As in the examples above, we want something to happen (or not happen) and our child or teen is saying, "No way!" That's when respect can go out the window. Our patience is stretched too thin; we shoot from the hip and wield our power. We don't know what else to do. (Besides, power has some tempting payoffs: in addition to getting our way, we have a chance to vent our feelings and feel big and mighty.)

But respect can also get lost in situations where there *is* no stress. Too often, we talk to children in ways that fail to model respect. We hold attitudes that have negative effects—and we don't even realize it. It happens because we're not aware that certain "loving and helpful" ways of relating actually communicate the opposite of respect.

That's what the rest of this chapter is about: becoming aware of how you communicate in your family—discovering the attitudes you hold. That awareness will reveal areas in which you can grow. Then you'll be prepared for the chapters ahead: learning how to express mutual respect more consistently.

Sending the Wrong Message

Since none of us is perfect, we tend to communicate in ways that are less than ideal at times. It isn't pleasant to see that; it takes courage to recognize our own shortcomings. But that's what it takes to grow—and to create a family that encourages cooperation, independence and responsibility. The rewards are more than worth the effort. So take a deep breath. Here we go.

Do you ever find yourself using some of these communication styles?

Ineffective Communication Styles
(Aggressive)

- Order
- Threaten
- Reassure
- Flatter
- Divert (others)
- Advise
- Analyze
- Probe
- Lecture
- Label (others)

Each of these ways of relating reflects an attitude of *inequality*. Believe it or not, each one is actually *aggressive* behavior. Though our intentions may be good as gold, using these communication styles sends a deprecating message to a child: *You don't deserve my respect.*

Many parents find that hard to accept; some of these approaches seem benign or even positive. So—let's take a closer look at each one.

We can all agree that to *order* or *threaten* sends a message that fails to model respect. Would you want someone to say to you, "Don't talk that way!" or "Do it now or else," or "No TV for you tonight!"?

But what's wrong with *reassure* or *flatter*? Aren't these respectful ways to communicate?" Yes, they are—when your child is feeling comfortable and no problem exists. When she proudly shows you her schoolwork, there's certainly nothing wrong with offering honest praise. The problem occurs when a child is upset—and we ignore those feelings:

> *Cary comes home from school, sinks into a chair looking miserable and moans, "I've blown it. I think I bombed out on my geometry test." Mom keeps moving as she does her chores, saying, "Oh, you probably did fine. You always do better than you think."*

How does Cary feel? Dismissed, not believed. She's worried and concerned, but Mom's comments suggest that her feelings don't count. Has that ever happened to you when you're having a hard time? Friends quickly quiet you ("I'm sure it'll be fine"), without hearing your feelings. You feel cut off: not really heard.

Mom has good intentions, but her quick attempt to *reassure* seemed to say, "You're making a fuss over nothing; just exaggerating." Real communication is blocked; an opportunity for closeness is missed.

Flattery has a similar effect, when children or teens are upset with themselves or a situation. Jill stares in the mirror dolefully and says, "I look awful!" Mom replies cheerfully, "Don't be ridiculous; you look great, honey." Instead of feeling reassured, Jill may scream inside, "I just said I feel awful about myself. Won't she ever hear my feelings?" Jill learns that Mom isn't someone who will listen when she's feeling down.

It's hard for us when our children have problems; we hurt as we sense their pain. To make them—and ourselves—feel better, we may try to *divert* them by dismissing their feelings: "Oh, it's nothing. You worry too much." Or we change the subject: "Let's rent a video." Children sense that powerful parts of themselves—their feelings—are not accepted. And so they stop coming to us when they're upset. Or, even worse, they shut down and close off their ability to feel.

Other times, we try to help by giving *advice* that deprives children of the opportunity to work out their own problems: "You should change your study habits. Crack the books as soon as you're home from school; that's what I did." It may be good advice, but when we put in our two cents before children have a chance to think for themselves, we're being aggressive by interfering. We do it because we're anxious to protect them from mistakes—but mistakes are valuable opportunities for learning.

When we interject advice too often, the message a child or teen may hear is, "You're not capable of handling that on your own. I don't trust you." That doesn't help a young person's self-esteem.

Sometimes we go even further. We ...

- *Analyze:* "You did that to upset me."
- *Probe:* "What did you say that made her so angry?"
- *Lecture:* "You should learn to plan your time better."

Once again, we try to work out their problems, without giving them a real chance to struggle and find their own answers. Despite our genuine caring, they receive that same negative message: "You can't handle it; I'll take over."

Remember, the way children gain strength and become independent is by grappling with their own problems. Our job is to support and facilitate them in this process. We support them by trusting that they can find their own solutions and giving them the time and space to sort out their ideas. We facilitate by caring and showing interest, by respecting their process and reflecting without judging. For example: "So you're saying it's a good idea to study with Pat, that you'll help each other stay focused."

One of the least effective ways of communicating is to *label* a person: "Don't be lazy," or, "You're so selfish." Instead of complaining about their behavior, we label their whole *character* as faulty. We might as well say, "You're a defective person." What we mean is, "Your behavior is not acceptable; please change it."

The Hidden Message

We noted earlier that when parents use these aggressive communication styles, they send an *unintended* message to a child. Children are highly sensitive to the attitudes—the judgments and feelings—behind our words. Each style sends a different, specific message:

What's the Hidden Message?

Communication Style (Aggressive)	Hidden Message
Order, Threaten	*It's my way or else!*
Reassure, Flatter	*I can't tolerate negative feelings; you should always be happy.*
Divert	*I won't listen to that; you can't talk about it.*
Advise, Analyze, Probe, Lecture	*I'll take charge; you're not capable.*
Label	*There's something wrong with you.*

Obviously, messages like these discourage open communication and hurt the relationship. They deprive us of opportunities to have a real exchange of ideas, to know our children in greater depth and to help them learn and grow. They undermine our child's self-esteem—and ultimately our own.

Often we don't intend to send those messages. When we use ineffective communication styles, we may have no idea we're doing it. And that raises a serious question: how can we change something if we're not aware of it?

The answer, of course, is to become aware: each of us needs to discover the unique ways in which we use these aggressive styles, thus slipping into an attitude of inequality. Then we'll have the choice to find better ways.

So let's take an even closer look, to get a clear view of what needs improving.

Mighty Parent

Look again at the communication styles in the previous chart. Can you imagine how each might be experienced by a child as aggressive? Despite the parents' good intentions, the child hears Mom or Dad saying, *You must respect me, but I don't have to respect you.* Children easily sense that and feel diminished. Though the parents are often well meaning, these aggressive styles reflect the attitude I call *Mighty Parent.*

Mighty Parent

For example:

> *Martin comes home from school complaining, "Mrs. Peters is so mean! She kept me in for recess!" Dad says immediately, "What did you do <u>this</u> time?"*

Dad has every right to be concerned; it looks like Martin has misbehaved—again. But if you were Martin, how would you feel? He came home bursting to let out feelings—dying to tell his side of the story. But Dad sounds like his mind is closed: his son is guilty. Martin will probably clam up. He's likely to feel bad about himself and angry with Dad. Sadly, he may decide that he can't count on Dad to listen when he's upset.

A more effective approach would be for Dad to acknowledge Martin's feelings and say, "You really sound upset. I'd like to hear what happened." By doing a lot of listening—and no judging—Dad would learn more about his son: not only how he feels, but how he looks at the situation and *how his mind works.* Martin would have a chance to air his feelings and would feel respected; he would then be more open to hearing Dad's thoughts. In this open atmosphere, a useful dialogue could occur. Martin would have an opportunity to release his feelings, sort out his thoughts, hear another perspective and gain some insight—a chance to grow from the situation.

Here's another example:

> *Seven-year-old Margaret gives her mom a list of friends she wants to invite to her birthday party. Mom looks it over and says, "You've left out Jennifer; you can't do that. You'll have to include her; she invited you to her party."*

So what's wrong with Mom's approach? She means well; she's trying to teach her daughter etiquette and empathy. Doesn't she have a right to do that? Of course she does. But imagine you're Margaret and it's your party; then look again at Mom's response. She *orders* you to take the "right" action. She *lectures* you. She leaves no room for *your* point of view to be heard. You're wrong. Period. *Mighty Parent, mini child!*

Mom will be far more effective if she treats her daughter as she would want to be treated herself. In any disagreement, wouldn't Mom want *her* point of view to be heard?

Suppose Mom was to say, with genuine interest, "I see you didn't include Jennifer. I'm curious about that." If she really listened to Margaret's point of view, she would learn how her daughter thinks and why she excluded Jennifer. She might discover a new perspective on the girls' relationship, seen through Margaret's eyes. As they talk it over, Mom might comment, "In my view, it's polite to invite a friend if she invited you to *her* birthday." And—in a discussion in which *two* points of view are truly heard—Mom could also add, "I'm concerned about Jennifer. I'm wondering if you've thought about how she'll feel if she's not invited."

In an atmosphere of respect, mother and daughter can have an open and candid discussion. They have an opportunity to learn more about each other and about life, and to strengthen the mother-daughter bond.

What about Spanking?

We've been talking about destructive messages hidden in verbal communication. But, what about spanking? Is that a *Mighty Parent* approach?

Parents have a responsibility to discipline their children, to teach that some behavior is unacceptable and to help the child learn right from wrong. What happens when they use spanking to accomplish these goals?

A child who is spanked may get the message that certain behavior is unacceptable—but *other* powerful messages come through as well. One of them is, "My parents will hit me if they want to." Some children may conclude, "I'm not safe in my family." Another message spanking can send is, "It's okay to hit someone if you have a good reason; this is a way to solve problems." Children who are spanked often can become convinced that it's their right—or even their obligation—to hit others who have done wrong. And so they hit siblings, friends and even parents. We perpetuate violence as a way to handle conflict.

Another unintended effect of spanking is that it can close down communication. A child who is afraid of you is less likely to come to you with problems and difficult feelings; opportunities for closeness, learning and growing may be lost.

Some parents are convinced that spanking works: "My folks did it to me and believe me, I needed it. It taught me a few things!" And it probably did. The problem is that spanking teaches through fear and pain. Children may avoid the forbidden behavior—at least in the short run, when they're afraid of us, or when we're watching. But they may also decide to continue the behavior and try to avoid the punishment by sneaking and lying. In the long run, fear and pain have limited value. Children grow older and more powerful physically. They spend more and more time out of our sight. Will they learn the lessons we want to teach when the fear of pain is removed?

Parents often say they spank only when they're calm, solely to teach right from wrong. Despite those good intentions, the unpleasant truth is that parents are sometimes angry or out of control when spanking; it becomes an outlet to vent their feelings. Not only does that send a stronger message about lack of respect, it opens the possibility for losing more control and slipping into physical abuse. Many parents express worries about this. One of the ways to help prevent abuse is to avoid spanking in the first place.

The bottom line is that spanking—even by a calm parent with good intentions—sends the wrong message; it models hitting as a way to deal with problems and feels to the child like domination: the exact opposite of the attitude of mutual respect.

What Works Better?

A far more effective approach is to allow children to experience the consequences of inappropriate behavior. Tommy is careless at the table and spills his milk. Give him a sponge and let him clean it up. That's a logical consequence for his behavior. We'll explore this approach more fully in Chapter Nine.

We also need to help children *understand* why we insist on some behaviors. Jennie tries to run away from you when you ask her to hold your hand as you cross the street. Take her aside and insist she look at your eyes as you explain, with concern in your voice, why she must hold your hand. Let her know how you love her and care about her safety, how you want to protect her and how upset you'd be if she got hurt.

Suppose Tim takes Jake's new toy out of his backpack. We can say to Tim, "Can you imagine how sad Jake feels when he finds his new toy is gone?" Lessons like these help children develop empathy and internalize values. We engage their minds and their feelings as we help them understand why certain behaviors are wrong—and how they can find more appropriate solutions. We show our children we care about them and want them to be more responsible and respectful.

How Children React to *Mighty Parent*

How does a parent's aggressive style affect the children? Since many of us fall into this behavior at times, it's important that we take a look.

Imagine you were a child with a parent whose attitude seemed to say, "I've got the upper hand; you have to conform to my world, but I don't have to take in yours." How would you react?

Some children attempt to cope by *fighting back*; others *withdraw*. Either way, it doesn't feel good. Children are either angry and rebellious or anxious and insecure.

Why does Miriam pick on her little brother, agitating him until he cries? What makes her behave that way?

This same mom often yells harshly at Miriam when she moves too slowly or doesn't set the table on time. What's happening? Mom's aggressive behavior is mirrored—practiced on little brother. Miriam directs her frustration toward friends and teachers, too.

Children find a variety of ways to fight back: yelling, bullying or blaming others, even telling lies, stealing or cheating. These are paths that can lead to more serious trouble during adolescence.

Some children fight back by competing: becoming overachievers or "workaholics." Those behaviors have positive elements, but when driven by feelings of insecurity or low self-esteem, there's a price to pay later in life.

Instead of fighting, other children and teens give up: they withdraw into submission, fantasy and isolation. Afraid to "make waves," these youngsters become passive, trying, in effect, to make themselves invisible. These quiet, self-effacing children are the ones whose problems are most likely to be overlooked. Adults may see them as "well-behaved," yet their problems could be serious, requiring our attention and support.

The Opposite Extreme

Just as children have different ways of coping with stress, so do adults. Sometimes we tend to become aggressive. Other times we go to the opposite extreme: giving in, ignoring our own feelings and needs or becoming a doormat—letting the child or teen run over us. That's the attitude I call *mini parent.*

mini parent

When we're afraid of losing our child's or teen's love and approval—or afraid of confronting them—we give in too readily. We try to please. We give them far more power than is reasonable, more than they can handle. Psychologically, we make ourselves small and look up to a child who towers above us: *mini parent, Mighty Child.*

For example:

> *Ed's mom buys cookies and states clearly, "You can have two, no more. The rest are for company tonight." Ed eats two and asks for another. Mom says, "No." Ed begs, "Please, Mommy? Please! I really love them. I promise I'll be good all day if you just give me one more. Okay?" And Mom gives in.*

Does that make Ed happy? In the short run, yes; he got an extra cookie. But if this continues over time, he's learning that he can make Mom do what he wants. A strong message is coming across to him: *I am more powerful than my parent.* And in many situations, he is. Mom's afraid of the consequences if she displeases him. She'll do what it takes to keep the peace.

Imagine being a small child and seeing those giants you depend on—your parents—acting afraid of you. *They're* the ones who are supposed to keep *you* safe! If they're acting scared or uncertain—how safe can you feel?

Can you remember what it's like to be a teen, grappling with the uncertainties of adolescence? How would it feel if the most important adults in your life reacted to you by cowering?

Our children feel less safe and secure when we *yield* to unacceptable demands, *ignore* unacceptable behavior or *deny* our personal needs unreasonably in favor of theirs. When they see that we don't respect ourselves—that we model powerlessness or low self-esteem, *how can they respect us*—or learn about self-esteem?

Of course, none of us really wants to become a doormat and slip into the role of mini parent. We often do it without realizing it. Frequently, we're not aware that our attitude has become *nonassertive.* And if we don't know it's happening, how can we ever change it?

So what's a parent to do? The best way I know to discover whether you've slipped into mini parent is to become aware of how you communicate with your children—verbally and nonverbally. That's when your attitudes are revealed.

Children feel the impact of your attitude in your tone of voice and body language, more than in your words. Mini parents have voices that hesitate, stammer or fail to speak with clarity. Their gestures are tentative or nervous—shoulders shrug, posture droops. Body language says, "I'm insecure."

Look at the list of nonassertive communication styles on the next two pages. These are the opposites of the aggressive styles we saw earlier. Each reveals an attitude that says, in effect, "I matter less than you."

Do you ever find yourself using any of these styles? If so, you've discovered an opportunity to grow.

You're Not Alone

If you catch yourself using any of these styles, you know you've moved away from the attitude of mutual respect, toward nonassertion. And you have lots of company. Mothers often imagine that the fathers won't understand how it feels to be nonassertive. They're in for a surprise! Men say they find themselves slipping into these styles too—and feeling quite uneasy about it. They wish the women would understand that they, too, can lose themselves around the children.

There's always a lot of laughter when we go a little deeper and talk about the payoff: what we gain by being passive. That's an important step for any of us who want to change—to take an honest look at what we gain from that behavior. One woman sums it up with tongue in cheek: "Look at the plus side. When I'm passive I get to avoid confrontation and conflict. No hassles. Oh yes, I also avoid rejection. And responsibility! Not bad for a start." Heads shake all around the group; we understand—all too well. A father chimes in, "Some of us are people-pleasers; everyone likes us. And why not? We're great company; we go along with whatever the other person wants." But a young mother makes us all stop and think when she expresses a sobering truth: "Yes, everybody loves me—except me."

Recognizing how we go off track is the first step toward change. Awareness is always the beginning. In the next chapter, you'll find help in transforming a passive attitude into the attitude of equal respect. But first, it's important to see *why* change is so important. That is, to see how being nonassertive affects our children.

Ineffective Communication Styles

(Nonassertive)

Comply: Accept demands without considering options.

- "Make my lunch, Mom. I'm late 'cuz I had to do home-work." Mom complies, "Okay, I'll take care of it, but I don't know why I do things that are your responsibility."
- "If I have to bring your soccer shoes to school, I guess I'll do it."

Concede: Give in to threats out of fear.

- Fourteen-year-old Marla says, "I could have made up a story, but I told you the truth about the party. If you don't let me go out, I won't tell you the truth any more!" Fearing his daughter's threat, Dad concedes: "Alright, I'll let you go this time."
- "Okay, okay, you can have it; just stop yelling."

Seek Advice: Ask others to solve personal problems instead of taking responsibility.

- "I give up. How can I get you to listen to me?"
- "I told you not to run around in the supermarket; tell me what am I supposed to do with you?"

Blank Out: Lose touch with one's own feelings and needs.

- "I need to make a two-minute stop at the store to pick up something for my meeting tonight." Latisha refuses, "No, Mom! I'm sick of running around!" Mom negates her own needs, "I guess I can come back later, though the traffic will be terrible."
- "I feel so defeated, I don't know what I want anymore."

Ignore: Overlook one's own share of responsibility.

- "I don't know why you kids are so cranky this morning. Is this the thanks I get for letting you stay up late last night?"
- "My child is afraid of the teacher and won't speak up in the classroom. I guess there's nothing I can do about it."

More ...

Ineffective Communication Styles
(Nonassertive)

Yield: Accept other person's point of view in order to avoid confrontation.

- "Put more butter in the mashed potatoes, Mom. Don't be such a health freak." "Well, okay, if you want to; I was just trying to watch our cholesterol."
- "I don't really agree, but I guess I'll go along."

Label (self)**:** Judge mistakes or inadequacies as if they were a reflection of personal worth.

- "It was so stupid of me to forget the felt pens; I'm such an air head."
- "I can't talk to the kids about our trip to the Indian reservation; I'm just too awkward in front people."

Dismiss: Convince self that feelings or thoughts are not real, important or valid.

- "Oh, nothing. It's not important anyway."
- "I guess I'm being silly to worry about Jason. His grades have really slipped, but he says he's doing fine now. I should probably just believe him."

Discount: Reject or ignore positive feedback and approval.

- "The kids said my apple pie was the best, but I told them it was easy, that anybody could have done it."
- "Mom! That was the perfect birthday gift; you must have looked everywhere for it!" Mom disregards the compliment, "Oh, I was just lucky."

Divert (self)**:** Distract self from feelings that signal unmet needs.

- "I read a lot or watch TV so I don't have to think about Chad's rudeness."
- "I've gained twenty pounds since Pam began dating that boy."

Children of Passive Parents

Children feel an enormous loss when their parents are nonassertive. They want a parent they can admire, emulate and look to for guidance; someone they can depend on to be strong and keep them safe—even from their own impulsive behavior. It's like having a teacher who lets the classroom drift out of control—who's too weak to insist that students behave and live up to their capabilities. How much can you really learn? How much can you respect the teacher? And what happens when your parents, the most important people in your life, fail to give you a feeling of confidence and clear direction? You feel less secure. A family like that feels like a ship without a rudder.

When parents fail to assert their needs, they often keep their feelings hidden as well. Their children feel a loss of closeness with Mom or Dad; having a nonassertive parent feels like having a friend you can never really know—a person who keeps you at a distance and remains a mystery. That leaves children feeling empty and incomplete. How can they learn about feelings and intimacy?

When nonassertive parents give in to children, they often ignore their own needs—and later feel resentful. Children sense that resentment and feel less loved.

Because passive parents ignore their own needs, they often fail to make their own lives rich and rewarding—to fulfill their own potential. Yet children need strong models they can learn from and look up to. When parents are afraid to follow their own dreams—to create satisfying lives—their children also lose out. They miss the joy and satisfaction that a fulfilled parent brings into the home.

Nonassertive ways of communicating may seem harmless—at first glance. But children hear a powerful message behind our words and tone of voice: *I am not worth much. I don't respect myself. I demonstrate low self-esteem. I feel powerless. I don't stand up for my needs.* How can such children learn about self-respect and self-worth?

Living with a nonassertive parent, children may take advantage and become aggressive, just as students do with a weak teacher. Other children mimic their parents and become self-effacing. They train themselves to deny their feelings and needs; they fail to develop a positive sense of self or to realize their potential.

We Flip Back and Forth

We noted earlier that most of us play the role of Mighty Parent sometimes and mini parent at other times. In fact, one often leads to the other.

As a young mother I would sometimes deny my own needs, playing with Derek long past the time that was comfortable for me. I was being a nonassertive mini parent. The longer I ignored my own needs, the more pressure built up inside—until Bang! Out burst Frenzied Franny, my anxious, aggressive lower self. And that's typical; self-denial holds in the pressure until we discover we can't contain it any longer. Then we explode.

A parent tells about the reverse flip:

> *I'm rushing to make dinner after a hectic day when my daughter runs in and begs, "Can Gina stay over tonight?" "No! Forget it!" I bellow. Then I start to feel guilty for being mean. My daughter pleads a little more and I end up giving in—when I don't really want to.*

And that's typical, too: we feel guilty about being aggressive—so we roll over and become nonassertive.

Some of us flip several times a day; others may take weeks or months. A mother "confessed," "I act like a timid mini parent for about six months. Then I get fed up. At that point I find any convenient target for my pent-up anger—usually my son's table manners—and blow up."

Different children can bring out different roles. One father explained, "When I'm challenged by my ten-year-old son, I become aggressive. With my flirtatious five-year-old daughter, I collapse and become nonassertive. Both feel out of balance; I'd like to find a better way."

Summing It Up

Despite our best intentions, we hold attitudes at times that reveal a lack of respect for our children—or for ourselves. And we don't even know it's happening! If we care enough to change, we can "catch ourselves in the act" by noticing the ways we communicate. Whether we're being aggressive or nonassertive, Mighty and mini are simply two sides of the same coin. Both send negative messages to our children. Neither reflects the attitude of mutual respect—the golden rule—that is the hallmark of the centered self and the foundation for a family that brings out the best.

In the chapter ahead, we'll learn how to spot these behaviors early on and replace them with more effective ones. We'll meet a tongue-in-cheek cast of characters, which can make it easier to recognize when we're off track—and show us the way toward mutual respect.

CHAPTER 7

How to Gain Respect:

Attitudes Make the Difference

*Treat your loved ones as you do your pictures,
and place them in the best light.*

—Jennie Jerome Churchill,
Mother of Sir Winston Churchill

WE CAN BE GOOD PARENTS without being perfect. Thank heaven for that; otherwise none of us would make it.

We don't have to be saints. We all find ourselves advising, lecturing or issuing orders at times—or giving up and caving in. The very best parents make their share of mistakes. The difference is that they view mistakes as opportunities to learn. What matters is that we stay *aware* of what we're doing and look for ways to improve.

Our goal is to create a family that consistently encourages children to respect themselves and others, develop self-esteem and become responsible and independent. In other words, we want a family that models mutual respect. We know that mutual respect is an *attitude*—a mindset that says:

> *However different our age and experience, you are a
> fellow human being; your needs, feelings, perceptions and self-
> knowledge deserve respect. I will treat you accordingly. I also
> will respect myself—and expect you to do the same.*

139

In the last chapter, we looked at ways we tend to go off track, slipping into communication that is aggressive or nonassertive. But what makes us do that? Why does it happen?

Why Do Parents Become Aggressive or Nonassertive?

We've all experienced some degree of personal pain as we grew up, inevitably leaving us with a few emotional scars. We all have "buttons" that can be pushed, and these affect the way we relate to our children.

Another trigger can be our fears as a parent: we worry that our children will get out of control, and we try to cope by becoming aggressive. Or we're afraid to confront our kids and face their rejection—and we become passive.

Yet there is more than our personal experience to consider. We're also shaped by the culture in which we live, and its influence is potent. In a thousand indirect ways, our culture sends us messages about how to treat children. As we noted in the Preface, many of those notions about parenting are left over from earlier eras.

Those traditional beliefs and parenting styles can remain firmly rooted in our psyche, even when we think they're gone. And especially when we're under stress—when our ability to think clearly is compromised— those old, familiar patterns rise to the surface.

Whether it's personal or cultural, those attitudes communicate a lack of respect, either for our children or ourselves. And *lack of respect* is the mindset of the lower self.

Oh No! Not the Lower Self, Again!

Yes, it's true. Whenever we use ineffective communication styles, we're modeling attitudes of the lower self. We may feel perfectly calm and in control; we have *no sense that there's a problem*. We might even feel *good* about what we're doing. After all, isn't a parent supposed to take charge? Isn't it right to make sacrifices? This is not that out-of-control subpersonality we met earlier; this is the lower self in more refined, genteel form. But it *is* the lower self because it holds a mindset of *inequality*. By contrast, when we're centered, we treat others as we would want to be treated. The very essence of the centered self is that it reflects the attitude of mutual respect.

An attitude of inequality takes its toll on family relationships, on children's self-esteem and their willingness to be responsible and cooperative. So what can we do? The key is to become acquainted with the many faces of the lower self. We need to recognize our attitudes—to be aware of our thinking and beliefs—if we're ever going to change.

To help you do that, I've created a set of humorous characters that personify the attitudes we hold when we communicate in aggressive or nonassertive ways. These are archetypes that occur in many cultures; they're a part of being human. Becoming familiar with these characters can help you recognize the lower self when it appears. Later in this chapter, I'll show you how to transform each one into the attitude of mutual respect.

Meet the Cast: *the Lower-Self Characters*

In the chart below, you'll meet the aggressive characters—one for each of the five relationship issues. Each one shows us the kind of aggressive thinking we can slip into when confronted with that issue.

Most of us play all of these roles at one time or another, but favor certain ones more often. Look over the cast of characters and see which ones most resemble you. The descriptions are extreme and tongue-in-cheek, yet they tell a basic truth. Try to see yourself objectively. Above all, hold onto your sense of humor.

Aggressive Lower-Self Characters

CHARACTER	ISSUE

 KNOW-IT-ALL   Authority

The world's greatest expert possesses vast and superior knowledge. When facing the issue, *Who knows best?* the answer comes with certainty: *I know. You don't.*

 V.I.P.   Needs

"I'm more important than you," claims the V.I.P. When the problem is, *Whose needs will be met?* the message is clear: *My needs come first.*

 GURU   Perception

The wise and all-seeing one perceives reality with greater clarity than ordinary mortals. When the question arises, *Whose point of view is right?* there is no hesitation: *I'm right. You're wrong.*

 DICTATOR   Control

The powerful one rules by decree. When we face the question, *Who should decide?* the command is clear: *I decide. You follow.*

 ROYAL HIGHNESS   Expectations

How do we deal with expectations? From high atop a lofty throne comes the royal proclamation: *I show respect only if you meet my expectations.*

Sound Familiar?

Can you recognize any aspect of yourself in these characters? Most of us can ... and do!

Once again, keep in mind *the reason* these aggressive characters come out. It tends to happen when we feel fearful: afraid our authority, needs, perception, control or expectations will be denied, dismissed or diminished. If we don't find a better way, we try to cope by becoming aggressive: getting tough and using power.

All of the same characters show up to interfere in our adult relationships as well. Learning to recognize them can be helpful at work and with friends, as well as at home.

The Opposite Extreme

The same fears may provoke us to flip the other way and become nonassertive. Let's take a look at the passive branch of the family (below) and see if your attitudes ever resemble theirs. They deal with the same five relationship issues—in the opposite way.

Nonassertive Lower-Self Characters

CHARACTER	ISSUE

KNOW-NOTHING   Authority

Awed by the question, *Who knows what's best?* this humble character bows low and says, *You know. I don't.*

MARTYR   Needs

Suffers quietly in the corner so as not to disturb anyone. When the question arises, *Whose needs will be met?* this self-effacing character whimpers, *Your needs come first.*

MUTE   Perception

Anticipating defeat, this character refuses to stand up for its feelings, thoughts or opinions. When there's disagreement about *Whose point of view is right?* the safe response is, *I'm wrong. You're right.*

SHEEP   Control

When the question arises, *Who should decide?* this obedient follower mumbles, *You decide. I follow.*

PEOPLE PLEASER   Expectations

Hungry for approval, this character hides real feelings and puts on a happy, compliant face. When considering, *How do we deal with expectations?* the response is, *I do what you expect, even if I don't want to.*

While we may not be as blatant as these characters, we all slip into lower-self behavior that echoes these attitudes at times, perhaps more often than we'd like to think. But we can change those habits and create a better climate for our children and ourselves—*if* we tune in and become aware of *when and how we slip.* To help you do that, I recommend you take the time to do the exercise below.

Exercise: Roles I Have Played

Purpose: To sharpen your familiarity with the characters and their communication styles, so you're better able to *recognize when you're going off track.*

Directions: You might find it helpful to do the exercise with a spouse or friend with whom you feel safe.

Look again at the lower-self characters in the preceding charts. Choose one or more that you identify with most readily.

For each character you choose, think of specific times when you play that role. Then write answers to these questions:

When I'm playing that role:

> *How do I act?*
> *How do I feel?*
> *How do I think?*
> *What do I say?*

Come back to this exercise in a few days or weeks. Read what you've written again. Add to it if you like. The more awareness you have, the more choice you gain.

When you've completed the exercise above, you'll be more familiar with your lower self, even when it acts out in more subtle ways. You can be on the lookout for the attitudes it holds and the ineffective communication styles it uses. Eventually you can catch this culprit *before* it goes into action.

You can use this awareness in your continuing practice of the Three-Step Process. The exercise above can deepen your ability to take step one. You'll be able to recognize not only your blatant subpersonality, but more *subtle* lower-self behavior as well.

You can use this awareness as you practice step two, using the relaxation exercise to become calm and the bridge exercise to remind yourself that you can make a different choice.

Later in this chapter, you'll find an illustrated *Help Chart* designed to assist you in transforming an aggressive or passive attitude into a centered one.

It's useful to recognize that children respond to our subtle subpersonalities just as they do to our more blatant ones: when they feel stressed and helpless, they cope by developing subpersonalities of their own.

Children's Lower-Self Characters

When children become aggressive or passive, their lower selves are on stage. You'll see the same cast of characters as in adults, expressing the attitudes I call *Mighty Child* and *mini child*. If we learn to recognize when and why that happens, we can gain new insight into our children's behavior.

Like us, children and teens feel powerful when they're aggressive, and later feel guilty or ashamed. Like us, they enjoy avoiding confrontation when they're nonassertive, and then suffer from low self-esteem.

Here are some examples of children in the role of aggressive Mighty Child:

Children's Aggressive Characters

KNOW-IT-ALL:	*I already know that.*
V.I.P.:	*No! I should be first!*
GURU:	*You're wrong. That's not what happened.*
DICTATOR:	*Give it to me now!*
ROYAL HIGHNESS:	*You're so mean. I hate you!*

Sound familiar? How about these typical quotes from nonassertive mini child?

Children's Nonassertive Characters

KNOW-NOTHING:	*I don't know. (Shrug)* *What do you think?*
MARTYR:	*Oh, it doesn't matter;* *I can wait until later.*
MUTE:	*I'm sorry. It's my fault.*
SHEEP:	*Okay. I'll do whatever you say.*
PEOPLE PLEASER:	*Oh sure, that's fine. Really.* *It's no problem.*

When you see behaviors like these, remember that your child or teen is trying to cope. Underlying these behaviors there is a legitimate need; your child requires your help to identify that need and find a better way to meet it.

In the chapters that follow, you'll learn skills that will help you to assert your own needs—meet them in more constructive ways—and assist your children to do the same.

Some lower-self behaviors are typical at certain ages; I encourage you to read about stages of development. The more informed you are, the easier it is to understand what's happening and remain calm. In any case, keep perspective: some of these attitudes are virtually inevitable.

When our children slip to the lower self, we don't have to take it as a personal affront. Instead of becoming upset or defensive, we can help them—and ourselves—to grow beyond those behaviors.

If we create an atmosphere of mutual respect in the family, subpersonalities will be active less often. We become positive models, as well as guides for our children. But how can we do that more consistently?

How to Turn It Around

The kids are over the top. You find yourself growing frustrated and then angry; you start to yell. They resist everything you say and you become even madder. Some part of you realizes you're headed nowhere fast; the kids are acting from the lower self and so are you. What can you do?

The truth is, you've already taken the most crucial step: you've become aware that the lower self is on stage. Part of you is frustrated and angry, but another part is objective enough to observe what's happening and realize it's not effective. Being able to observe yourself is the "dual awareness" you want. Regular practice of the relaxation and bridge exercises (in Chapter Four) will keep your awareness sharp.

What do you do next? Here's how some parents tell us they've handled it:

> I just stop right there and say to the kids, "This isn't going
> well. Let's talk about it later." And we take a break until we're
> able to talk reasonably.

I take a moment to cool down and say something like, "I'm feeling really upset. I don't like yelling at you and you don't deserve that. Let me explain what it is that I want and need. And I want to listen to you as well."

When I know I can't deal with it on the spot, I take a short "time out." I excuse myself, go into the bedroom and close the door. I do the relaxation exercise—take a deep breath—and remind myself that I can make a different choice. It takes a couple of minutes. Then I'm ready to go back and talk.

Once I realize what's happening—that I have a choice and can handle it differently—I'm able to shift gears and change my attitude.

When our children are fighting, we can help them to recognize that there are other options:

I can see you're both upset. I'm wondering if you'd like to try another way. Do you think it could be helpful if you both agreed to stop yelling and cool down for a moment—and then listen to what each of you has to say? Maybe then you can begin to sort out the problem.

Some parents become so angry that they don't *want* to behave differently, even though they recognize their behavior is ineffective. That *dual awareness*—the ability to see what they're doing and to be aware of the results—will help them stop eventually. That's what I refer to in Chapter Four as the "magical key" to parenting; it can open the door to growth and change.

Likewise, if we recognize our *children* are acting from the lower self, we can remember it's a cry for help; our role is to help them find a better way to meet their needs. The skills you'll learn in the chapters that follow will make that job easier.

Mutual Respect—a Personal Guide

Earlier, we introduced a set of characters that personify the attitudes of the lower self. Now we can use those characters to offer you some personalized guidance.

Look at the Help Chart (page 151) and find the drawing of the character(s) you slip into most often. Then think about which characters your children or your spouse may regress to. Aggressive characters are on the left; their nonassertive counterparts are beside them. Beneath those characters you'll find the relationship issue you're dealing with.

On the right you'll find a more effective approach for that issue: the symbol and mindset of a centered-self character that models mutual respect. That's the attitude you want to adopt—or the attitude you want to help your children and spouse adopt. For example, if you catch yourself expressing the attitude, *I know. You don't.* you know that the Know-It-All is on stage and you're dealing with the issue of Authority. You can address that issue effectively by adopting the attitude expressed by the Listener.

Which lower-self character do you most resemble?
Which centered-self character would be a good model?

Help Chart

LISTENER

| KNOW-IT-ALL | *I know. You don't.* | *We respect each other's* |
| KNOW-NOTHING | *You know. I don't.* | *knowledge.* |

Authority—*Who knows what's best?*

HUMANIST

V.I.P.   *My needs come first.*   *We respect each other's*
MARTYR   *Your needs come first.*   *needs.*

Needs—*Whose needs will be met?*

OBSERVER

GURU   *I'm right. You're wrong.*   *We respect each other's thoughts,*
MUTE   *You're right. I'm wrong.*   *feelings and perceptions*

Perception—*Whose point of view is right?*

PRAGMATIST

DICTATOR   *I decide. You follow.*   *We respect each other's desire for*
SHEEP   *You decide. I follow.*   *autonomy.*

Control—*Who should decide?*

REALIST

 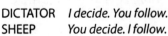

ROYAL HIGHNESS   *I show respect only if you meet*   *We respect each other's*
                    my expectations.   *expectations and create*
PEOPLE PLEASER   *I do what you expect even if I*   *family agreements.*
                    don't want to.

Expectation—*How do we deal with expectations?*

If you're not sure which character you resemble or which issue you're dealing with, don't worry; the chart can still guide you. Choose any character described on the far right; every one provides a model of mutual respect.

The more we practice these attitudes, the more they become a part of us. With ever-greater consistency, we can treat all family members *as we would want to be treated*—and teach them to treat us and each other in the same way—building positive family relationships based on mutual respect.

How Do You Adopt an Attitude?

We noted earlier that an attitude is partly a picture you hold in your mind. To adopt the attitude of mutual respect, picture yourself and your child or teen as two human beings who are equally deserving of respect.

Read the description of the appropriate centered-self character; can you comfortably adopt that attitude? Try to make that mindset your own.

An attitude is also what you believe and expect. Expectations are powerful. Remember the research (Chapter Two) in which teachers were told that certain students had exceptional potential—and those students performed better, even though they were chosen at random? The teachers treated those students differently because they believed and *expected* they would excel. And the students responded to those high expectations.

What beliefs and expectations do you hold about your child or teen? What expectations do they have of each other? Those beliefs affect the way you treat them—and the way they respond to you and each other.

You can create a positive, self-fulfilling prophecy if you hold these beliefs about your children:

- They are capable and competent.
- Their worst behavior is a cry for help; they're trying to meet legitimate needs.
- They want to express their best.

All of those are true for all normal children, no matter how difficult their behavior. Hold those beliefs and you'll be more patient and trusting. You'll have the confidence and courage to persist—to help them learn to meet their needs in more effective ways. *You'll expect them to become their best and believe they can do it.* Your children or teens will respond accordingly.

Changing behavior is a journey; it doesn't happen all at once. If you're patient, you will see changes, week by week. It's important to appreciate improvements, even small ones. Recognize and honor your own growth and your children's. It's helpful to keep a chart of situations that go well; it can keep you motivated and provide perspective on difficult days. You will continue to improve if you hold on to your commitment. Every parent I've known—if he or she had the desire and stayed with it—has been able to change and grow, and to see that growth reflected in the family.

Attitudes in a Nutshell

Even when we're not under stress we can slip into attitudes like, *I decide. You follow,* or *You're right. I'm wrong*—attitudes that are the opposite of mutual respect. Without being aware of it, we become the Dictator or the Mute. If we learn to recognize our personal styles—which character we resemble—we can "catch ourselves in the act." Then the Help Chart will show us the issue we're dealing with and a way of approaching it with a mindset of mutual respect. Recognizing when our children hold lower-self attitudes can remind us that this behavior is a cry for help; they need our support to find a better way to meet their legitimate needs.

What's Next?

In this chapter, we've been talking about the power of adopting— simply holding—an effective attitude. To put it into action fully, to express the attitude of mutual respect, we need appropriate skills. In the next few chapters we'll look at valuable skills you may already use—see how to polish and improve them—and learn new ones that can make a difference in your family every day.

CHAPTER 8

Speak from Your Heart:

The Skill of Assertion

*The influence you exert is through your own life
and who you become yourself.*

—Eleanor Roosevelt

ASSERTION HAS CHANGED MY LIFE—as a parent and as a person. There was a time when I felt uncomfortable saying no to people, including my children and husband. It took me a while to figure out the true reason: I was afraid they would become upset with me and withdraw their love. I made sure to care for everyone else's needs; it didn't dawn on me that I could say *what I want and need* as well. I didn't realize my children *needed me* to stand up for myself, to set limits and to express fully who I am. How else could they learn about self-respect and self-esteem?

When I learned the skill of assertion, I became effective in setting limits, but I gained other rewards as well: I learned more about who I am and how to express myself. I learned to say what I want for our family.

What Are Your Goals?

As parents, we're all different, but we share the same fundamental goals: we want the kind of family that nurtures every member—that helps children to grow into capable and caring adults. But how do we create a family like that?

If your children feel deeply respected—and can see that you and others are also respected—they're likely to emulate that attitude. If you set clear boundaries and require discipline along with respect, they will learn responsibility. If you show them the things you care about—what you value, your goals and how you try to achieve them and the qualities you admire and respect—you'll be on the road to creating the family you want. Assertion is a style of communicating that can help us reach those goals.

What Is Assertion?

Assertion is an effective way to say what you feel, need and want. It helps you tell others who you are and what you value. It's a way of communicating that is more likely to produce cooperation, because it does not blame or judge. It is neither aggressive nor passive.

Assertive statements often begin with (or include) the pronoun "I." That's because an assertive message is about the person speaking: what *I feel, think or want.*

Assertive statements are ...

- Revealing
    You disclose yourself.
- Straightforward
    You speak clearly and directly, preferably face to face.
- Honest
    You are sincere; your ideas are well thought out.
- Congruent
    Your verbal and nonverbal messages match.

Parents learning this skill sometimes *believe* they're being assertive because they begin with the pronoun, "I"—until they discover their statement is actually aggressive: it labels the child, issues orders, etc. Others are so indirect or disguised, their message is unclear; their statements are actually nonassertive.

Consider these examples; they'll give you a feel for the difference:

Aggressive	Nonassertive	Assertive
I don't like sloppy habits.	*It would be nice if you cleaned up.*	*I'd like you to leave the kitchen clean; I'm concerned about germs and I like a neat house.*
I want you to hurry up.	*The boys are waiting.*	*It's important to me that we arrive at the Scout meeting on time.*

Remember that assertive statements are "clean": they do not imply criticism. If you find yourself beginning with the word "You ..." stop and consider if you are about to pass judgment. Again, limit your statement to yourself: what *I* want, need or feel.

When Assertion Works—and When It Doesn't

Like any tool, assertion works best when used in appropriate situations. A fork is a great utensil, but it's not very useful for eating soup. We should use assertion when we're calm and centered —when we're under stress, we're vulnerable and in danger of slipping to the lower self. Once that happens, we become aggressive or passive, these are the *opposites* of being assertive.

When should we use assertion? It's the perfect tool for dealing with situations we face every day:

- when we respond to a child's request
- when we set limits
- when we express a concern
- when we want to express our feelings and values

In this chapter you'll learn how to be effective in the first situation: responding to a request. In the process, you'll master the principles of assertion. You'll also learn how to be effective when the inevitable happens:

when children or teens resist. For that purpose, you'll acquire a companion skill, called reflection.

Daddy, Can I ...?—Responding to a Request

> *Can I watch the special tonight? I'll do my homework in the morning. I promise.*

> *Can we buy Sugar Pops? We <u>never</u> get to have them! Please?*

> *I need a new dress for the party. If I don't get one I'll feel left out for sure.*

> *Will you advance me next week's allowance? There's a CD I really want to buy.*

Sometimes it feels as if you need the wisdom of Solomon to be a parent. How do you respond to requests that are expressed with such urgency, yet test your judgment and resolve?

The first thing to keep in mind is that you don't have to decide right away. It's fine to say, "I need time to think about it," or "I need to check my schedule." Don't make a decision until you feel comfortable with it. When I first realized that was true, it felt like a huge weight was removed from my shoulders; I didn't always have to be quick and think on my feet!

Is This a Need Or a Want?

When a child makes a request, it's important to figure out whether he or she is expressing a *need* or a *want*. "I'm thirsty; may I have some water?" is very different from, "Can I have another scoop of ice cream?"

Needs *deserve to be met* whenever possible. Wants deserve respect, but may be granted or refused. Distinguishing between them will help you decide what to do.

For example:

> *Sure, I'll get you some water; after so much running, I'm not surprised you're thirsty.*

No, one scoop of ice cream is enough.

It's Okay to Say No

When you're deciding whether to grant a request, consider whether you're being respectful of your child's needs—but don't forget to respect your *own* needs. It's okay to say no if a request violates your values or needs. No is a way to define your boundaries.

Below are some examples of parents using assertion to say no. Notice that each one gives a reason, explaining how the request conflicts with the parent's needs or values.

> *No, Damon. The rules are clear: homework must be completed before bedtime.*

> *No, Tim, I won't buy Sugar Pops. I'm unwilling to buy cereal that has so much sugar.*

> *No, Susan. I'm not willing to give you your allowance in advance. One of the reasons we give you an allowance is to help you learn how to plan your own spending.*

One good reason for saying no is to discourage dependence: "No, I won't bring you water; you're able to get it yourself," or "No, I won't look up that word in the dictionary; that's part of the homework you're supposed to do." A no in these situations is actually a yes: "Yes, I will help you learn to be responsible and independent."

Another assertive way to teach responsibility is to say yes—and explain the conditions that are necessary to earn it. For example, "Yes, you can watch a video, after you complete your homework." Children and teens may accept the boundary more readily, knowing their request will be granted if they do what is required of them.

Why Give a Reason?

Whether you decide to grant the request or refuse, children will be more receptive if you give a reason. Think about how it would feel if your spouse or boss simply said, "Sorry, the answer is no"—and left it at that. Wouldn't it feel better if the boss said, "Sorry, I'd like to say yes, but that would interfere with the meeting we've planned"? We all feel more respected when decisions don't seem arbitrary.

When you give a reason, children are more likely to understand and accept your decision. They might still complain if you say no, but their negative feelings aren't likely to last as long.

For those reasons, an *assertive response* to a child's request has two parts: an *assertion* and an *explanation*. Some examples:

Assertion: *No, I can't help you with your homework right now.*
Explanation: *I need to prepare dinner. I'm free at seven if you still need me then.*

Assertion: *I'm not certain if I can give you a lift to Jenna's house on Thursday.*
Explanation: *I'll check my calendar and tell you at dinner.*

Assertion: *Yes, I'm happy to take you to the park.*
Explanation: *I've been looking forward to going outside all day.*

Parents often ask, "Why give a reason when I *agree* to a request?" It isn't essential, but it is helpful; children want to understand your thinking. And it's also good prevention: an identical request may get a yes today and a no tomorrow. For example, Jimmy asks for a banana at three-thirty this afternoon. You say, "Sure, that's a great after-school snack." Tomorrow at six, you deny the same request: "No, we're having dinner in fifteen minutes and I want you to save your appetite for the meal I prepared."

By offering a reason, we teach our children that we respect them; we show we're not being arbitrary. We think about their requests and, in response, we share our thinking and our values. We pay attention to them and take them seriously. Children and teens value that.

What If I Can't Come Up with a Reason?

Parents often find it difficult to state a reason. That usually happens in two kinds of situations: either parents need time to discover or formulate their reasons, or they don't *have* a solid reason.

So give yourself time. If you're saying no and you don't have a reason— except that something doesn't feel right—what can you do? Simply say, "This doesn't feel right to me," and explain, "I need time to think about it." That's the truth, isn't it?

If your children or teens push for a reason, it's fair to tell them, "I don't have a clear explanation right now; I need some time to think. But I'm not going to change my mind right now. It won't help if you continue to press me."

Often, when we give ourselves time, we discover feelings we didn't know were there.

> *No, I can't give you permission. I feel that's not appropriate for someone your age.*

> *No, I can't buy that for you. I'm not comfortable spending that much money.*

When the reason becomes clear, you can let your children know. Taking time to find a reason has an extra value: we uncover feelings we weren't aware of before.

You can also help your children to provide explanations when they refuse each other's requests. For example: "Can we play dolls together?" "No, because I want to be alone now." Or, "Can I play with your Lego?" "No, because you wouldn't help me put them away last time."

It's Okay to Change Your Mind

Sometimes, when you think about why you said no, you discover there is *no good reason*. Maybe you were busy and didn't want to be bothered. Or you were in a bad mood. When that happens, it's perfectly fine to admit it and change your mind. Children would certainly prefer that. You might fear they'll lose respect for you if you change your mind. That could happen if you did it often, but it's more likely they'll appreciate your honesty.

For example, one mother confessed to her son, "I said no because I was busy paying bills and felt interrupted. But when I think about it, there's no reason why you can't have Steve over on Saturday. I'm sorry I was so abrupt." Parents are not perfect and should not pretend to be. When you admit a mistake and apologize for it, you're modeling behavior children can emulate. One day, you might be amazed when your child or teen apologizes *to you.*

Children, too, can change their minds. If their sibling thinks about the explanation and renegotiates the request, it may be accepted. "When you've had enough time alone, then can we play together?" "If I promise to help you clean up, will you let me play with your toys?" Siblings might reply with something like, "Yes, but you better mean it!"

Practice Responding to a Request

Write down four typical requests your child or teen might make: two that you find acceptable and two that you find unacceptable. Be sure they are typical and involve different kinds of situations.

Write an *assertive response* for each request; remember to include a reason. Unacceptable requests include those that interfere with your needs, break family rules, foster dependence or are impractical due to limits of time or money.

When you've finished, look at your responses. Are your replies about "I" rather than "you"? Did you include an answer and a clear explanation? Are they free of criticism and blame?

When Children Challenge Us

What happens when your son or daughter says, "No! That's not fair," or, "You're just being mean"? Or worse, slams a door or throws a tantrum? How can you stick to your principles and stay centered? Now *that's* the real test.

No matter how skillful you are at being assertive—or how perfect you become at explaining yourself—you will, at times, meet opposition (as if you didn't know). Children or teens will get angry, refuse, ignore or delay. And that's to be expected; we're all human. We all have different needs, moods and points of view. Perfect agreement is not our goal, since we're not raising robots.

Our goal is to remain centered as we deal with inevitable confrontation, to handle it skillfully and avoid slipping to the lower self.

But I Need Help!

We *all* need help when children confront us. We can even find ourselves saying yes when we really mean no, just to avoid that confrontation.

So how do we prepare ourselves? One way is to anticipate their disagreement. Every human being is unique, with different perceptions and needs; we should hardly be surprised to encounter conflict. Children or teens *will* resist at times. If we keep that in mind, it will be less upsetting when it happens.

One of the most effective ways to deal with resistance is to adopt an appropriate *attitude*. Being challenged with opposition can certainly be frustrating. But you can choose to see it through the eyes of the Pragmatist, viewing resistance as the child's desire to assert autonomy.

It's also the best opportunity we parents have to demonstrate equality—by respecting the child's right to express a different point of view—without losing sight of our own. After you respond to your child's concerns, you'll have an opportunity to educate your child to your needs, feelings and values. Instead of seeing opposition only as a problem, notice that it also presents opportunities.

Another way to be prepared for disagreement is to be aware of the different forms it takes. Most of us are all too familiar with reactions like these:

- Complaint: *That's not fair!*
- Questions: *What are you talking about?*
- Denial: *I never said that!*
- Put-down: *That's ridiculous.*
- Threat or dare: *You can't make me.*

All of the above are *aggressive* ways of resisting.
Passive or *nonassertive* styles of resisting include:

- Making faces: *Kids give you "that look."*
- Silence: *Kids don't answer.*
- Delay: *I'll do it later (meaning never).*
- Agreement: *Okay, I'll do it (but no action follows).*

And any number of other favorites we all know and love.
So what's a parent to do?

Handling Opposition

You could regress to Mighty Parent and say, "Because I said so!" and enforce your will—except for the slight problem that an aggressive response is likely to create more confrontation. Or you could shrink down into mini parent and give all the power to the child, "Okay, whatever you want." But we've seen where that leads. So what's a better way?

We want to avoid adding more stress to the scene. If we provide only an unyielding opposing force, that will heat up the emotional temperature and encourage conflict.

Instead, we can begin by truly *listening*—and then acknowledging what we've heard. It's very satisfying for any of us to have our feelings heard. Children are like adults in that way: *they want to be listened to; they want their ideas and feelings to be understood and acknowledged.* That helps them cool down and become available to hear *us*. When children (or adults) are all steamed up, full of their feelings, they have no room to take in someone else.

I can't emphasize this enough. When emotional temperatures run high, we're unable to hear each other or think rationally. The lower self reveals its limitations; frustration increases and the discussion escalates.

Another reason to begin by listening is that we really do want to hear. We need to understand what our children or teens are experiencing and feeling. How else can we learn to understand them better? How else can we build an atmosphere of mutual respect?

Listening takes time and effort, but it's one of the most important ways we give children what they most need: our love and attention. The skill of listening well to a child's opposition—and acknowledging what we've heard—is called *reflection*.

Using Reflection

Reflection may be the most valuable skill for improving human relations. As we noted earlier, we all have a powerful need to be heard— to be taken in and understood—to have our thoughts and feelings acknowledged and respected. That need is especially strong when we're in disagreement. For those reasons, you'll find the skill of reflection enormously helpful, not only with your children, but in all relationships.

Here's how it looks in action:

Timmy:	*Will you play with me on the computer now?*
Dad:	***Not tonight, Timmy; I promised Mom I'd go shopping.***
Timmy:	*That's not fair! You never want to be with me!*

At this point Dad puts his own feelings aside, just for a moment, and really listens to Timmy.

Dad:	***Sounds like you're upset; you think I don't care about being with you.***

Notice that Dad tries to put himself in Timmy's shoes—to understand his experience. He listens for Timmy's *feelings* as well as his thoughts. Then he reflects or mirrors them back to Timmy, so his son will recognize he has been heard and understood.

That's the skill of reflection: to put aside your own feelings—just for a moment—and reflect the other person's thoughts and feelings, to show you truly understand. It may sound simple, but it's a powerful way to improve communication and relationships.

Remember that reflecting doesn't mean you *agree* with what was said; it simply means you've heard and understood. This is a key point.

Please rest assured that reflection equals *acknowledgment,* no more, no less—and certainly not agreement.

When you use reflection, your child or teen receives this message: "Even when I'm mad at my parents, or don't want to do what they ask, they're willing to hear me out; that means they care about me." Often that's more important to children than getting what they want. When they sense we care about them, children tend to calm down. If they're calm enough, they may even recognize we have a good reason for saying no.

Here are some more examples of parents using reflection to respond to a child's opposition:

Child:	*You never listen!*
Parent:	***You feel I don't really hear what you have to say.***
Teen:	*I don't buy it; that's ridiculous.*
Parent:	***You don't think I'm making any sense.***
Teen:	*Okay, okay, chill out! I said I'd do it.*
Parent:	***Seems like you want me to relax and believe that you'll take care of it.***

"I Feel Like a Parrot"

Parents often misunderstand at first, and complain that reflection seems mechanical. As one father put it, "I feel like a parrot, just repeating what's been said."

But reflection is not the same as parroting. We don't listen in order to *repeat* what was said. We listen as an act of respect: to demonstrate to our children that they have the right to state opposing opinions and feelings and we will hear them out. We let them know we've heard and understood them by reflecting the *essence* of what we hear: their *feelings,* most of all, and then their *thoughts.* Our tone of voice and facial expression show respect.

Reflection often feels awkward at first. Like any new skill—learning a new golf swing or tennis serve—it takes a while before it feels natural.

Don't be discouraged; using reflection will convince you that it works. You'll gain confidence, learn to use your own words and begin to feel comfortable.

If you have a tendency to avoid confrontation by giving in to your children or spouse, reflection can help you feel stronger; it provides an effective tool to help everyone slow down and remain calm. If you tend to become aggressive because you fear your child will get out of control, using reflection can bolster your confidence; you have a way to handle the problem with respect, yet remain assertive.

You can use this skill when your children are quarreling with each other. Simply comment on the information each child provides. For example, "You want to show Daniel a magic trick, and you're disappointed because he doesn't want to watch it right now." When you describe the situation without judgment, your children are more likely to calm down, providing them an opportunity to create their own solution.

Reflection is an invaluable tool in *any* relationship. Example: Your spouse says, "You're too lenient with the kids. Why don't you send them to their rooms?" You reply, "You think I should take a tougher stand and insist they separate from each other." Instead of responding by saying, in effect, "Your way is wrong!" you remain centered and acknowledge your spouse's point of view. That doesn't mean you agree with it; it means you're willing to show respect—even when you disagree. A calm and productive discussion can then follow.

Practicing Reflection

To gain some practice with reflection, look at the statements below; each is a quote from a child or teen resisting. How would you reflect each one?

Write down what you'd say. While there is no "right" answer, you can learn by comparing your answers to those at the end of this exercise.

How would you reflect each statement?

1. *Why can't I? Susan's mom said okay.*

2. *You always say no.*

3. *That's not fair!*

ABOUT THE ANSWERS: Sometimes you have to guess about the feeling behind the statement; your child or teen will let you know if you're on target. What's important is your attempt to reflect accurately the opinions and feelings you've heard—while remaining neutral emotionally. Be sure there is no hint of upset or judgment in your tone of voice.

Here are some possible answers:

1. *You want me to agree like Susan's mom.*

2. *You feel I refuse you all the time.*

3. *You think I'm not being reasonable.*

Summing It Up

Healthy relationships are supported by good communication. We assert ourselves and let each other know what we really feel, think and want, without putting anyone down, including ourselves. Sometimes, assertion will be met with opposition. When it is, use reflection: respectfully listen to the objection. That will help everyone to calm down, truly hear each other and create an atmosphere for useful dialogue. Assertion and reflection show respect for everyone concerned—and so they encourage cooperation.

When children ask, demand or beg us for something, it helps to remember these guidelines:

- Consider if this is a need or a want.
- Consult your feelings to be clear on what feels comfortable.
- It's okay to say no—or yes—or explain that you'll decide later.
- Give a reason.
- It's okay to change your mind.
- When children disagree with you, reflect their point of view. Showing you've understood will help everyone to calm down.

Now that you know the skills of assertion and reflection, you'll find it easier to take on the challenging task of setting limits. You'll learn how to do that effectively in the next chapter. And you'll discover how valuable it is to allow your children to learn from the natural consequences of their own behavior. Both will help you to create an environment that brings out the best.

CHAPTER 9

Life's Lessons:

Setting Limits and Natural Consequences

Fear should never prevent you from doing what you know is right.

—Aung San Suu Kyi

HOW CAN WE GET children and teens to *listen*—to cooperate and accept the limits we set? The answer lies in knowing what we want, feeling confident in our decisions and staying centered—holding an attitude of respect for our children and for ourselves. In other words, using the skills of assertion and reflection. In this chapter we'll discover how to use those skills to set limits effectively.

We'll also discover that life itself has a way of setting limits—of creating consequences—if we allow our children to experience them. We'll learn about times when *natural consequences* are the most effective teacher.

Setting Limits

No question about it: setting limits is a challenge for most of us. How can we know where to draw the line and how to hold it? If we're too rigid, we encourage rebellion; if we're too flexible, we invite chaos. We all need help with this one!

Remember that children depend on us to set limits—to teach them what is acceptable and what is not. That's how they first learn self-control, right and wrong, positive values, respect and responsibility. Without limits, there is chaos for them (not to mention for us!) and they cannot feel safe; they need to experience freedom, but within clear, firm, protective boundaries.

Setting limits helps children grow. Remember the two core principles (Chapter Two): children *yearn* to become their best and they *depend on us to help them*. They need and want our help in gaining self-control and growing beyond their lower-self behavior.

When we say no and children cannot accept it, their subpersonalities often show up. They whine, beg or try to manipulate. They're not proud of these behaviors, but the lower self is impulsive and has little control. Children haven't yet developed the resolve to act maturely and accept a legitimate no. Sometimes they don't know a better way. Though they might not admit it, children realize at some level that this routine serves them badly. When we hold our resolve firmly—and with respect—we create a boundary that helps them gain self-control. A part of them feels relieved: now they're free of the chaos that comes with lower-self behavior. We help our children to mature and earn their own respect.

Still, it takes courage to say no and stick with it, especially when children or teens pressure us. As you learn more effective ways to set limits, remember that it takes *time* to master a new skill; awkward moments and frustration are a natural part of the process. Keep perspective and be gentle with yourself. Toward that end, it will be useful to take a brief look at the feelings you might experience as you move through the learning process.

Stages of Learning

Each time we learn a new skill—using a new computer program, learning long division or mastering an assertive skill—we move through certain predictable stages. The better we understand that process, the more able we are to relax and support our children and ourselves.

Over time, learners are, in turn:

Stages of Learning

Unskilled and unconscious
At the beginning, we lack skills but *aren't aware* they're missing. "Blissful ignorance" provides comfort.

Unskilled, but conscious
At this stage we still lack skills—but now we're *aware* of our inadequacy. How do we deal with this discomfort? Here are some typical coping styles:

Learners:
- put themselves down
- devalue the skill
- give up because of unrealistic expectations

Skilled, but self-conscious
We know how to use the skills now, but they still feel awkward and unnatural. It's an uphill battle and we tend to complain. When frustrated, we feel like giving up—and sometimes do, temporarily. This stage usually lasts the longest.

Skilled and instinctive
The final stage is the most satisfying. We use the skills without conscious effort; they have become "second nature." We reap the rewards of persistent practice.

Each of us learns at a different pace. If we accept and respect that, if we honor the persistence and courage required to master something new, we can help our children and ourselves to become more confident and successful learners. Patience and compassion, rather than pressure, give us the strength to carry on. Hold on to that perspective as you learn the skills in the pages ahead.

How to Set Limits

Fortunately, you've already learned most of what you need to know in order to set limits effectively:

- Decide what's appropriate and what is not, according to your own values and what you feel is best for the family.
- Distinguish needs from wants.
- Respect your own needs as well as your child's.
- Use assertion and reflection together, to help you set limits and follow through.

We call this skill *assertive limit-setting*. Here's one example:

Child's request:	*Can you help me with my doll clothes now?*
Assertion:	***No. I told you Daddy and I needed to talk for a while and that I would come to your room when I'm free.***
Complaint:	*You never have time to help me.*
Reflection:	***You feel I'm always too busy, with no time for you.***
Child's reply:	*Yes!*

Now you've listened, reflected and received confirmation that your child feels understood. Emotionally, she's more available to listen. It's time to follow through on your original purpose: to set limits.

Assertion:	***I hear you're upset, but that was our agreement. I'll be available when Dad and I have finished our discussion. It'll probably be about fifteen minutes.***

If a child continues to be upset, you may want to use reflection once more—to help the child calm down. But don't use reflection beyond your comfort level. Once or twice is often enough. Remember that your purpose is to set limits. When there's nothing new to add, it's time to *end the discussion.*

To continue with the example:

Child:	*Fifteen minutes is too long!*
Reflection:	***You don't want to wait; you wish I could be with you right now.***
Assertion:	***But now is my time to be with Dad. I'll come to your room when we're finished.***

If the child remains upset, you might reflect once more and then end the discussion. Repeating your exact words makes it clear that your comments are final:

Reflection:	***I hear that you're very unhappy having to wait.***
Assertion:	***(Pause.) I'll come to your room when we're finished.***

Notice that Mom truly took in what her daughter said, but she held firm to their agreement. Too often, when parents begin listening and empathizing with their children, they tend to give in, losing sight of their *own* needs. It's fine to change your mind *when appropriate.* But parents who are overly permissive—and they have been in the majority recently—are robbing their children of the opportunity to learn self-control, respect and responsibility.

Tips for Success

Parents *want* to set limits, but using the skill under fire can be difficult at first. "When I'm challenged, I don't know what to say," is something I hear often. To help you find the words, I've collected some limit-setting phrases parents have found successful. They're all different ways to say the same thing. Become familiar with them when you're *not* under stress; then you can call on them when you are.

- *You don't want to accept my no, but I'm not going to change my mind.*
- *I've been very clear; there's no need for me to repeat what I've already said.*
- *You've been asking me again and again. Do you think I'm going to change my mind? I can assure you, I'm not going to.*
- *I see we're going over the same territory; since there's nothing new to say, I'm going to end the discussion.*

In certain situations, it can be easier to eliminate words completely and communicate nonverbally:

- Hold up your right hand firmly in a stop position; remain silent and firm.
- Place your hands in a T position (time out).
- Hold your hands up; take a breath; ease them down.

Three Guidelines

To be successful in setting limits, there are three points to keep in mind:

First, don't lose sight of your original purpose; remember to shift back to assertion after you reflect what your child said. You can identify with how your child feels—and not lose sight of your own purpose. If your answer is no, make it clear that it remains no.

Second, remember you have every right to meet your own needs. Children respect parents who respect themselves. By setting limits, you model an attitude of equality and mutual respect.

Third, be consistent. Carefully think through what you feel is appropriate and what is not; establish clear guidelines and stick to them consistently, no matter how challenging that may be.

Whenever you set limits, keep those three points in mind:

- Keep your resolve.
- Respect your needs, too .
- Be consistent.

Are You Really Listening?

A father in my class confronted me with a direct, but fair question: "Is reflection really mutual respect—or just a clever way to manipulate the child?" The answer depends on whether you really listen to your child. If you truly take in the child's feelings and point of view, you're demonstrating respect. And if you do that, you'll be open at times to *modifying* your point of view when you feel that's appropriate. For example:

Request:	*Can I go to Carlos's house tonight?*
Assertion:	**No. You know it's never okay to go to a friend's house on a school night.**
Complaint:	*Why are you so strict, Dad? This is really important.*
Reflection:	**Seems like this means a lot to you and you'd like me to make an exception.**
Assertion:	**I'm willing to listen.**
Response:	*Carlos called; his dog is having puppies. I really want to see them being born.*
Assertion:	**How exciting. No wonder you want to go there. I agree with you; that's worth making an exception.**

The key is to be open and flexible, rather than rigid. Once again, you weigh the child's needs and wants as well as the family's and your own. If you feel there is good reason to change, be open to doing so, but don't give in just for the sake of avoiding conflict. Check to see if you've slipped to the nonassertive lower self. It's important to be centered when you make a decision.

Knowing What You Want

Parents make good decisions when they have clarity, when they know what they want. In the example above, there was a clear family agreement: no visiting with friends on school nights. When Carlos asked to change the agreement, Dad held firm and said no. But when he heard all the facts, Dad felt there was reason to make an exception. He did *not* change because he was afraid to confront his son or feared losing his love. He felt the request was legitimate and decided to support what his son wanted. He remained assertive.

In the earlier example, the parents had taken time to make a plan. Realizing they needed time to talk, they had discussed the plan ahead of time with their daughter and made an agreement with her. As a result, they had no hesitation in refusing their daughter's request. It's much easier to handle a child's discomfort when we've thought ahead and are clear about what we want.

Children more easily wear us down when we're not sure of what we want or deserve. If you don't feel you have the right to have your needs met—if you're not clear about what you think or feel— they're more likely to get to you.

For instance, imagine that the mother in the first example wasn't really *comfortable* with the agreement made earlier. Suppose she thought it might be unfair to her daughter, leaving her alone that long, but had kept those concerns to herself. She would have made the agreement feeling half-hearted about it. Inevitably, when her daughter interrupted, she would feel torn. Then she might weaken, shortening the discussion with Dad and probably leaving him frustrated. The unintended message to her daughter: "I don't keep my agreements and I don't expect you to." The moral of the story is obvious: be clear about what you want, then you can stick to it and be consistent.

It's not always easy to be fully in touch with our own feelings and thoughts. And if we're not clear with ourselves, how can we be clear and consistent with our children? A simple formula can help; write or say aloud an assertive statement. Begin with "I," then fill in the blank:

> "I feel _____"
> "I think _____"
> "I want _____"
> "I value _____"

Using that formula helps us clarify what we're feeling and thinking, and enables us to express ourselves assertively. That's important; the actions we take have powerful effects. When parents respect their own experience—which demonstrates self-esteem—their children learn to model this behavior as well.

The more consistently we use the skills of assertion and reflection to set limits, the more our children come to expect that we will be fair, but firm. They may not like the limits, but they will respect us and feel respected themselves. The result: their opposition will diminish.

Let It Be: *Natural Consequences*

What happens when children or adults *exceed* limits? Well, life has a way of reminding us to do the right thing; it's called *consequences.* If you forget to take your raincoat when a storm is coming, you're likely to get wet. A child who forgets her homework has to face consequences at school. Experience is a great teacher, the most effective one we know. But learning comes to a screeching halt when parents are too softhearted and shelter children from the lessons life teaches.

> *Jacob forgot his soccer shoes this morning—again. He called me in a panic; the coach wouldn't let him take part in practice. I had to miss an important appointment and drive all the way down there.*

> *Arianna waited until the last minute to write her big report; then she was too tired to proof it. She asked if I would do it. I found myself making corrections late into the night.*

Guess what the children in these stories are learning: "I don't have to be responsible; Mom or Dad will rescue me." These well-meaning parents are acting as *enablers,* helping their children remain immature and dependent.

When a family maintains some regular structure and routines, children know what's expected of them. When they're forgetful or irresponsible, allow them to experience the natural consequences. Jacob will have to sit on the bench this time, while his buddies play; Arianna will turn in a late paper, compromising her grade. Natural consequences make a direct, and often immediate impact on our children's lives, providing a powerful opportunity for growth. By refusing to interfere, you help your children become responsible and independent, building their self-respect and self-esteem.

Here's what Jacob's mom could have said when he called about his shoes:

> *I hear that; you're <u>really</u> upset that you can't play without your soccer shoes. But I can't bring them. I need to stay at work.*

In that way, Mom would have been clear: Jacob had his responsibility and she had her own. She understood his pain, but felt no obligation to change the situation. The problem was his—and self-imposed.

Arianna's mom could have walked into her room and said simply:

> *I'm always available to help when you're having a problem understanding something. But, I'm not willing to do your work.*

That approach would have been appropriate—but it's not easy. To strengthen your will, remind yourself: You're actually showing your child that you know he or she *is* capable of being responsible. That message is a great gift! Just hold onto yourself when you feel like rushing in to rescue your "baby." Don't interfere with life's lessons.

Allowing natural consequences sends another valuable message: *You can count on me to be consistent.* Suppose you arrange with your kids that you'll wash their clothes if they put them in the laundry basket. When you find dirty clothes on the floor and not in the basket, simply leave them there. Wash only those clothes in the designated place. Children then experience the unhappy, and natural consequence of their actions. They receive your powerful, nonverbal message: you mean what you say. You're consistent.

Letting children experience natural consequences is more effective than talking. Especially when we're learning new communication skills, parents tend to talk too much and children can tune us out. While words are certainly important, children respond best to something they experience.

It's Not a Punishment

Remember that we're talking about consequences—the natural results of behavior. That's different from punishment, which is a penalty *we* impose. If a parent were to say, "You left your clothes on the floor, so no TV tonight," that would not be a natural consequence. It would be a penalty we create—not the natural result of the child's behavior. Mighty Parent imposes punishment, often a knee-jerk reaction that grows out of our frustration. You'll find far more effective ways to deal with difficult behavior in Chapter Ten, Problems Happen.

Mighty Parent

Despite the fact that we're centered when we allow our children to experience natural consequences, it's no surprise that they don't appreciate us—and will do whatever they can to avoid them. Often they make excuses: "I was going to do it in a minute." Or play Martyr: "I can't do everything; I was studying for my math test." Or they might lash out: "You're so uptight." But these are just lower-self reactions, a "tap dance" that has probably worked for them in the past. But you know, and they know, it's not about you. They're responsible for the consequence. And deep down, believe it or not, they respect us for towing the line.

That is, *if* we can follow through.

For many of us, it's painful to let our kids experience natural consequences:

> *Our agreement has always been clear. Beverly knows I'll drive her to school if she's ready at seven. If she runs late, we've*

agreed that she'll take the bus. Still, nearly every morning, I coax and plead because she's dawdling—and I end up tense as a tightrope while I drive her to school.

What keeps a system like that going?

In discussing this dilemma, Mom discovered many reasons that keep her from holding the line:

- *I don't want to confront Beverly.*
- *It takes more energy to be tough and I'm already exhausted.*
- *I like to be a helper.*
- *I feel like a good person when I sacrifice for her.*
- *I don't have to yell.*
- *I don't want my daughter to be mad at me.*
- *I don't want to see her fail so I intercede.*
- *If she's late to school or acts irresponsibly, it reflects poorly on me.*
- *Part of me likes to see her as a young child who still needs me.*

mini parent

Mom is not unique; I've heard much of this thinking before and have been guilty of it myself at times. Mini parent is running the show, afraid and unwilling to confront. When we shelter our child from consequences, we send this message: *I don't trust that you can be responsible.*

What to do? Remember in Chapter Three when we identified our own lower selves and met a subpersonality? Whether Mighty or mini, a subpersonality surfaces when we're under stress. In Chapter Four, we learned the relaxation exercise and the concept of loving wisdom.

And finally, we practiced the bridge exercise to identify with the centered self. This is a perfect opportunity to practice these techniques and become centered.

Centered Self

Then gather your courage. Resist the temptation to rescue. Allow your children to experience natural consequences. Despite their protests, they will grow to become responsible and capable. They will gain respect for you and feel good about themselves.

What *Is* the Natural Consequence?

It's not unusual for parents to say, "In that situation, I couldn't figure out what a natural consequence would be." Sometimes it's not so obvious, until we get used to thinking that way. The question to ask yourself is this: *What's the natural result of the child's behavior?*

To gain experience in identifying natural consequences, look at the examples below. First consider what the child has done; then speculate on what the consequences might be. After giving your answers, look at the consequences I'm suggesting (below) and the lessons the child might learn.

Example 1. Jayden loses his allowance money.
    Consequences: _____

Example 2. Ashley leaves her science project on the floor within the baby's reach.
    Consequences: _____

Example 3. Brandon forgets to write down a math assignment.
Consequences: _____

Example 4. Austin's parents discover he has cut school.
Consequences: _____

Example 5. Abigail refuses to take her antibiotics.
Consequences: _____

Example 1:
Consequences:
  Jayden can't buy something he wants.
Lessons:
  Jayden may learn to keep his money in a safe place.
  Jayden may consider creative ways to earn the money he lost.

Example 2:
Consequences:
  Ashley's project may get damaged.
  Ashley may have to redo parts of her project.
Lesson:
  Ashley may learn to take better care of her things.

Example 3:
Consequences:
  Brandon may have some points deducted from his grade.
  Brandon may have to complete his project at recess.
Lesson:
  Brandon may be upset and become better organized.

Example 4:
Consequences:
  Austin's parents contact all his teachers.
  Austin's teachers inform his parents if he misses a class.
Lessons:
  Austin learns that his parents take cutting school seriously.
  Austin learns that the school will cooperate with his parents.

Example 5:
  Consequence:
    Abigail's parents remain firm: she must take her medicine.
  Lessons:
    Abigail learns that health issues are non-negotiable.
    Abigail learns less painful ways to take pills.

When we allow a child to experience natural consequences we need to be centered. And we need to be courageous. Recognizing the wider perspective can help us do that. While it can be painful to watch our children suffer, we can find comfort in knowing that we're helping them learn lessons and skills that will serve them for a lifetime.

In a Nutshell

Children need limits in order to feel safe and cared for, to gain self-control and to learn sensitivity to others. Assertive limit-setting allows us to set boundaries in ways that model mutual respect and encourage cooperation. If children protest, we reflect their concerns. If appropriate, we can change our minds. If not, we maintain our limit and end the discussion.

You'll be effective when you set limits if you:

- Feel clear about what is appropriate.
- Listen to your child's objections.
- Remember to respect your needs, too .
- End the discussion when there's nothing new to add.

Natural consequences allow our children to learn essential lessons from life itself; often, minimal communication is needed.

To apply natural consequences skillfully:

- Don't confuse consequences with punishment.
- Ask yourself: "Are the consequences the direct result of the behavior?"
- Don't over-protect your child. Natural consequences

teach indispensable lessons: they help children become responsible and capable.

No matter how skillful we are as parents, problems will happen, of course. In the next chapter, we'll learn how to express our concerns effectively and how to solve problems with respect.

CHAPTER **10**

Problems Happen:

Expressing Concerns Effectively

Difficulties, opposition, criticism—these things are meant to be overcome, and there is a special joy in facing them ...

—Vijaya Lakshmi Pandit

PROBLEMS WILL HAPPEN; CHILDREN and teens are "works in progress"—and so are we, of course.

> *Hannah forgot to do her chores again; I had to feed all her fish and pets, even though I was late for work.*

> *Madison keeps tripping his little brother; Joshua nearly got hurt. It looks as if he does it on purpose.*

> *Alexis took a phone message from my boss—and never wrote it down or said a word!*

The last chapter helped us learn how to set limits and allow children to learn from natural consequences. But what happens when their actions affect *us*? How can we express our serious concerns and strong feelings while still modeling respect?

Expressing a Concern

When we're feeling frustrated, it's tempting to make quick negative judgments:

> *When Jimmy said, "Are you kidding? No way!" I shot back, "Don't be rude!"*

> *When I heard the bad news, I blurted out, "You lost your jacket again? Can't you take care of anything?"*

Responses like these may be understandable, but they're not likely to be effective. It might feel good to express those feelings, but when we blame or criticize, our children are likely to dig in their heels.

Children—and adults—are more willing to change their behavior when we avoid judging them. For that reason, the most effective way to express your upset is to be objective in describing the child's behavior and to say how it affects you:

> *I feel frustrated when you say, "No way." I start wondering whether you're willing to hear my point of view.*

> *It really upsets me to hear that your jacket is lost; I'm worried about how we'll pay for a new one.*

That approach gives children a clear message as well as an opportunity to respond to your concern. More often than you might think, children will suggest a solution or volunteer to change if you're skillful in expressing your discomfort. The best way to give them that opportunity is to avoid aggressive communication, such as name-calling, criticizing or lecturing. Those approaches only invite resistance. When you tell your children how their behavior affects *you*—how you feel about it and how it interferes in your life—it gives them honest feedback. They have an opportunity to take responsibility.

How to Be Effective When You Express a Concern

The format for *expressing a concern* has the familiar two parts—assertion and explanation—illustrated in the example below:

Assertion: *When you leave your clothes on the couch ...*

Explanation: *I feel frustrated and disappointed. It's hard to come home from a long day at work and see the house out of order.*

Let's look at each part separately to see how to make it most effective.

Assertion: Describe the *troublesome behavior.*

Simply describe what the child said or did, without labeling, judging or interpreting. Imagine that a microphone recorded the event. It would simply hear Jimmy say, "No way!" It would not label the statement as "rude" or interpret it as "impudence." It would record only those exact words. Similarly, a video camera would record that a towel was left lying on the bathroom floor. It would not label that as "careless" or "sloppy," nor would it decide that Sally is "acting like she doesn't care." Describe what was said or done objectively, nothing more.

Explanation: Describe your *feelings* and how the behavior *affects you.*

The idea is to focus on *your* feelings—in a sense, to take responsibility for your reaction. Stay with yourself; don't slip and analyze the other person. Parents often make the mistake of saying "I feel ..." and they make a comment about the *other* person ("I feel you're being selfish"). Stick with your own feelings, such as "frustrated," "disappointed," "let down," etc.

When possible, choose words that describe the way you feel precisely, to help your child understand. In the appendix, you'll find a list of "Words to Express Feelings," to help you identify the wide range of feelings you may experience (pages 309–310).

Avoid words about anger when possible. It's fine to be clear and forceful about how strongly you feel, but anger is often a secondary feeling, triggered by an earlier emotion. Talk about the feeling that came first, such as, "I feel frightened, worried, ignored, used ..." etc.

Also, explain how the child's behavior affects you. It might affect your time, energy or money. Chances are it affects the relationship: "It makes me feel less trusting," or "I feel like I don't want to put myself out for you now..." It's a personal and intimate statement that goes to the heart of your concern.

The idea of explaining how your child's behavior *affects you* may be unfamiliar; it might take some time to think it through. But that's the most valuable part of the skill. Expressing a concern invites your children to enter your world and understand how it feels to you, to go *outside of themselves* temporarily. As children learn to identify with another person, they acquire *empathy,* which is the foundation for ethical behavior. Empathy helps people become sensitive, kind and caring. It will be valuable to your children in every relationship, throughout their lives.

Here are some examples of using assertion to express concerns. Note the lack of blaming and the focus on how the problem affects *you*:

Assertion:	*When you came home after curfew and didn't call ...*
Explanation:	*I felt worried and scared. I didn't know if you were in an accident or what, and there was no way I could find out. I waited and waited, just pacing around. There was nothing I could do. Now I find myself wondering whether I can count on you to keep our agreements.*

In the case of the lost jacket:

Assertion:	*When you tell me you left your jacket at the park and it got ripped off ...*
Explanation:	*I feel frustrated and annoyed. I know you can't go without a jacket and it'll be hard to find the money to buy another one; we've already used up the clothing allowance for this month.*

To sharpen your skills, I encourage you to practice what you've just learned, using the exercise below.

Using Assertion to

Express Your Concerns

Divide a piece of paper into three columns.
Label the columns as below.

ASSERTION   +   EXPLANATION

Description	*Feelings*	*Effects*
Example: *When you leave your clothes on the living room couch ...*	*I feel frustrated ...*	*because I care a lot about how the house looks, and I get upset when I see things out of place.*

_____
_____
_____
_____
_____

   Think of two or three concerns you might want to express. Write assertive statements to express them, putting each part in the appropriate column.
   Remember that when we express concerns, we're often upset. It takes more self-control to stay centered and avoid slipping to the lower self, with its aggressive or nonassertive ways of communicating.
   When you've completed the blanks, check your answers. Have you followed the guidelines in this chapter for using assertion to state a concern?

How Will Your Child Respond?

Now comes the interesting part: your child's response. Lay out the red carpet and wait patiently to see what your son or daughter has to say. Always provide an opportunity for your child to take responsibility.

Be alert to how much your child is taking in your concern; it will tell you what to do next. If you meet opposition, that's your signal to use reflection.

For example, here are some different ways a child or teen might respond:

> *It wasn't my fault.*
> *I just can't be perfect.*
> *I didn't mean to do it; I'm sorry.*

The first step, as always, is to reflect the child's response:

Child:	*It wasn't my fault.*
Reflection:	***You're saying you're not to blame.***

Child:	*I just can't be perfect.*
Reflection:	***You feel kids make mistakes and I should be accepting; that's part of life.***

Child:	*I didn't mean to do it; I'm sorry.*
Reflection:	***You feel badly, like I do. You certainly didn't do it on purpose.***

It's Wasn't My Fault

Although the first two children are deflecting our concern, the first boy is unwilling to take responsibility. That tells us this child will not be available to respond to our concern in a way that would satisfy us. Our task is to help create an atmosphere that is safe enough for this child to look honestly at his own behavior. Several rounds of reflection may be necessary.

That conversation might go something like this:

Child:	*It wasn't my fault.*
Reflection:	***You're saying you're not to blame.***
Child:	*That's right. That kid shouldn't have taken it. Why are people so dishonest?*
Reflection:	***You think it's not right to take something that isn't yours.***
Child:	*Yes, then there wouldn't be a problem.*

The child still takes no responsibility, but reflection has helped him to calm down. Mom has created a safe environment.

Notice that this parent avoided a trap that's easy to fall into. When children talk about what other people did, it's easy to begin commenting on the *third party*. If Mom said, "He did the wrong thing," the conversation could have been about the "bad guy." When she simply reflected her son's belief—"You think it's not right to take something that isn't yours"— she helped him stay focused on his understanding or interpretation of the situation.

Now that the child is calm, the mom asserts herself again:

Assertion:	***I agree with you; it's not right to take something that isn't yours. But that child isn't here for us to tell. And I'm concerned that you left your jacket at the park and now there's a problem: we've already used up the clothing allowance for this month.***

At this point, the child *might* take some responsibility.

Child:	*I get so hot, I forget. I'll have to be more careful.*

If that happens, parent and child can continue the dialogue. Of course, the child might also find another way to avoid responsibility:

Child:	*Just borrow money from next month's allowance; it's no big deal.*

Again, we would acknowledge what's been said:

Reflection:	*It seems like you've found a simple solution and I don't need to fuss any more."*
Child:	*Yes.*
Assertion:	*But I'm still uncomfortable. I'm concerned that the new jacket might also get lost. I'm not sure what you might do differently in the future to help me feel more confident. I'm really interested in your thoughts.*

The parent stated her concern directly. Did you also notice the gentle way in which she invited her son to take responsibility? Expressions such as, "I'm really interested in your thoughts," can be thought of as *door openers*. Their purpose is to encourage self-reflection without imposing pressure. Throughout this chapter we'll identify several more helpful phrases you can use to calmly encourage your children to think about their actions.

I Just Can't Be Perfect

Once again, the way a child responds provides important clues that can help us be effective. In this situation, we would use the same skills, but express ourselves quite differently:

Child:	*I just can't be perfect.*
Reflection:	*You feel kids make mistakes and I should be accepting; that's part of life.*
Child:	*Yes, I usually take good care of my things. I'm sorry. I was having such a good time, I just forgot. And I had run around so much, I didn't need my jacket, so I didn't notice it was gone.*
Reflection:	*You want me to remember that you usually take care of your stuff and this was an exception.*
Child:	*Yes.*

Assertion:	*I know what you're saying is true. You do take really good care of your things and I value that in you. But we're still stuck with the dilemma: you have no jacket and we've used up the clothing allowance for this month.*

Once the child takes responsibility, parent and child can brainstorm together to find a solution that works for them.

I Didn't Mean to Do It; I'm Sorry

In this example the child accepts our concern. Still, it's important to reflect, to let the child know he's been heard—and to continue the dialogue, to find a solution:

Reflection:	*You feel badly.*
Child:	*Yes.*
Assertion:	*I can see that. Let's talk about how this problem could have been avoided in the first place. Then we'll figure what to do about the lost jacket.*

Again, once the child takes responsibility, parent and child work together to find a solution that meets their needs.

More Door Openers

When you're facing a problem, it's great to have some handy door openers to get things going in the right direction. We heard a good one in the story about the missing jacket: "I'm really interested in your thoughts." Door openers are helpful when your child struggles with taking responsibility.

I'm Curious

In many difficult situations, I'm curious is a great starter. When you suspect your child:

- has broken a family agreement
- may not be telling the truth
- has stolen something
- has violated the law

Obviously, we're entering touchy territory. You don't create a safe environment by accusing children of being guilty, or calling them a "liar" or "thief." Yet you have a strong suspicion that some heavy-duty, lower-self behavior may have occurred. To follow the guidelines of mutual respect, we know it's helpful to begin by stating the objective facts.

A mother told this story:

> *I had two ten-dollar bills in my wallet. I don't like to carry cash, so I keep a minimum amount in case of an emergency. I filled the car with gas, using a credit card, and ran to the bathroom while Haley remained in the car. On the way home Haley reminded me, "I need glue for my project." I asked her to run into the supermarket and opened my wallet to give her a ten-dollar bill. I was shocked to discover there was only one!*
>
> *To catch my breath and clear my head, I decided to wait until Haley returned with the glue before I spoke to her. Then I began, "Haley, when I checked my wallet before I picked you up from school, I had two ten-dollar bills. I haven't spent any cash since then and I paid for the gas with a credit card. When I gave you money for the glue, I found only one bill. I'm curious. Do you know what happened to the other one?"*

No matter what, Haley will be uncomfortable; that's inherent in the situation. But instead of accusing her, Mom provided an opportunity for Haley to volunteer the truth.

Sometimes children admit their mistakes, explaining why it happened and expressing regret. But Haley just shrugged her shoulders and said, "I don't know." Mom continued, stating the facts:

> *I saw both bills at 3:00 pm and at 4:00 pm one was missing. During that time I was either driving to pick you up, with you or in the bathroom.*

Soon after, Haley began to tell the truth. That doesn't always happen, of course. Children differ. But here's what matters: The child or teen knows that you're not ignoring the situation as mini parent might. Nor are you accusing her, acting like Mighty Parent. You're just presenting the facts and saying, "I'm puzzled; I'm curious." Haley would have a lot to think about.

If Haley still remained silent, you'd probably feel terribly frustrated; you'd need to say more. Calmly, from the centered self, you could add:

> *I see you don't want to talk right now. I don't feel finished, but I can accept waiting if I'm certain there will be a time when you will talk. I'd like you to agree that we talk before 8:00 o'clock tomorrow evening.*

You've set a boundary. Haley is given time. And you haven't neglected your own needs. You've taken a respectful approach to a challenging situation.

Help Me Make Sense of This

Two or more door openers can be used in combination. A father told this story:

> *The school principal called me at work and said, "Mr. Hamill, I'm sorry to have to tell you there was an incident at recess today. Ryan shoved Sam pretty hard and he's badly bruised." When I got home that night, I asked Ryan what happened. All he said was, "I didn't do it."*
>
> *I wasn't sure how to begin, but I thought I'd use a door opener to calm the situation: "I'm curious, Ryan. You said you didn't push Sam. Yet, the teacher on the playground says she saw you push him when Sam grabbed the ball out of your hands. And we both know that Sam has a big bruise on his knee. Can you help me make sense of this?"*

Dad did not use an aggressive tone, nor label his son. He stayed calm and centered, presenting the information and inviting his son to respond to it. After an uncertain start and a few tears, they had a long discussion that was honest and satisfying for both.

Help Me Understand

This door opener is similar to the previous ones, but even a slight variation helps us sound fresh. Teens, in particular, could find us irritating if we sounded too predictable (or even if we didn't, for that matter).

I'm Confused

This door opener and the two previous ones often work well together. In a sense, they say, "Something doesn't quite fit." For example:

> My seventeen-year-old, Kayla, is allowed to drive to and from her soccer games. But she's not allowed to drive her friends. So imagine how I felt when her friend's mom called to thank me for letting Kayla drive her daughter home!

Here's how Kayla's mom opened the discussion:

> Olivia's mom called. She thanked me for giving you permission to give Emily a ride home. I'm confused. We have a clear agreement that you aren't allowed to drive a friend. And we haven't spoken all day. Help me understand what happened.

Again, the door opener allows us to initiate a discussion respectfully. By avoiding an aggressive manner, we make it easier for our children to talk openly and take responsibility for their actions.

Here are some other ways to word a similar door opener:

- *I'm wondering how to put this together.*
- *I'm interested in exploring this a bit further.*
- *I'd like some help; this isn't clear to me.*
- *Something seems missing. Could you explain that further?*

To Invite Problem Solving

We've seen how door openers can help us initiate a discussion when the situation is tense. Once the tension is reduced, door openers can invite the child to think further about the problem. To see how that can work with care and respect, let's re-visit the lost jacket example.

Mother begins gently:

Assertion: *I'm interested in exploring this a bit further. I'm curious: Do you have any thoughts about how this situation could have been avoided in the first place? I imagine it would be a lot more fun for you to buy new clothes, rather than to spend your clothing allowance to replace a lost item.*

In the midst of a difficult situation, we can still be aware of our child's feelings and express empathy. We can let them know that we *do* care.

Remember the meeting at the principal's office? Ryan's dad said something like this after his son admitted that he pushed Sam:

Assertion: *I'm glad you told me the truth; that's really important, as you know. I also want you to realize that I understand why you were upset with Sam. I wouldn't want someone to grab a ball out of my hand. I was wondering if it might be useful if we talked about another way to deal with the problem. I imagine you'd be happy to avoid this scene and would much prefer to have more time to play.*

When we remain calm and deal with problems from the centered self, children feel our love and respect. That strengthens the relationship and helps them mature.

You won't be surprised to learn that I love door openers. And without question, I'm curious is my favorite. I use it constantly when I teach, in my family practice and in my personal life. It serves so many purposes and seems to have no negative repercussions, no matter the age or gender of the person. I think it's one of the simplest and most useful tools in parenting.

In a Nutshell

Problems happen. Children behave in ways that upset and disappoint us; that's inevitable. When we express a concern skillfully, we create an environment that invites our children to hear us. The skill has three parts:

- Describe the behavior objectively.
- Express your feelings.
- Explain how the behavior affects you.

When the child responds, it's always important to reflect what you hear—especially now, in an uncomfortable situation. The child might take some responsibility or not; door openers can strengthen the odds.

These gentle, yet powerful assertions can help cool things down, making it safer to face and solve problems. If we remain calm and centered, we can reveal to our children that we care. That can help them to mature and discover that growth and change can benefit them too.

CHAPTER 11

Dreams Can Come True:

Creating the Family You Want

The clearer your goals the better—like aiming at a target. The more focused you are on the target, the more likely your chance of striking it.

—Jeanny Chen

SOMEWHERE IN EVERY PARENT'S mind, there is a picture of the ideal family: how family members would relate to each other, the feeling and tone in the home and the way the household would run. The vision may be incomplete or cloudy, but it's there. The skill of assertion can help you to create a real-life family that moves closer to that ideal in your mind.

You are, in effect, drawing the boundaries of your ideal family as you set limits and express your concerns; you're describing what you *don't* want. But assertion can be used in more direct ways to create the family you *do* want. Sharing something of yourself—your feelings, values, hopes and frustrations, is one of the best ways. When you're open emotionally, you plant the seeds for better understanding and closer family relationships. That kind of assertion provides a model for children, demonstrating self-respect and open communication.

Assertion can also help shape the family when you use it to recognize positive behavior, make a request or prevent a problem. This

199

final chapter on assertion will show you how to be effective in all of those situations.

Picture the Family You Want

One of our most important jobs as parents is to "build" the family we want: the way we share work, the things we value most, the way we treat each other and so on. But any builder is lost without a plan—a specific idea of what is to be built.

So how do we get a clear picture of the family we want to create? One way is simply to sit down and give it some thought. Look at the exercise below; it can help you to clarify your picture of the ideal family. By "ideal" we mean that it is realistic and possible, yet requires a stretch.

Exercise: The Family I Want Is …

Find a time when you feel relaxed and free to daydream. Allow yourself to muse as you imagine an ideal family.

The questions below are a useful guide. Choose the ones that interest you; add others if you like. Jot down a word—or a few words—in response to each one you choose:

- What is the atmosphere in this family?
- Describe the attitude or feeling tone when family members talk with each other.
- Describe what each member does on a weekday morning, at bedtime.
- Name some household chores (cooking, clean-up, etc.) and describe how work is distributed.
- What values are most important to this family?
- What rules or principles guide this family?
- What rituals or ceremonies (including playful, informal ones) does this family practice?
- Describe ways in which this family differs from your present family or the family in which you grew up.

This exercise will give you a more complete description of the family you'd like to create. You might want to keep a notebook or journal by category, adding ideas whenever they occur to you. If you have a spouse or partner, ask him or her to do the exercise as well. It will help each of you to clarify your own thoughts. At some point, you'll want to work out differences and create a plan you both fully support. If you're a single parent, you can brainstorm with a friend; that could help you clarify your own ideas. Once your vision is clear, you'll be able to make it come alive, day-by-day, using the powerful skill of assertion.

Making the Vision Real

If you know what you want, assertion can help you achieve it. Every time you assert your values, preference or feelings, you're influencing an impressionable child or teen: "I want us to divide the chores in a way that's fair," or "This is how I prefer we treat each other in our family." Day by day, you can set the guidelines and model the behavior—bringing your family ever closer to the picture in your mind.

Here are some examples from parents as they teach their children what kind of family they want:

Learning manners

I'd like you to wait until everyone has been served before you reach for a second helping; it's a way to show each person respect.

Learning family rules

It's okay to be mad at your sister, but it's not okay for you to hit her.

Learning to work as a family

If you and your brother want to trade chores this week, I'd like you both to inform me, so that I know what to expect.

Learning how to follow society's rules

The law says we have to wait for a green light before we cross the street, even if no cars are coming. It's meant to keep us safe.

Learning self-control

I'd like you to allow your brother to finish what he was saying before you tell us what's on your mind.

Learning patience

I know you want me to help you find Tamara's telephone number right now, but I need to watch the eggs so I don't overcook them. I'll be there in five minutes.

Learning the family's values

I'll find out more about that movie before I decide; I want to make sure it's not violent.

Sharing Yourself: *Children Want the Real You*

> *This above all: to thine own self be true.*
>
> —Shakespeare

Most of us want families that are loving and close and supportive. A good way to achieve that goal is to provide a model—to share our feelings openly. Intimacy grows when people let their feelings show; we can choose to "be ourselves" with our children and teens. I learned that lesson the hard way, many years ago:

> *As a family therapist, I provided support and guidance for teachers who were my clients. Though they were pleased with their growth and became more effective in the classroom, I had misgivings. How could I continue to guide these professionals when my own experience was so limited?*

To be authentic, I felt I should first become a good teacher. So I went back to the classroom.

The first year I felt stiff and uncomfortable. I tried to emulate the best teachers I knew, but I couldn't quite create the open and stimulating environment I wanted. Three years later I was still trying! Not until the fourth year did it suddenly "click"; at last I felt at ease, having a wonderful time. The students were more cooperative, creative and alive. I had finally found the "secret": instead of trying to act the image of "teacher" I carried in my head, I became myself. I was simply Ilene—with all my feelings, quirks, likes and dislikes—who happened to be in the role of teacher right now. I was open and spontaneous with the children; I enjoyed them more because I was more comfortable with myself. And they responded as never before.

The same truth applies to parenting: too often, we limit ourselves by "playing the role" rather than being ourselves. We do best when we're open with our feelings, honest and authentic. From that genuine and centered place we can be most effective. Though we take on the responsibilities of family leader or disciplinarian, we can still be *ourselves*. The grandest part of parenting is being alive with your own personality, humor, interests, creativity and spontaneity—sharing yourself whole-heartedly. When you parent in that way, you reap many rewards:

- You model honesty, openness and intimacy.
- Your children know you better.
- You express and become more aware of what you think, feel and want.
- You model self-esteem and experience self-respect.

How to *Express* the "Real You"

Once again, the key is assertion. That word implies that we're expressing ourselves in a way that is direct, clear and forthright—free of ambiguous messages—verbal or nonverbal. For example:

- *I'd like to have dinner outdoors; the weather is so delightful.*
- *I enjoy helping you with your homework; it gives us a special time together.*
- *I was so mad at myself when I forgot to put stamps on the outgoing mail!*

"But those are just simple statements!" parents often say. "What makes them assertive?" "Because they reveal what you want, how you feel or what you think," I reply. That's what assertion *is*: expressing yourself and saying, in effect, "This is who I am." Assertive statements are self-revealing.

Since the concept is simple and we already use it often, why bother to learn more about this skill? The problem is we often veer *away* from assertion when we feel less secure: when we're anxious to be accepted or fear rejection. Sometimes we become less direct—and so less clear. That limits our ability to create the family we want. For example:

1. Indirect: *I don't know what you think about this new recipe I cooked.*

   Direct: **I hope you'll like this new recipe; I made it as a special treat.**

The first version asks a question instead of revealing something personal. There's nothing wrong with that. Yet this indirect message hides more intimate and valuable information. When we're open with our children, they learn to know our values and more of who we are.

2. Indirect: *I need you to clean up your room.*

   Direct: **I'd like you to clean up your room. I want you to learn to take care of your toys by putting them away after you use them.**

Parents often say "need" when they mean "want." The first version fails to tell the whole story. The second is clearer: "I want you to develop habits I value."

3. Indirect:	*I want you to find something to do for a little while.*
Direct:	***I want to practice the exercises I'm learning in my parenting class; I'll need fifteen minutes alone to complete them.***

The parent in the first version tells the child what to do without revealing the *reason* for the request. Children feel more comfortable when they understand what's happening.

All three indirect examples reveal a common shortcoming. Although they begin with the pronoun I, they focus on asking something from the other person, ("What do you think ...") rather than revealing something about themselves. Why do we tend to do that? To protect ourselves. We feel vulnerable when we reveal our own thoughts and feelings. We fear that others might judge, criticize or belittle us in some way. Yet our children cannot know us fully—our values and approach to life—unless we're willing to be open. We can express our feelings every day, with simple statements like these:

- *I look forward to Friday dinner all week long. I love it when we're all together and relaxed and can really enjoy each other.*
- *I feel really proud of myself. I finished my report at work without having to put in overtime. That took a lot of planning and it really paid off.*
- *Finally, I'm exercising three times a week. It hasn't been easy to get into this routine, but I'm getting used to it and actually enjoying myself!*

In the examples above, parents share their positive feelings; it's also useful to share when you're having a difficult time. That's just as real. For example:

- *I feel exhausted by those chores. Everything took longer than I expected.*
- *I don't feel very well today. I'm worried that I might have a short fuse and take it out on you.*

Statements like those allow you to share the struggles, goals and values in your own life. Revealing what's on your mind and in your heart—whether it's a simple statement about flowers or a difficult relationship issue—requires courage. It exposes you and could make you feel vulnerable. But it also builds stronger and closer families.

There is another significant way in which assertion can help us to shape our families: by giving recognition to positive behavior.

Water the Flowers, Not the Weeds

Kind words can be short and easy to speak,
but their echoes are endless.

— Mother Theresa

One of the great joys of parenting is taking delight in a child's finest qualities and behaviors: a sunny disposition, a sense of humor, an open show of affection. Making sure to notice—to really take in and acknowledge these qualities and behaviors—enhances our lives and nurtures the best within our children.

Too often, we give our children attention when we disapprove of their behavior. While it's part of our job to address problems, it's equally or more important to "catch our children doing something right." We want to acknowledge qualities and behavior we value—a child's enthusiasm for learning, an inclination to be kind and helpful, a willingness to say, "I'm sorry" and an ability to see two sides of an issue. Water the flowers, not the weeds!

We give a precious gift to our children and teens when we let them know how much they delight us, how much we appreciate their uniqueness. Parents are the child's most influential "mirrors"; the images we reflect, day after day, help our children discover who they are. When we reflect their strengths, children are more able to see these fine qualities and integrate them into their own self-images: "I have something to offer; I'm worthwhile."

The skill that helps us show our delight is *assertive appreciation*. Parents in class often say it's their favorite way to use assertion. It certainly is mine.

Using Assertion to Express Appreciation

The format for assertive appreciation is the familiar two-part statement: an assertion plus an explanation. Include your *feelings* in the explanation (as you would in an assertive concern). Some examples:

> *When you offered to bring in the groceries without my asking, I felt so good. It feels great to have your help.*

> *When you helped your sister with her homework, I was really touched. She's having a hard time with division and I imagine your gentle manner made it easier for her.*

The key is to be alert: to *notice* when your child or teen does something you value. And then express your appreciation clearly.

Whatever we nurture with attention will grow. Assertive appreciation is an important way to encourage the best in our children. And, like every skill in this book, it can benefit *all* your relationships. As one mother told us shyly, "That's one of the skills that keeps our marriage so alive."

Appreciation

Divide a piece of paper into three columns, labeled as below.

Think of two or three appreciations you would like to express; write each part in the appropriate column.

Assertion   +   Explanation

Description	***Feelings***	***Effects***
Example: *When you finished your homework before you turned on the TV …*	*I felt delighted;*	*it makes me feel so good that our talks make a difference.*

_____

_____

_____

_____

Now take the final step: *express* your appreciations to your children. Notice their reactions; that should encourage you to express appreciation more often!

Asking Children to Help

Assertion can help us to transform the family in still another way: encouraging children to share in family responsibilities. When we're skillful in making requests, we discover some unexpected benefits:

- Our children are more likely to cooperate.
- Our needs are met more often.
- We feel less tension.
- Our children become more competent and responsible.
- We feel closer to our children.

Take a moment now to ask yourself: How much do you expect your children to contribute to the household? Many parents have minimal expectations—and end up exhausted, feeling like martyrs. If that sounds like you at times, the *assertive request* can make a positive difference in your family.

Children cannot learn responsibility and grow to become independent unless we expect them to share in caring for themselves and the family. They can learn to cooperate even when they're still very dependent, as we change diapers, put on shoes and feed them. Their responsibilities should increase as they become more capable. They gain a sense of competence and mastery as they help us prepare meals, maintain the household, care for themselves and family members. They need to feel they make an important contribution to the family. And you need and deserve their support.

But what if they don't want to cooperate? Children have very different dispositions, of course, and some are naturally more conscientious than others. If you have friends whose children are happy helpers, maybe they are just lucky. But as parents we play a key role—whether we're aware of it or not—in creating an environment that encourages cooperation or resistance.

Do You Deserve Help?

More important than anything else is the *attitude* we hold as we ask for help. Do you believe you *deserve* help from your child? Are you convinced your child *needs* to contribute to the family in order to learn responsibility, cooperation and independence? If you're unsure of the answers, the first step is to look at your beliefs. Can you adopt the attitude that you do deserve help rather than doing it all alone—and that your child does need to have responsibilities in order to mature?

Have you ever known children who've had everything done for them? When they go to college or leave home, such children are ill equipped to face independence. It's unfair to deprive children of opportunities to develop a sense of capability.

When you feel comfortable and secure about the requests you make, your child or teen will sense that attitude and be more likely to cooperate.

Remember too, no matter how much they complain, there is a core part of every child and teen that really wants to cooperate. They need your help to insure that contributing to the family becomes a regular part of their lives. When you make a request, keep that in mind: you're helping your child to bring out the best. You're on the same team.

> *"I feel sorry for some of my friends," Derek said casually one night as we peeled potatoes. He was fifteen. I had no idea what he was talking about so I asked, "Why do you feel sorry for them?" "Because they can't do anything; they don't know how to cook chicken or spaghetti. They don't even know how to make their beds." That answer delighted me; Derek's help had made a real difference to me over the years. Though he dealt out his share of resistance, he could see a different perspective now: sharing in the family work had helped him feel more capable and independent.*

Requests and Mutual Respect

Another key to gaining cooperation is to hold an attitude of mutual respect. It's easy to see why that matters: just imagine for a moment you're a child. Listen to these two requests from Mom. Which one makes you feel more like cooperating?

Version 1:	*Chris, get me Billy's diapers.*
Version 2:	*Chris, I'd like you to get me Billy's diapers. I thought I had a bunch downstairs, but I've run out. The baby's nursing and I need some help.*

In version two, Mom shows Chris more respect. She says, in effect, "I care enough about you and your time to explain why I need to make this request."

The why is important, as we noted earlier; even adults don't like requests that seem arbitrary. We feel respected and more willing to cooperate when we're given a reason. A father in one of our classes admitted,

> *I felt resistant when my wife would tell me to give Chloe a bath. Although I always enjoyed our time together, I felt like I had no choice—like I was a kid, having to do whatever my mother said. Only when my wife explained, "This is a great time for me to relax, turn on some music and enjoy cooking," did I feel we were working as a team.*

Making Requests Effective

The format for making an *assertive request* is simple. It has the same two parts as the other assertive skills: assertion plus explanation.

Assertion:	States the request
Explanation:	Provides the reason

Either part can come first. The combination gives you an effective way to ask for what you want and respond to resistance. Just be sure your statements are free of implied criticism.

While the format is familiar, it's worth taking some time to set it in your mind. Try the exercise that follows:

Request

Think of two or three typical requests (any physical action) you might want to ask of your child or teen. Write the words you'd say, including a clear explanation.

Assertion   +   Explanation

Example: *I'd like you to put all your toys away before Sasha comes over.*

I want her to know that we expect the room to be in order before she leaves.

_____   _____

_____   _____

_____

Now imagine that your child refuses. Write what he or she might say.

Then write your reply. Use reflection plus another assertion, if necessary.

Child's Concern   Reflection + Assertion

Sasha won't help me.

You're worried she won't pitch in. We'll need to teach her that in this house we expect everyone to help with cleanup.

_____   _____

_____   _____

_____   _____

Educate Your Family

An assertive request can go far beyond teaching children to help. I use it all the time to educate my husband and children about my feelings and needs—and the kind of family I want. Here's a personal example:

> *Early in our marriage, I'd come home from the hairdresser all excited about my new hairstyle—and then feel let down. My husband hadn't noticed!*
>
> *At first I thought, "There are some things you just can't change." But then it dawned on me: "Why not ask for what I want?" My husband was sweet, but his answer was revealing: "I guess I just don't notice things like that."*
>
> *I realized I had to educate him about what it meant to me, so I said gently, "Honey, there's a little girl inside of me who is hungry for attention. She feels very sad if you don't notice a new hairstyle. If I tell you that I'm going to the beauty parlor, would you try hard to remember to notice—and fuss over me?"*
>
> *And that's exactly what he did! I enjoyed the attention and he enjoyed my appreciation. On one occasion when he knew he'd arrive home after I did, he played our "game" magnificently. He left a huge note on our bedroom mirror that said, "Hi. You look great. I love your new hairdo!"*

As a therapist, I tell clients to educate their spouses or lovers: "Teach them how to be good partners for you." When you tell people exactly what you would like, they're often more than willing to give it to you. And that includes children. For example:

Assertion:	*I'd like everyone to support me in making each of our birthdays a memorable experience.*
Explanation:	*When I was a child, my parents often forgot to make a special day of our birthdays; that really hurt.*

The mother in this example invites the family to be sensitive to the pain in her past. Being open with your feelings—having the courage to say what you really want—allows the family to know you intimately.

That's a step toward creating a close and loving relationship. Day by day, this is how to create the family you want.

But here's a caution: sometimes we *intend* to say what we want, but without meaning to, we criticize or attack. The mother in the example above would be far less effective if she said,

> *I'm disappointed and upset because you don't get excited enough about the children's birthdays.*

That might look like an assertive message because it starts with I, but it's actually aggressive. Mom criticized and blamed ("... you don't get excited enough ..."). She would be far more effective if she came from center and simply stated what she wanted and why.

Remember: an assertive statement tells what you feel or want, without judging others. Again, it has two parts: the assertion and the explanation. For example:

Assertion: *I'd like you to tell your sister why you're so mad at her.*

Explanation: *Hitting is not okay in our family because I don't want anyone hurt. You can learn better ways to express your anger.*

Here's another example, with the order reversed:

Explanation: *I care about your grades because I believe they reflect your study habits. I see those habits as a foundation for success in life.*

Assertion: *I'd like you to think seriously about what I'm saying. Then I'd like to talk with you about your grades on Saturday, after your game.*

The examples above illustrate making a request—asking for what you want—as well as *educating* family members by revealing your values.

Though the format is simple, again I encourage you to write down a few examples, to fix the concept in your mind. The brief exercise that follows can help you do that.

Use an Assertive Request to

Educate

Think of three things you'd like to explain to your family—things you'd want them to do—to meet your needs or your picture of a more cooperative family. Write a request for each, using the two-part format:

Assertion   Explanation

_____   _____

_____   _____

_____   _____

_____   _____

The warmth and love that is possible when we educate our children about our world is evident in this mom's story:

> *Two nights a week I go to a community college where I'm learning interior design. I worked for hours at home on a project to design a special bed. The children hovered around my worktable making comments and asking questions. I took the time to explain what I was doing, why I made changes and discussed their comments. They knew the project meant a lot to me.*
>
> *When the design was well received and put on public display at the school, the children were excited for me. They were so proud; they wanted to bring their friends to see their mom's work! I really felt supported.*

This mother didn't have to ask her children for support; by sharing her interests and feelings, she created an atmosphere that encouraged it. When she asked them to help more than usual with dinner, or explained that she couldn't read to them as much during the last week of the project, they were cooperative.

One reason children fail to help out in our world is that we often exclude them from it, without thinking. When we share our interests and include them, they're more likely to root for us and offer support when we need it.

All Sorts of Help

You can get all sorts of help—if you have the courage to ask. Here's another example, this time from a dad in class:

> *I hate to admit it, but I used to yell quite a bit. My wife and kids complained all the time. I've been working hard to change that—and have improved greatly—but nobody notices! My family was quick to complain, but where are the pats on the back?*

I reminded the class that we can educate our families with assertive requests. I encouraged this man to tell his wife and children how hard he'd been working to control his temper. "Let them know it isn't easy for you, that you want them to notice and acknowledge the change." Adding to my suggestion, Dad said, "I'll let them know that their recognition will make me feel good and motivate me to keep on trying."

At the next class he reported the results with a heartwarming grin:

> *The family made me a surprise cake that said, "Dad Is Cool." They had noticed the difference the whole time; they just hadn't said anything!*

This father received even more than he asked for, while the family enjoyed giving. And there was an added bonus. Dad provided a model worth emulating—working hard to improve self-control. The moral is obvious: tell people what you need and you'll be more likely to receive it.

By now I hope it's more than clear: assertion is an all-around tool you can use in many situations, with everyone in your life. There is still another important circumstance in which this skill can help you to create the family you want: when you have an opportunity to *prevent problems.*

Using Assertion to Prevent Problems

Imagine that Grandma will arrive for a visit tomorrow and you dread what might happen. Your stomach was in knots the last time she came for dinner. The children were wild at the table, and raspberry jam got on her white, hand-knit dress.

What can you do to prevent problems this time? Try using an *assertive request*:

Assertion:	*I'd like you to use your best table manners when Grandma visits tomorrow ...*
Explanation:	*because she cares a lot about good manners. The last time she came was a difficult visit for me and I want to feel relaxed.*

Having a problem with the family morning routine? Use an assertive request to plan a discussion:

Explanation:	*I'm not satisfied with our morning routine; I feel uncomfortable rushing so much.*
Assertion:	*I want to talk about it after Sunday brunch. I'd like each of you to think about it; maybe we can all come up with ideas.*

Here's another example of a parent intercepting a potential problem:

Explanation:	*When we're planning a party for your friends, I can easily get stressed. I like to buy everything in advance. That helps me stay calm.*
Assertion:	*I'd like you to give me a complete list by Friday, so we can discuss it and shop on the weekend.*

I encourage you to use assertive statements for prevention as often as possible. Children don't want you to be stressed or frustrated; they prefer that you ask them for help. Remember, they're not shy about asking *you*!

To review the format and create a new habit, take a moment right now to write three assertive statements you might actually use *to prevent problems.*

Use an Assertive Approach to

Prevent Problems

Think of three things you'd like to explain to your family—things you'd want them to do—to help prevent problems.
Write a request for each, using the two-part format:

Assertion   ### Explanation

_____   _____

_____   _____

_____   _____

Keep in mind that you might get what you want, simply by asking. On the other hand, you might get resistance. Be ready and willing to use reflection; that's your key to success. Assertion and reflection are your basic skills; like a needle and thread, they're meant to be used together.

Summing Up

Whether we realize it or not, we influence our families in important ways every day. Every interaction is an opportunity. Step-by-step, we can support and encourage the family to move closer to the ideal in our minds.

The first step is to clarify that ideal, to make it so specific and detailed that we can describe it and see it as a goal we can reach. Then assertion can help us to be effective in moving toward that goal by:

- setting limits to encourage cooperation and teach responsibility
- expressing concerns skillfully when behavior falls short
- modeling closeness and trust by revealing our true selves
- giving recognition to qualities and behavior we appreciate
- making requests in ways that encourage cooperation
- educating the family about what we want
- providing clear guidance to prevent problems

In all its forms, assertion is simply good communication. Its purpose is to reveal something about the speaker: to share thoughts and feelings. Assertion is direct and honest, neither aggressive nor passive; it contains no hidden resentment. Most assertive statements include an explanation. Requests and concerns are even more complete: they say how the behavior affects the speaker. The hallmark of assertion—and every other skill of the centered self—is that it reflects an attitude of mutual respect.

Yet no matter how skillful our communication, we can expect resistance at any time. That's when we use reflection, an effective way to acknowledge we have heard and understood our child's concern. In the coming chapter, we'll learn a more sophisticated form of listening, one that deepens understanding and empowers children and teens to find solutions to their own problems.

CHAPTER 12

Empowering Your Child:

The Art of Listening

*It is the province of knowledge to speak and
it is the privilege of wisdom to listen.*

—Oliver Wendell Holmes

ONE OF THE GREATEST gifts we can give our children is to invite them, on a regular basis, to share their feelings and tell us about their worlds. To have our feelings heard in an atmosphere of *complete acceptance* is enormously healing; it is so beneficial that virtually all therapists provide it. Yet it's surprising how often children grow up without that opportunity—without the sense that their thoughts and feelings are valued.

Providing a quiet time when you "roll out the red carpet" and show your interest helps children to know and appreciate themselves. It helps them learn the skills of friendship and intimacy; it creates a bond of trust between you. The more you listen to your children, the more they will listen to *you*.

We use the skill of listening every day, of course; it's a natural expression of mutual respect. We know it's an effective way to respond when children or teens resist. But skillful listening offers so many other rewards—and is so often overlooked—that it deserves special attention.

Together with its sister skill, assertion, conscious listening is a powerful tool for creating the family you want.

Getting to Know You

To invite our children to help us know them better, all we need to do is show genuine interest. So long as they sense our complete acceptance, they will feel safe to share their worlds. Specific questions are more helpful than general ones. "What's happening at school?" is less effective than, "What are you learning in social studies?" or, "How are you feeling about the new soccer coach?" Our purpose is not to pry, but to become better acquainted. In an atmosphere of trust, we can forge a bond that may last a lifetime.

In addition to listening on a regular basis, there are special situations in which skillful listening can make a great difference: when children or teens bring us problems, and when they're filled with delight.

Mom! Dad! Something Great!

Most of this chapter deals with listening when children reveal problems. But it's equally important to take the time to listen—to give ourselves fully—when our children or teens are excited about something. Why is it beneficial to listen and show our delight when children are excited or enthusiastic? Because they want us to *embrace their happy feelings*—to celebrate with them.

When you have great news, don't you want to share it? Don't you want someone close to you to celebrate your joy? When friends smile, when their eyes light up, when they genuinely enjoy your pleasure, they give you the gift of love. It's so easy to celebrate your children's joy, yet it means so much to them; you touch their hearts.

What's more: these special moments are golden opportunities to learn more about our children and their worlds.

If Johnny comes bursting home from school and screams, "Mom! Kevin invited me to his birthday party!" Mom could miss the boat by being only half there, saying mechanically, "That's nice. When is it?" An opportunity is lost: Johnny may not always share his exuberance. And Mom would miss his joy, his aliveness.

But if Mom were more fully present, she might truly enjoy—and reflect—her son's delight: "Johnny, you're so excited. Seems like this invitation means a lot to you." Johnny would experience Mom's sincere interest, encouraging him to tell the whole story. And he probably would. "Peter's invited too. We're going to bring our games. He has some I don't have and I can't wait to play with them. Oh, this is going to be great, Mom. I'm really excited." Seeing our children delighted and joyful is one of the great rewards of parenting; sharing happy moments brings us closer. Don't let those moments slip by unnoticed! Take the time to listen well and reflect, so you can share them fully with your children or teens; *they want the opportunity to express those feelings of joy and feel your love!*

It's equally important to tune in and listen well when our children's moods are more subdued.

When Children Reveal Their Problems

Nearly every day, our children or teens reveal their problems: "The kids at school are so mean …" "You won't believe what happened today …"

Our hearts go out to an unhappy child or teen; we want to help, to solve the problem and make it better. We want to share our experience and wisdom and teach our values.

Those are natural reactions but, the truth is, our advice is more likely to hamper growth than to foster it. There is a far more effective way we can help.

For example, here's what one mom did:

Susan:	*The kids at school are so mean!*
Mom:	*You're really hurt.*
Susan:	*Jennifer and Lisa were teasing me the whole time we were painting. They said my flowers looked like toads. I hate them!*
Mom:	*You're really mad at them.*

That's right: Susan's mom *listened* carefully to her daughter, without adding any advice or comments. The result was that Susan had the opportunity to work through her own problem:

Susan:	*That's not the worst part. You know that Jennifer invited me to a movie on Saturday, right? Well, now she says I can't come!*
Mom:	***You're disappointed that you can't go!***
Susan:	*Jennifer is supposed to be my best friend; I don't get it. Why would she do that to me?*
Mom:	***That surprises you.***
Susan:	*I would never treat her so mean. I bet it's that awful Lisa who's making her act that way.*

If you're feeling impatient reading this dialogue, you're not alone; parents often express concern about how hard it is just to listen. It's *so* tempting to ask questions or offer advice. But watch what happens when a parent has faith in her child and gives her plenty of space to "hear herself think":

Mom:	***You think maybe it's Lisa's fault.***
Susan:	*Jennifer never did stuff like that until Lisa got into it. Before she met Lisa she was saying things like, "You're my best friend; I wish you were my sister."*
Mom:	***You feel Jennifer has changed since she met Lisa; she used to express a lot of love for you.***
Susan:	*She also said she never wanted to hurt me. I told her the whole story about how Jessica hurt me.*
Mom:	***Seems like she understands you well and doesn't want you to be hurt again.***
Susan:	*You know, I think I should talk to her and tell her how I feel.*
Mom:	***Uh huh.***
Susan:	*Yes. Jennifer and I were pretty mad at each other once before, but we were able to make up.*
Mom:	***You've had success in the past and you believe you can have it again.***
Susan:	*I think it will work. I'm going to call her right now.*

| Mom: | *Sounds like you have a plan.* |
| Susan: | *I have to go now, okay? Thanks, Mom.* |

Children *can* work through their own problems—and often find more appropriate solutions than we could—*if we give them the opportunity.* Only by grappling with their own problems can children learn to make decisions, become more capable and independent and thereby gain confidence and self-esteem.

Here's another example:

As Dad drives Jonas home from practice, the conversation grows more personal than usual:

| Jonas: | *I don't know if I really want to ask Jill to the game or not. I guess the truth is, I'm afraid she might turn me down.* |

A silence follows. Dad is tempted to say, "Don't be silly; there's nothing to be afraid of," or to offer advice. Instead, he says ...

Dad:	*You'd like to invite Jill to the game, but you're afraid she might not accept.*
Jonas:	*Yeah. She's so pretty and all the guys really like her; I'm scared she'll turn me down or just laugh or something.*
Dad:	*You're worried she may say no or even laugh at you.*
Jonas:	*Yeah, I guess. I'm sure a lot of guys feel the same way.*
Dad:	*You imagine you're not alone in this one.*
Jonas:	*But you know what? I'd probably feel worse if I didn't even try. I promised myself I wasn't going to lose out because I didn't "go for it." I'm a little uptight, but I'm still going to call.*

Dad allowed Jonas to sort through his feelings without interruption. Yet he was fully present—showing his interest and implied faith. What a great gift! Dad's listening helped his son figure out how he really felt and what he wanted to do. Jonas had a chance to find his courage and his own solution.

Skillful Listening

In previous chapters you learned reflection, a basic technique for listening. There, the main purpose was to deal with resistance, to listen well and help a child become calm—and available to hear you. In this chapter, our purpose is to be a good *facilitator*—to support children in working through their own problems, without our input. You'll discover your children can manage their own problems, providing essential growth for them and a new kind of freedom for you.

Since our purpose is different, we'll use a slightly different way of listening. It's similar to reflection, but more sophisticated and refined; we call it *conscious listening*.

Conscious Listening: How to Do It

As always, the attitude we bring is fundamental for success. We've said that our goal is not to solve the problem or teach; it is to *support the child* in grappling with it. Responsibility for working out the problem stays with the child or teen. Our attitude is one of trust: holding the belief that our child is capable of working through it.

How can we do that? These are the guidelines to keep in mind:

- Be "invisible."
- Be sensitive.
- Be succinct.
- Be supportive.

Let's take a brief look at each one.

Be "Invisible"

Being "invisible" means simply *observing* the child's problem-solving process, without offering comments or suggestions. Even if we believe our input would be helpful, we refrain. We keep the focus on the child.

Here's an example of a parent who slipped and became visible:

Child:	*I've decided I'm too upset; I'll just avoid Sandra for a while.*
Mom:	***I'm not sure that's such a good idea.***

Notice that the mother's comment interjects her own point of view; she takes the spotlight. A better response would have been to reflect the child's decision:

Mom:	***You don't feel ready to deal with her.***

Another way to keep the focus on the child is to avoid referring to another person. Don't talk about the friend she's mad at; talk about *your child's feelings and thoughts.*

Avoid:	*Sandra's acting mean again.*
Instead:	***You want to keep some distance for now.***

Above all, don't make suggestions! Whether we're children or adults, the solutions we accept rarely come from someone else; they are the result of sorting through our own inner experience.

For example:

Child:	*I'm so mad at Kathy. I'd like to tell all her friends she's such a phony. I was so upset I could hardly concentrate in class. I feel so angry!*
Mom:	***You're really revved up about this!***

Be Sensitive

Listen for what the child is experiencing: thoughts *and* feelings. Remain *patient;* children may need time to get in touch with their emotions and thoughts. Give them space to sort through the layers of feelings and ideas that may surface gradually. A moment that feels like an awkward silence is often a time when a child is doing valuable work.

The general rule is to speak only when necessary:

- When there's a *natural pause,* you can provide a brief recap to summarize what's happened so far. After a child reveals several options, you might recap by saying:

    You can see different choices, but aren't sure which one feels best.

- When a *new idea or feeling* is presented, you'll want to acknowledge the shift:

    At first you were upset, but then you felt comforted when James said he had the same complaints about the teacher.

- When children convey nonverbally that they *want reassurance,* you can provide it by saying something like:

    I'm very interested in what you're saying; I'd love to hear more.

Watch your children's eyes and expression. Sometimes you'll see uncertainty, as if they're asking *nonverbally*: "Is it safe to continue? Are you still with me?" You can show your support and create a safe environment by staying quiet and remaining present, by being patient and reflecting what you've just heard or by saying words of encouragement such as, "I'm here; it's okay to continue." More than anything, children need to feel our acceptance.

Be Succinct

Unnecessary detail may detract from the child's focus. Keep your responses brief. Mirror only the *essence.*

For example, suppose a child says,

> *Rebecca teased me in front of the kids again in the cafeteria.*
> *She called me a pig when she saw how much food I packed in*
> *my lunch bag.*

The parent need only reflect the child's experience. Something like:

> *That really hurt your feelings.*

Repeating all the details could be annoying—and counter to our goal of being invisible. Often, we may need to say nothing at all; silence contains a rich, warm quality when we are truly present and open.

Be Supportive

Listen with genuine interest and acceptance. Comments that show empathy, such as "Um hmm," "I see," "Really," and "Oh," assure our children that they are being heard and understood. Empathetic facial expressions and body language also show that we care.

The bottom line is that we create a safe environment through our *attitude:* by trusting that our children or teens can solve their own problems. And by remaining patient and accepting—allowing children the time they need to get in touch with their own feelings, thoughts and solutions.

What Else Should I Know?

Simply listen well. That's the heart of it. Give your child or teen the stage.

But in order to listen well, we first have to do something else that is much more difficult: *put aside our own feelings and reactions*—and put aside that impulse to jump in and solve the problem. Empty your head;

be receptive; become a "blank page." In other words, adopt the mindset of the Observer.

Then tune in, with sensitive ears, mind and heart. Listen for what your child is feeling as well as thinking. Imagine yourself as the child in those circumstances; what would it be like? Reflect or mirror the essence of that experience, without judging it in any way.

For example:

Child:	*This homework is too hard; I can't do it.*
Parent:	***You think it's too tough for you.***

Now—after you reflect—listen for your child's response; it will give you more information about what's going on in his or her world.

Child:	*This teacher is impossible. She talks and talks and I don't know what she's saying. Then she puts problems on the board for us to solve, calls on all the smart kids—and then goes onto something even harder. I'm lost!*
Parent:	***You don't understand the material and before you have a chance to get it, the teacher is on to something else.***
Child:	*It's so frustrating! I want to raise my hand and tell her to slow down, that there are some of us who don't get it. But that's embarrassing; it's hard to do.*
Parent:	***You have an idea about what to do, but you don't feel comfortable doing it.***

It isn't easy to put aside your impulse to judge or question. You might be dying to ask, "Are *you* really concentrating? I know you're smart; why are some of the students getting it and you're not?" Or to praise: "That's a great plan. Don't worry about what others will think." But it's important, when we're listening, not to impose *our* agenda. The goal is to stay out of it, for now—to give the child or teen all the space he or she needs to think it through.

When parents have the patience, skill and wisdom to listen well, they're often rewarded. Here's what happened next:

Child: *You know what? I'm calling Serena; she's a math genius. She'll help me catch up.*

Children often surprise us by finding their own solutions. When you think about it, that makes sense; they know so much more about their situation. As a parent, would you have known that Serena is good at math and willing to help? Even when we have good ideas, they may not be solutions that the child feels comfortable in accepting. Children and teens know more about their worlds and are more able to find solutions that work for them.

The Patience of a Saint

Sometimes children find solutions that sound great to us—and then reject their own ideas. Suppose, in the situation above, the child had concluded, "This is hopeless." You might be tempted to jump in and ask, "Why? It sounded like a good idea to me." Or you might even lose your patience and say, "Don't be dramatic." But in the problem-solving process, when children are stuck, they need us to remain calm and accepting.

For example, you might then say,

Parent: ***You don't feel comfortable with your plan and now you feel really frustrated.***

I call this "tracking." You simply reflect what's happening at the moment—how the child is feeling during the problem-solving process.

At this point, we have no idea what will happen next. The process seems at a standstill; the child feels uncertain. That's what I call a "pregnant pause"; it might feel uncomfortable, but be patient! That moment is ripe with possibilities.

It's important we not break the silence. That shows our children we know it's *their* problem, not ours—that we trust they can work it out. By leaving the responsibility with our children, we give them the opportunity to develop "backbone"—to persevere in the face of a challenge—to develop faith in themselves. And that helps them build self-esteem and confidence.

Did I Get It Right?

As you reflect the essence of your children's thoughts and feelings, listen for their feedback. Your child or teen will tell you if you got it right—or missed the target.

Our children may tell us we've heard them accurately:

Yes, that's right. I'm scared that this semester could be really tough.

Or they may agree only in part and clarify what was incomplete or inaccurate:

Yes, I'm scared, but I'm also excited because I have some of the best teachers.

Or disagree:

No, I'm not scared. I'm anxious. When I'm scared I feel wasted and have no energy; being anxious revs me up.

Tuning in to their feedback helps us know and understand our children as they change and develop day by day. For our children, the act of giving feedback helps them clarify their thoughts and feelings. Our supportive listening helps them to hear their own internal dialogue. That's a great gift, made possible by our skill and patient interest.

It's Not Just About Finding Solutions

Every stage in the problem-solving process has value. For example:

Children May Define the Problem

Sometimes children choose to stop talking, once they define the problem. For example, the teen in an earlier example might have ended the conversation by saying, "I want to ask Susan out, but I don't want to risk her rejecting me." He might want to leave it at that for a while.

When a child successfully defines a problem and doesn't want to talk further, parents often feel incomplete. They may imagine that nothing has changed and think, "What good was that? The problem is still there." But in the child's world, a great deal was accomplished. Once the problem is clearly defined, a barrier is broken; new options can appear. The children or teens may think more about it, talk with friends or decide to accept things as they are for a while. It's *their* decision, not ours; the problems are *theirs*. Allow them to gain strength by working them out in their own ways, over time.

Never minimize the importance of your contribution. If there was any progress toward defining the problem, you've helped your child take a valuable step in the process of problem solving.

Children May Establish a Plan

When we help them by listening, children sometimes discover steps they can take to move toward a solution: "Maybe I'll call Aunt Liz; I know she helped Jolene learn to study better."

Children May Find a Solution

Sometimes children do solve the problem, right on the spot. Here's a story that's typical:

Three-year-old Oliver ran to Mom, tears welling up as he complained bitterly about his friend, Michael.

| **Mom:** | *Sounds like you're really mad at Michael.* |

Within a few moments, Oliver perked up and announced ...

| Oliver: | *I want to play another game anyway. Michael said he'll let me play with his truck tomorrow.* |

With younger children, the process may be complete in seconds. As children get older, expect it to take more time. Be aware: once teens begin talking, they may not want to stop.

But I Want to Teach My Child!

We all want to teach our values and share our experiences with our children and teens; obviously, that's an important part of being a parent. Chapters Eight, Nine and Ten showed how the skill of assertion can help us do that. But there's a time to be assertive and a time to listen. When children bring us a problem, it's far wiser to begin by listening.

But what if the child or teen *asks* for our input? "What do you think I should do?" Our silence, at this point, could be interpreted as withholding, rather than as providing a space for self-discovery. When asked for advice, we have two practical options.

The first is to mirror the child's request and explain your hesitancy, "I'd be happy to share my thoughts with you. But, in truth, you know more about (name the situation) than I and I'm concerned that my suggestion might not be appropriate." Sometimes simply putting the ball back in their court is all that's needed. Then they're on a roll again.

The second option is to offer your suggestion. But don't become attached to it! Sometimes children accept what we have to say, but generally they don't. Here's what I've observed: The greatest value of our input is that it helps children break through their own block. Rejecting our suggestion seems to free them to come up with their own ideas.

I can't help but laugh as I write this. It doesn't exactly feed our egos to discover that our silence and discarded ideas are great assets. It takes time to appreciate the larger truth: they're gifts of empowerment!

As you practice conscious listening, you'll gain a sense of when to offer input and when to listen.

For example, suppose Terry comes in looking troubled:

> *I just don't know if I should join the yearbook committee.*
> *I'm not sure what to do. What do you think, Mom?*

Since our job is *not* to solve the problem, but to support the *child* to grapple with it, you might simply reflect:

> *You're wondering what my opinion is.*

The child's next comment will guide you:

> *I'm so confused. I'm pretty sure it would be a lot of fun and*
> *I'd love doing it—but I think it'll take a lot of time and I really*
> *want to study for the S.A.T. exam.*

That comment tells us Terry is torn, weighing his priorities. Asking Mom's opinion was probably an attempt to reduce his discomfort. But it's likely that another opinion would only complicate the matter. We want to support our children to get "unstuck"—to struggle with their problems in their own ways. Conscious listening can help by mirroring our children's thoughts:

> *You think you'd enjoy working on the yearbook, but you're*
> *worried that it might interfere with studying for the S.A.T.*

We can continue reflecting, so long as it helps the child move through the process. But sometimes the child *asks* us to tell our own experience? Suppose Terry had said,

> *Mom, you said you worked on your school yearbook. What*
> *was that like for you?*

Then, of course, Mom would share her experience. But still, parents need to be cautious. Often, when we share our stories, we learn that the child is still sorting out his concerns.

For example, suppose Mom said the following:

Mom:	*Working on the yearbook was great for me. That's when Suzanne and I got really close. It was a lot of fun and we became best friends.*

And then her son responded ...

Terry:	*How much time did it take?*

That's your cue that Terry's time concerns have resurfaced—and it's time to do more conscious listening.

Our children love to know us, but when they ask questions that show they're still struggling, it's wise to give the spotlight back to them rather quickly. They're not really available for a true dialogue at that time.

When to Use Conscious Listening—and When *Not* to

We've seen that conscious listening is a wise response when children or teens show us they're struggling with a problem. Sometimes children say plainly, "I have a problem." But often we have to infer a problem exists from indirect clues. Aggressive, lower-self behavior, for example, often indicates there's a problem that needs attention. To cite a blatant example:

I'd like to hit Billy in the nose.

Clearly, this boy has a problem with a friend; conscious listening can help him clarify it and think it through. But another child might give us a clue about similar problems in a subtler, nonassertive way:

I don't want to play at recess; I like helping the teacher instead.

A child having a problem with a parent might express it aggressively:

You're so unfair! (Slams door.)

Or nonassertively:

> *Sure, I'll go. It doesn't matter anyway.*

A child might let you know there's a problem by saying something completely out of character, such as this child who loves ice cream:

> *I don't want dessert tonight.*

Listen well and you'll pick up clues that tell you when there's a problem—and when conscious listening can help.

But there are times when it's wise *not* to use conscious listening. One of them is when you're not centered; you can't be objective and available to another person unless you're calm and at ease with yourself. Wait for a time when you're centered before supporting your children to solve their problems.

Making an assertive comment to describe your situation would model respect:

> *I hear you're upset and I want very much to listen to you, but right now I'm consumed with sorting out problems with medical bills. I'd like to finish this first and clear my head; it should take about half an hour. If that's okay, I'll come into your room then, and I can give you the attention you deserve.*

Another time not to use conscious listening is when you're in a hurry. Wait until you're relaxed and can give your child your undivided attention. It can take time to complete the process, especially with older children; don't begin a session unless you feel confident you have time to complete it. Again, an assertive statement would be helpful:

> *I'm expecting a call from my sister in a few minutes. I want to know more about what's happening, but I don't want us to be interrupted. I'm wondering if you'd be willing to wait until I complete the call with Aunt Josie?*

It's also not appropriate to use conscious listening when you have an agenda—when you decide there's a problem or when you want to request a change in behavior. That's when you use assertion to express your concern. The essence of conscious listening is acceptance—accepting and trusting our children as they work through the problem-solving process. Advising and judging interfere with that process; they are the opposite of acceptance.

Choose a Skill That Fits

We know conscious listening is appropriate when the child has a problem; but if the child is upset with us, conscious listening is not a wise choice. When children are angry with us, they want a response. They want to know they're making an impact on us, and what that impact is. They want an honest, forthright answer—an assertion—a direct response to their upset. It's useful to begin with reflection, to acknowledge our children's feelings, but if we continue listening to hide our own feelings, they could become infuriated. And rightly so! It would be wrong to conceal what we feel while mechanically mirroring them—as if to imply they have a problem. They think we are the problem! And they want us to take responsibility!

A mom shared this story:

> I agreed to pick up my eleven-year-old daughter from school at 3:15 pm and arrived thirty minutes late. Emily was angry. I reflected her feelings, "You're mad at me for coming late." Then shared my own, "I'm really sorry. Traffic was jammed; it took twice as long to get here. I felt awful knowing you'd be waiting."
>
> I thought Emily would understand and cool down, but she didn't. So I reflected again, "You're still mad, even though I explained what happened." At that point Emily spelled out the problem: "Now I'm late for dance class and the teacher will be mad at me, when really it's your fault." I repeated how sorry I was and offered to tell the teacher that I was to blame. Only then did Emily feel better.

Be aware of what's happening from moment to moment and use those skills that fit. Remember to use conscious listening only when:

- the child expresses enthusiasm
- the child provides cues that a problem exists
- the conflict doesn't involve you
- you're feeling centered
- you have ample time

Tips for Better Listening

We noted earlier that conscious listening is an art; you'll find yourself improving with time and practice. The more skilled you become, the more you can help—and the closer your relationship grows.

Here's a tip I find useful: *lean back* as you listen; it'll help you stay detached. It's a simple idea, but useful. Our children's problems stir up our own feelings, and it's not always easy to keep quiet. I've learned from experience that when I'm too involved, my body leans forward. I get wound up, ready to talk, when it would be more productive to listen. Over the years, this trick has helped me: I lean back and focus my attention on the support the couch or chair gives me. That reminds me to back off! I do it with my clients too; it helps me remember to behave!

Different Styles for Different Children

To be most effective, you may need to alter your style of listening to accommodate children of different ages and personalities.

The Infant

Numerous research studies affirm the importance of creating a strong bond from the very beginning; that attachment has a positive impact on the child's intellectual and emotional development. Here are some comments from parents on the value and joy of practicing conscious listening with infants:

It's a wonderful way to be fully present to my baby—to talk with her as I try to meet her needs. But mostly, I love to use conscious listening to respond to her joy—the brilliant smile that spreads and animates every inch of her body.

Honestly, I feel as if he understands everything I'm saying. Either his sounds or his movements convey, "You got it, Mom," or "No, that's not it, try again!"

I feel as if I'm in basic training. The more practice I gain now, the more skillful I'll be when my daughter is able to talk.

I'm a model for my husband. He loves the baby, but feels awkward around her. He doesn't have the female hormones that make me melt just looking at her! But he's starting to mimic the way I talk with her. I see them bonding and I'm thrilled.

Typical things parents say to infants:

You're really hungry, aren't you? You want me to feed you right now.

You love when we play tickle; your face just lights up.

You're just not comfortable today; you're having a hard time.

Babies benefit in more ways than we initially understood. Research shows that when we "tune in" to infants, they relax and appear to feel safe and secure. That frees them to do what's natural and vital at that stage: ravenously explore the world around them. When they face frustration and we respond with a peaceful, steady presence, we help them learn the lifelong lesson of calming their emotions.

Think about what that also means: by helping to create a serene world, we're minimizing their need to create subpersonalities! That's truly a gift to our baby—and the whole family.

The Toddler

Younger children are very responsive; they delight in your attention. You don't have to be very skilled; they seldom complain about your communication, even if you parrot them (though you don't want to develop bad habits).

These children often need little more than your acknowledgment that they're upset or sad. A few words may do the trick—and they move on to something else. Their worlds are simple. For example, a child gets a bruise and comes running to you: "Look!" With compassion in your voice you might simply say, "You got hurt!" Suddenly he or she slides off your lap and runs back to the sandbox. Parents sometimes feel they've failed because the interaction is over in a flash. Quite the reverse; with young ones, brief interludes are often a sign of success.

The School-Age Child

At this stage, conversations vary considerably. Girls generally talk more about problems than boys do. But there are many exceptions. What matters most is that our children know we are available to listen when they need us. Remember that the length of the conversation does not necessarily reflect on the quality. Some children sort through their issues quickly, while others take more time. Some need to tell you every detail, while others say it briefly. (We'll talk more about that later in this chapter.)

Keep in mind that problems at school and relationships with peers are very important in children's lives. Research suggests that peers play an even more crucial role than we thought. Be aware of your attitude. If their stories sound "childish," can you put yourself in their shoes and see how serious those problems feel to them? By working out their age-appropriate concerns, they're gaining maturity. We can be a big help by appreciating their perspective and facilitating their process.

Teenagers

Caution! When teenagers feel insecure or unsafe, they're likely to attack *us*. They don't allow us much room for error or for the awkwardness that's a natural part of learning a new skill. To protect your ego, it's a good idea to practice conscious listening with others first. Gain some confidence and skill before using it with your teen. And be sure you're centered when you do.

Then be prepared: teens can be quick to criticize. If they sense you're doing something different, paranoia may surface and you'll hear, "Don't use that stuff on me." If you're wordy or sound like a parrot, they're likely to shoot back, "Don't repeat everything I say." But once they get going, you'll be reminded that teens can talk for hours! They have so much going on inside; they're hungry for your time and attention. Teens truly relish the opportunity to sort out the many thoughts and feelings that bombard them every day. Using conscious listening can help you gain insight into their stormy world and deepen the bond between you.

The Nonassertive Child

For reserved children who are reluctant to talk, it's especially important to create a safe environment. If we pick up cues suggesting the child might have a problem, it helps to offer encouragement. An invitation to talk about a specific topic might provide some needed safety.

For example, you might say,

I'm interested in what you said about the teacher.

I'd like to listen if you'd like to talk more about what happened on the playground.

I'd like to hear more about your science test.

Showing your interest in a supportive way often helps the nonassertive child to talk. Helping to "draw out" a quiet child so he or she can think through a problem is a legitimate use of conscious listening. That's very different from a situation where a parent has an agenda—to "get the child to talk" in order to gain information or persuade the child to change. In those situations, conscious listening would not be appropriate. When a child indicates there's a problem, but has trouble expressing it because he or she is nonassertive, then we can use this tool to help facilitate the process. Instead of pursuing our agenda, we're following the child's cue.

Once these children do begin to talk, they benefit from consistent and regular feedback. Nonassertive children easily withdraw into silence. They need our encouragement and obvious interest in order to feel safe and continue sharing their feelings. As we noted earlier, a simple comment of acknowledgement, like "Oh," "I see," "Ah ha," makes it clear you're still listening. Attentive body language adds to their assurance.

Nonassertive children might show obvious upset, but may not be able to find words to express it. Especially with younger children, I've found it helpful to ask if they'd like to draw a picture to show how they're feeling. Often this right brain activity frees them. Once they've completed the picture, they're often able to talk about their concerns with greater ease.

The Verbal Child

Verbal children need lots of freedom to express themselves fully. Unlike nonassertive children, they value deeply our attentive silence. These children need lots of time to sort out their rich inner worlds—out loud. They like to do that without interruption. Long periods might pass without the need to say a word. Only when there's a natural pause do they find our feedback useful. They appreciate the space you create by listening in an interested and supportive way.

When you're new to this skill (or any other), it can feel uncomfortable. A father once said to me, "What use am I? I'm just standing there, not offering advice—and barely giving any feedback!" But he was missing the larger picture. Even though his son spoke openly about his feelings and thoughts, this might well have been the first time he articulated them. When the words flow readily, we might imagine that these ideas are familiar to our children, when in fact the content may be brand new. By listening in an interested and supportive way, that father was giving his son a great gift: an opportunity to understand himself more fully.

When Children Quarrel

He started it! No, she did!

Sibling rivalry drives parents right up the wall. Conscious listening can help. You don't have to play referee. You don't have to figure out how to solve their problems. There are other options!

> *Oliver won't let me play with his cars. He's so mean.*
> *That's not true! I said Amy could play with some of them,*
> *just not my new ones.*
> *But those aren't any fun!*

Sound familiar? Let's *not* do the familiar and put yourself right in the middle. Instead, step back and act as the witness: just comment on what you hear and what you observe. Acknowledge, without judgment, each child's experience:

> *Amy, you want to play with Oliver's cars, but not with the ones he's offered. Oliver, you're willing to let Amy play with some of your cars, but those don't interest her. I can see you're both upset.*

Sometimes, simply acknowledging the situation allows a new idea to emerge. Amy might change her mind: "Okay, I'll play with these." (No guarantee, but you could be surprised; it *does* happen.)

Sometimes, it's useful to invite the children to brainstorm:

> *I'm wondering if you can come up with an idea that would work for you both?*

It's not unusual to hear children negotiate their own solutions:

> *I'll let you play with one of the cars, if I can pick out the book Dad reads us tonight.*

The solutions children create often fall outside our radar screen. That's one reason we want to encourage them to come up with their own ideas. The other, of course, is that we want to support them to gain experience in problem solving. Have faith; they really can do it!

If your children don't readily accommodate each other or can't find workable solutions, don't worry. There are steps we can take to help them gain more skill.

Initially, you can acknowledge their objections by using reflection. Then, you can calmly encourage them to talk to each other, to find a solution they're both comfortable with. If they appear stuck, you might then offer a suggestion, which they might accept. More often I've discovered our suggestions best serve to remove a "block"—helping them discover their own solutions.

After your children have experienced success under your guidance, you can reduce your role by giving them more responsibility for solving their own problems. Now, you become a facilitator. Instead of restating each child's feelings and thoughts, you can guide the children to do that themselves.

Suppose Heather and Penny are fighting. After they've told each side of the story, you might help them hear each other. You can begin by saying,

> *Penny, can you tell Heather what you heard her say—what's making her so mad.*

After Penny speaks, can you say to Heather:

> *Did Penny hear you correctly?*

If she missed something, ask Heather to repeat what Penny missed. Then ask the question:

> *Do you feel she understands your position now?*

Once Heather gives the okay that she's been heard, it's her turn to acknowledge Penny's point of view:

> *Heather, now you can tell Penny what you heard <u>her</u> say—what's making her so mad.*

Again, check to make certain Penny feels heard and that she has a chance to correct any misunderstandings. Once the girls have heard and understood each other, invite them to problem solve:

> *Do you have any ideas about how you can work out this problem, so that you both can feel better?*

By encouraging your children to listen to each other and acknowledge what they've heard, you're giving them an opportunity to learn conscious listening. As they become more skillful, you can go even further and make an additional suggestion:

> *I'm impressed with how well you can listen to each other and find creative solutions; I'm wondering if it would be alright if I leave while you sort through this issue yourselves? If you need me, I'll be happy to come back. Or if you want to tell me your solution, I'd love to hear it.*

That transformation is truly possible: you begin by imagining you're responsible for solving their problems and end as a proud parent, watching your children become more skillful and mature. As they gain greater independence, you gain more freedom as well!

The Key to Success

Whether we're using conscious listening with one child or angry siblings or with friends, the key to success is our *attitude*. If we're genuinely interested and accepting—children and teens will feel that and appreciate it. They'll be forgiving of technical errors and happy to correct us without a fuss. They sense we want to help and trust that they're capable. The opportunity to be supported in an atmosphere of acceptance is rare; children and teens soak it up like sunshine.

When we accept that our children have problems, that we're not to blame and that they're just fine, we become more calm; we can hear more accurately what they're experiencing. We become better facilitators and create the supportive environment they need to wrestle with life's problems.

It's when we're not centered and accepting that common errors occur. That's when we become judgmental, ask questions or analyze what we hear. Though we don't realize we're doing it, children and teens are supersensitive to being analyzed or judged.

Of course, it also helps to polish our skills: to be accurate when we reflect. To understand why, imagine yourself in your child's place. Is it easy to admit to someone that you're having a personal problem? For most of us, that's uncomfortable. When you tell someone about your problem, do you feel vulnerable? That's how children feel! In that vulnerable position, they need to trust that we're right there with them—that we really understand what they're experiencing.

While younger children are more forgiving, as they grow older they become more sensitive to the accuracy of our reflection. Teens may feel less safe if we misinterpret their thoughts. Again, they'll be forgiving if they sense our interest and acceptance. It's worth some time to sharpen our skills.

Accurate Listening: *Hitting the Target*

When an archer shoots an arrow at a distant target, he or she aims to hit the bull's eye. In conscious listening, a bull's eye is when you accurately reflect the essence of what the child said: feelings as well as thoughts.

You don't have to be perfect; no one is. But after you reflect what you've heard, it's important to listen for the child's response, to see how close you came. A child may say, "No, I wasn't angry; I was disappointed." That tells you that you didn't hit the bull's eye—but now you know where it is. Making your feedback more accurate increases your ability to support your child as he or she works through a problem.

The most common errors in listening are *overshooting* and *undershooting*. Overshooting means going beyond the child's message to add your own interpretation or insight. For example:

Child: *Tommy keeps taking my toys.*
Parent: ***You're angry that he doesn't care about your feelings.***

Mom overshot by going beyond the child's comment. A more accurate response would be,

Parent:	*You're upset that Tommy takes your toys without asking.*

Undershooting happens when we leave out something important. We'll use the same example to demonstrate the other extreme:

Child:	*Tommy keeps taking my toys.*
Parent:	*You're upset with your brother.*

Here Mom failed to acknowledge that the upset was focused on the child's toys, clearly a very important part of a child's world. Again, the more accurate response would be,

Parent:	*You're upset that Tommy takes your toys without asking.*

Here's another example of undershooting:

Child:	*I'm horribly worried; I think I failed the test.*
Parent:	*You don't think you did very well.*

The parent greatly understated the child's concern. A more accurate response would be,

Parent:	*You're scared you really blew it.*

Sharpening Your Skills

No one ever mastered a tennis or golf swing solely by reading a book; skills have to be practiced. The chart that follows provides an opportunity to sharpen your listening skills; it reveals four areas in which errors occur, and offers tips to help you hit the bull's eye in each one.

How to Hit the Bull's Eye

When You're Listening

Here are two areas to consider when you reflect:

1. Intensity

How you would reflect this statement?
I'm so frustrated with the teacher. Her tests are so hard!

> TIPS: Don't *overshoot*—increase the emotional intensity:
> *You really hate the teacher.*
> Don't *undershoot*—decrease the emotional intensity:
> *You think Mrs. Smith is a hard teacher.*

Now write *your* response before reading further.

Hit the bull's eye:
You're having a rough time with her tests.

(Many other answers also may be accurate for all examples.)

2. Accuracy

How would you reflect this statement?
I don't think I'm getting a good education.

> TIPS: Don't *overshoot*—expand on the information:
> *You don't think you're being prepared for college.*
> Don't *undershoot*—eliminate pertinent facts:
> *You don't like school.*

Now write *your* response before reading further.

Hit the bull's eye:
You're concerned about your education.

LISTENING: Hit the Bull's Eye
continued

Two more areas to consider when you reflect:

3. Pace

How would you reflect this statement?
You always side with my brother.

> TIPS: Don't *overshoot*—anticipate the child's next thought:
>
> *You think I love him more than you.*
>
> Don't *undershoot*—respond to an earlier comment versus the current one:
>
> *You're upset with me.*

Now write *your* response before reading further.

Hit the bull's eye:
You think I'm unfair; that I favor your brother.

4. Sensitivity

How would you reflect this statement?
Mom, any normal kid hates school!

> TIPS: Don't *overshoot*—interpret or "psychoanalyze" the child's underlying motives:
>
> *You're always trying to build up your case.*
>
> Don't *undershoot*—repeat or "parrot" the child's exact words:
>
> *You think any normal kid hates school.*

Now write your response before reading further.

Hit the bull's eye:
You're convinced that all kids feel that way.

Listening to Adults

Children aren't the only ones who appreciate a skillful listener when they have a problem. Conscious listening is valuable in any relationship. Couples report greater intimacy when they use it. We all want someone to listen to us—to truly understand. It's all too rare when others give us supportive attention and space, without interjecting advice or judgments or related experiences. Try it with your spouse, parents, boss, co-workers and friends; they'll tell you what a wonderful, caring person you are! And they'll be right.

Here's an example from the daughter of an aging mother:

> When I heard my mom complain that Dad wasn't feeling well, and he refused to let her call the doctor again, my immediate impulse was to lash out and complain about his stubbornness. But I thought for a moment and realized my reaction would only make matters worse. "Mom has a problem," I reasoned. "If I can listen, maybe she can think through her options." Then I used conscious listening, "You're worried and want to contact the doctor, but Dad won't give you the okay." I continued listening and after a short while, Mom figured out exactly what she wanted to do.

Here's an example from a husband listening to his wife:

> I used the skills when my wife, Sandra, began to cry, "I'm having a really rough time. I love work, but I feel as if the company saps my creative juices and there's not much left for the kids." I had strong, pent up feelings about this topic and was ready to sound off when I heard an internal, "Whoa". Thankfully, I put on the brakes and used reflection, "It's tough for you to see yourself being so creative at work, with very little left for the kids." Soon my wife hugged me. "I was so scared to talk with you. I thought you'd go off on me again. Please just continue to listen. I really want to make some progress on this one." As I listened, I realized I had seldom allowed Sandra to express herself so fully before. The truth is, I had been too angry. Now I discovered our feelings were not that far apart.

In a Nutshell

Listening is one of the most valuable skills for strengthening any relationship. It's one of the best gifts we can give our children.

In this chapter, we've focused on two key situations when skillful listening is appropriate: when our children are delighted with an experience and when they're having problems. In the first situation, we want to give them an opportunity to express their delight fully—to share their experience and celebrate their joy. When our children are having problems, we want to support them to find their own answers: to become more capable and independent. In the process, we have an opportunity to grow closer and learn to know them better, as we observe the way they view themselves, their worlds and the dilemmas they face. And, by modeling conscious listening, we empower our children to become skillful listeners themselves.

We've also seen that these skills are valuable in our adult relationships. All of us want our joys celebrated and our concerns supported. A caring ear brings us closer, whatever our age.

What's Next?

So far, we've explored three essential skills of the centered self: assertion, reflection and conscious listening. In the next chapter, we'll explore a skill you already know but may not be using fully; it's a skill that can make a surprising difference, helping family life to run smoothly and preventing problems before they happen. It's the simple, but potent skill called planning.

CHAPTER 13

Preventing Problems:

The Skill of Planning

A goal without a plan is just a wish.

—Antoine de Saint-Exupery

IT SOUNDED LIKE A deep psychological problem when the parents first came for therapy:

> *We're both worried sick. Sean hits his baby sister all the time, now he won't even let her be in the same room. We're afraid he'll really hurt her. We're at the end of our rope!*

Yet, when we looked closer, the central problem turned out to be quite simple:

> *"Do you have some 'quality time' with Sean each day?" I asked. "Well, every day is different. Most of the time it's so hectic..." The picture soon became clear: morning, dinner and bedtime were a mad scramble just to keep up—and every day <u>was</u> different. Mom and Dad felt they were running as hard as they could—and still falling behind. Moment to moment, no one in the family knew exactly what to expect. Sean could never count*

on getting the undivided attention he wanted—and vented his feelings on the baby. The whole family was unhappy.

And so we began to talk about planning:

> *Together, we looked at each person's needs: Mom needed some breaks and a more manageable family; Dad needed a clear role in child-care that felt significant; Sean and the baby each needed "quality time" with Mom and Dad they could count on each day. We set about creating a schedule to provide for these needs.*
>
> *We planned a daily routine for morning, play times, shopping, cooking, errands, dinner hour and bedtimes. There was a regular time for Sean to be alone with Mom, doing things they loved together. And also a time for Sean to play alone, right near Mom, as she paid bills and handled chores. Everyone's needs were considered: Mom had a time when she could be alone and a time for visits with other mothers at the park. She realized she could sometimes trade baby-sitting with friends, freeing up a precious hour or two. Dad would play with the kids while Mom fixed dinner; each would put one of the children to bed, alternating nightly.*
>
> *In time, each part of the day became a well-organized routine. Now everyone knew what was expected. Sean's tirades eventually subsided; the family began to function with far less friction. What began as a serious behavior problem demonstrated—once again—that lower-self behavior grows out of unmet needs. What made it possible to meet those needs was the skill of planning.*

Even if you're a single parent or have a more challenging situation, you can adopt the principles of planning. Real life cannot be mechanized, of course; children get sick, cars break down and the best-laid plans go awry. We have to expect the unexpected and be flexible. Still, we can create systems that give the family more serenity, order and harmony.

But a family that functions smoothly and meets everyone's needs doesn't happen by chance; in fact, it doesn't happen at all without some skillful planning.

How Planning Helps

Planning can prevent a surprising array of problems; we just have to think about doing it. It's one of the easiest skills to learn and use, yet the results can be remarkably rewarding.

A parent told this story:

> *Every morning I'd find myself nagging. "Pam! We're going to be late again!" I'd find her dawdling in the closet, casually considering—and reconsidering—what outfit to wear for the day. How could I speed up our mornings without becoming a witch? Finally, I sat down and thought, "There has to be a better way." And then I worked out a plan with my daughter: every school night Pam chooses clothes for the next day; she lays them out on the floor in the shape of a person—shoes, socks and all. She enjoys doing it and takes all the time she likes. And mornings are easier for us both.*

Another parent had this experience:

> *My son had a bad case of "The Gimmes." There was always something he wanted: new shoes, a new toy, more baseball cards. I gave eloquent lectures about the virtues of thrift. They had no visible effect. Then I realized we had no set plan for dealing with money. I offered a weekly allowance and we talked in detail about what we would pay for and what his allowance was to cover. He liked being in charge. Though it took a few weeks, "The Gimmes" diminished considerably.*

If so many family problems can be prevented with planning, why don't we do it more often? We plan for projects at home and work all the time. If we're making dinner for company, we plan out the menu and make a shopping list. At work, if we're responsible for part of a meeting, we think it through: what information we need to prepare, what's likely to happen at the meeting, what we need to bring.

Yet how often do we do prepare as thoroughly for family activities? We know the problems that come up—day after day—in the morning, after school, at dinner and bedtime. If we gave it some thought, we could predict problems that are likely to arise on trips, during family visits and in other situations. Yet we often grapple with problems only after they descend on us, rather than preventing them in the first place!

The mother in the story at the beginning of this chapter is a head nurse; at work, she had organized a dozen people into a smooth-running, efficient unit, with regular daily routines. Yet she never thought about applying those skills at home, where chaos—or a close relative of it—often reigned. She and her husband had carefully organized the space in their home: kitchen, nursery and bedrooms were models of efficient planning. But they had never organized the family's time in the same way.

We can make our family life so much more enjoyable—and remove so much destructive energy—if we apply the same mentality that we use for other projects. Think ahead, anticipate what's likely to happen and be prepared.

The benefits of planning can be rewarding:

- fewer frayed nerves, fights and hurt feelings
- more peace and calm
- more time for fun together

Not all problems will disappear, of course, but planning can dramatically improve the family atmosphere. When we hassle with problems, the whole family is in danger of slipping to lower-self behavior. Planning can help everyone stay centered.

Morning Madness

A mother shared this story. Does anything like this ever happen at your house?

"'Mom! My drawer is empty! I'm out of socks!' It was one of those mornings when we were running terribly late and I was trying to be efficient and stay calm. "Look in your backpack; remember we took an extra pair to the beach," I shouted from the kitchen, trying to rescue burning toast and assemble three lunches all at once. "Eric took my backpack!" Jenny shouted. "I did not!" "Yes you did!"

Dashing into Jenny's room, I searched in vain for the backpack until finally, crawling under the bed, I spotted it and fished out a wet pair of socks filled with sand. "Stay calm," I told myself. I glanced at the clock and my heart sank as I hastily rinsed the socks and tossed them into the dryer. "How come I get the same boring lunch every day?" Riley complained when I dashed back to the kitchen.

After interrogating three kids to make sure everyone had books, jackets and lunches, it seemed like a miracle at last: we were all in the car and nearly on time as we approached the school. I remember beginning to hope, "Maybe I'll only be a <u>little</u> late to work," when Eric got hysterical and started crying. "Go back! I don't have my homework. I can't go to school without my homework."

Sometimes we think scenes like these are inevitable, just part of bringing up children. Yet much of this chaos can be prevented—with a little thought and a few minutes of planning. Here's how the mother who told this story approached the problem:

I did a lot of thinking. Then we had a family discussion. The kids didn't like our morning routine any better than I did.

After a while, Jenny had an idea: "Why don't we pack our stuff the night before?" Eventually, that's just what we did. Now the children pack their backpacks and check off a chart on the wall before bedtime: books, school supplies and homework. The packs are placed by the front door each night, ready to go. They like to finish by 7:30, so they can have a bedtime story. Gradually, we worked out other routines, like making lunch together the night before. Now some mornings are actually calm. Everyone knows what's expected; we're relaxed enough to be in good humor and even enjoy each other.

Learning the Skill

As we look at planning to prevent different kinds of problems, we'll begin with simple solutions we can implement ourselves. Then we'll explore problems that require cooperation from the children and call on our assertive and listening skills.

Here's a typical problem that has a simple solution:

I'm going nuts! Jeffrey just sprayed water into the living room window. Yesterday he soaked his cousin just before we left for the christening. He was allowed to play with the hose only at certain times—but he wants to play with it <u>all</u> the time. I don't know <u>what</u> we can do! When my friend asked, "Have you thought of putting the hose somewhere else—out of sight?" a light bulb went off. Overnight, the problem was solved.

Sometimes we don't see the obvious. We think about "managing" the child, when the more effective solution might be to change the environment.

Simple Solutions

Remove an Object

Some problems are easily prevented; all we have to do is remove the troublesome object from the environment. If your children have reached the toddler stage, you've probably already "child-proofed" your home, preventing accidents by removing potentially dangerous or delicate items. The same principle can be applied to other problems:

Every time I walked into her room, Melanie was glued to her computer, playing games and messaging friends. I was tired of hearing myself say, "Have you finished your homework? We had an agreement." It took a while before I realized an obvious solution: remove the computer from her room.

The dentist warned us that Danielle had too many cavities. She was into the ice cream right after school, then skipping part of her dinner, anticipating another bowl. We thought of several plans, but the easiest was this: we bought only one pint of ice cream, once a week. When it was gone, that was it. Problem solved.

The third time my pliers were missing, I knew I was getting nowhere. Despite my complaints, Jason never broke the habit of taking my tools without permission. And he had a set of his own! Instead of another "discussion," I found a foolproof solution: a padlock on the cabinet.

Bradley has worn shoes with Velcro straps since he was three. When we shopped for school clothes, he insisted I buy shoes with laces; he wanted to be grown up. But Bradley still doesn't know how to tie his shoes, and he won't allow me to teach him. So, despite my pleas, the shoes have never been worn. Now Bradley's feet have grown and he needs new shoes again. And again he insists on laces! This time I thought ahead; I talked to him before we went shopping, "No shoes with laces until you learn how to tie them!" I simply removed that choice as an option.

Not only can we remove some troublesome objects from the environment, we can also remove or shift some activities that generate problems.

Reschedule an Activity

A father told this experience:

> *Every time I would put Caitlin to sleep it would take forever. We had a great time, but she just wouldn't settle down. But when my wife put her to bed, she'd go to sleep right away! I couldn't figure it out—until I joined them one night. With her mom, there was a calm, predictable routine: brush teeth, wash face, hear a story, then go to sleep. My style was to roughhouse and tickle—then say it was sleep time. For Caitlin, it was a sudden change of mood—like shifting from high speed to reverse. Now I make sure we roughhouse much earlier; at bedtime we follow a calm routine. And guess what: she goes to sleep more readily.*

A mother gave another example of rescheduling an activity:

> *"What's that awful smell," I'd wonder. And then I'd see the mess. Jimmy had failed to change the kitty litter—again! I was so tired of nagging that I thought, "I'd rather do the chores myself and not have to hassle." But I knew that would be a cop-out—and a real disservice to the children. So I sat down and thought about our week. We go out to dinner every Friday night and we all look forward to it. Then it dawned on me: why not schedule Friday afternoon for chores? They'd have a natural incentive to do them quickly! And that's what we do now: they always like going out, and they know we can't go until chores are done. Just changing the schedule made all the difference.*

Add Organization

Another way to prevent problems is to add something to the environment: something that will provide more order. A working mother told us:

> *By the time I got home, I was worn out. I was so tired of picking up clothes from the floor, hauling them down to the*

*washer, sorting out what belongs to which family member ...
Then I got a brilliant idea: we bought a different color laundry
basket for each child. They're responsible for putting dirty
clothes in their own baskets and bringing them downstairs on
washday. If someone forgets, sorry, those clothes are not washed.
Next morning the children pick up their own baskets of clean
clothes and bring them upstairs. Now we all know our jobs;
we're better organized and I'm less hassled!*

Adding something that helps to keep more order in the house—and
in our lives—can reduce conflicts and create a sense of harmony. There
are endless ways to apply the idea of adding something to organize:

*Garret lost keys faster than we could replace them. Then
we put a small basket right near the door; Garret takes the key
out of the basket when he leaves, and drops it back in when he
returns. By now, it's become a habit—and we seldom have to
replace keys.*

*Every day, Carey came home starving. "Mom, what can I
eat?" I'd list several snacks and she'd snub her nose at them. I felt
exasperated. Then I saw what her friend's mom did: snacks were
always kept on a certain shelf in the fridge. Now I keep things
like fruit, carrot sticks, nuts, celery and cheese on the snack shelf.
I also placed a "Request List" on the refrigerator with a magnet.
If Carey wants me to buy something, she can write it down. No
more hassles—and my husband likes this plan too.*

If you want to see a wonderful environment for children, look at a well-
run kindergarten classroom. Many materials are color-coded; everything
has a place. Children know where things go and what's expected during
each part of the day; they feel secure and comfortable. When the environment is well organized, there is less conflict and more time for fun.

Add Fun

Here's a familiar story—one that many of us experienced when we were children:

> *"Gary has his foot on my side of the car!" "I do not!" "You do too!" It was a long trip, and this was the third fight in the last ten minutes. Nothing could stop us from whining and bickering—until Dad said, "Let's play alphabet." Soon we were all focused on being the first to find objects that begin with each letter. Obviously, we kids had been "misbehaving" because we were cooped up and bored. The whole atmosphere changed when we had an activity to interest us.*

Creating a game—offering a challenge—making it fun, solved that familiar problem. Sometimes, that's all it takes:

> *The girls were taking forever to get their chores done, and my patience was running out. Then I had an idea: "First one done gets to be my first salon customer." They knew what I meant; they love to play dress-up and wear my makeup. The girls went into high gear to finish their chores, and we all had a good time. Every once in a while, I look for ways to create a fun reward.*

Snow White had the same idea when she suggested a way for the seven dwarfs to make their chores more fun: *Whistle While You Work.* Even when you're in a hurry, you can create a simple challenge:

> *Whoever is dressed and ready before this five-minute timer goes off, gets to pick the after-school treat.*

> *My kids like to race the clock when they're doing kitchen and laundry chores. If they're done by a certain time, they get to watch TV or we play a game together.*

The key, as in all planning, is to stop for a moment and take an objective look at what's going on. Try to see the situation as an outsider would, without judging anyone. Ask yourself, "What could make this go better?"

Exercise: Preventing Simple Problems

Think of problems that crop up repeatedly in your family: problems that are "simple," yet annoying, creating a negative atmosphere. Brainstorm (with the family, a friend or by yourself) about practical ways you might prevent these problems.

Divide a piece of paper into four sections and label them as below. Write your solutions in the appropriate spaces.

- Remove an object.

- Reschedule an activity.

- Add organization.

- Add fun.

The Key Is Your Mindset

All parents are busy; it's easy to feel we don't have time to stop and create a plan for simple, everyday activities. But the truth is, we often spend far *more* time fighting and hassling when we *haven't* made a plan.

The key is our willingness to believe that many problems *can* be prevented in this way. If our frame of mind is to wait and try to "put out fires" as they come up, we may never think about planning to prevent them.

What makes it work, once again, is the attitude that asks, "Is there any way our day could be improved? Without blaming or judging, "Is there any change that could make our life easier?"

Daily Routines

Does this story sound familiar?

> *"Dinner's ready!" I shout, rushing to get everything on the table. No sign of life in the house. In the next room, I discover Jimmy—glued to the TV. "Come on, food's getting cold," I urge. My son suddenly appears to be deaf. I'm disgusted. "Jimmy, I'm going to count to three. If you're not in here, you'll have no dinner tonight. One, two ..." Slowly, he flickers to life—with all the swiftness of a hundred-year-old tortoise. "It's about time!" his sister says with disdain as he arrives at the table. Dad gives her "that look." Now we're all upset. What a way to begin a meal!*

If the morning and evening routines at your house are not exactly models of peace and loving cooperation, you have lots of company! Most of the parents I meet simply groan when they're mentioned. Yet most aren't sure how to improve these daily events—or haven't considered the idea that they *can* be improved.

Begin by taking a few moments to:

- Think about what happens every day.
  and
- Consider how to make it go better.

When you do this, you'll be on your way; you will have identified a problem (the essential first step) and will be ready to think about a plan.

The mother who shared the story did just that. A few weeks later she told us:

> *I know this sounds like a dream, but it really happened. At five o'clock, Jimmy walks into the kitchen and sets the table, whether I'm downstairs or not! When I come in, he knows to ask, "Anything extra needed tonight?" At 5:30, Kimberly brings the food to the table. At dinner we talk about everyone's day and often share funny stories. After dinner, we all clear our own dishes; Kimberly puts the food away; Dad cleans pots and the table; Jimmy loads the dishwasher. I'm not exaggerating—dinner has become one of the nicer parts of the day.*

Too good to be true? It did really happen. I've heard dozens of similar stories. Not perfection, mind you, but daily routines that work a lot better. How do they do it? These are the steps:

- Ask yourself, "What could go better in our day?" Identify one activity, like the dinner routine.

- Be aware of what bothers you specifically (you have too much to do, kids don't do chores without a reminder, too much bickering, not enough fun).

- Break the problem into parts (cooking, setting the table, etc.).

- Ask yourself, "Is there a different way to do this?" Apply some imagination; create a detailed plan you can present to the family.

- Sit down with the family at a time when everyone is relaxed and feeling good. Use your assertive skills to explain the problem and your initial ideas for solving it. Practice your listening skills to take in everyone's ideas. Then, brainstorm and agree upon a plan.

- A good plan includes all the "W" words: *What* is to be done? *Who* will do it? *When* is it to be done? *What happens* if it isn't done well or on time?

Once again, think of outstanding teachers: whether elementary or high school level, they carefully structure tasks and time. Otherwise, the result could be chaos. In the family, structuring some parts of the day or week can help create harmony; there still may be plenty of time for freedom and spontaneity. Without any plan or boundaries, freedom can become chaos. Creating some structure provides focus; it allows a class—or a family—to work together smoothly and meet everyone's needs.

I finally got tired of fighting over my kids' messy rooms; they hated my nagging and so did I. So I sat down and did some serious thinking. The result was a big chart for <u>all</u> their chores—broken into small, daily tasks for each child. The kids check them off daily, and if all are done, they get to do something fun at the end of the week. Things work a lot better when they know exactly what's expected.

	Mon	Tues	Wed	Thurs	Fri	Sat
Sabrina	set table	feed cat	cat litter	feed cat	sweep	feed cat
Mark	feed cat	set table	feed cat	trash	feed cat	vacuum

Once you have a plan, put it into action and *follow through*. Make sure you carry out your part of the plan, and that the children do their part. If it works, the atmosphere in the family will be more pleasant for everyone.

If your plan doesn't succeed and problems persist, you might want to have a more formal dialogue to find a solution. Remember the Realist and the family agreement? A *family meeting* is an ideal format for creating family agreements. It's a place to talk about problems, and a time together to work them out. All family members participate and then brainstorm ideas until everyone agrees upon a solution. Since the process is democratic, resistance to the plan is minimized. A family meeting is especially appropriate when the solution includes a variety of tasks and participation by all.

Here's one way to create a successful family meeting:

- Days or hours before the meeting time, discuss the problem (as you see it) with each member; discover whether *they* think it's a problem—or have related problems. Ask each person to think about solutions beforehand. Encourage imagination.

- When the family gathers, create an atmosphere that is accepting and even light-hearted; humor is always a plus (if it's not at anyone's expense). Talk about one problem at a time (or maybe one to a meeting).

- Ask family members how they feel about the problem.

- Invite everyone to brainstorm to find solutions. Write down all ideas without judging. A list everyone can see is best. Explain that even unusual ideas should be accepted. Since we want to be creative and use our imagination, no idea is too "far out." As children witness their contributions being accepted, they gain trust that the family meeting is a safe place.

- When the group has run out of ideas, ask, "Which solutions do you think would work best?" Go through the written list until you find one —or a combination of solutions—that everyone thinks will work.

- Design and agree on a specific plan, clarifying each person's part. (At 7:30 Mom will have breakfast ready and Jana will be at the table.)

- "What if someone forgets their part?" Agree on consequences. ("Jacob will have his teeth brushed and be in bed by eight; if not, Dad won't read a story that night.")

While some problems are complex, many have simple solutions if we look at what's happening and ask, "How can we make it work better?"

As mentioned earlier, once you have a plan, put it into action and follow through. Make sure to do your part! If a child fails to follow through, allow natural consequences to happen. Or implement the consequences agreed on in the plan. I can't emphasize enough how important it is to show that you *honor the plan*. If your actions show that you don't really care, children learn quickly: "I can get away with far less than my best." How sad to imagine that this could be the lesson we're teaching our children. When we follow through, our message is clear: "I expect you to be responsible." Then we all share the reward: we feel good about ourselves and enjoy a more pleasant family atmosphere.

There is another kind of problem that can often be prevented with planning: the kind that happens when children face something new and unfamiliar.

When Children Face New Situations

> *It was the worst Fourth of July we ever had; the girls were three and five and they cried and complained, clinging to us the whole time. What made it worse is that the neighbors and their kids were at the beach with us; their children were almost the same ages—but they were having a ball! I felt so dumb when I found out how they had prepared their kids. The week before, they talked about what it would be like: the noise and smoke and confusion. They talked about firecrackers and sparklers; they knew there would be a long, long wait before the fireworks show began, and they brought toys and planned activities for that time. No wonder their kids had more fun!*

A surprising number of problems happen because children are not prepared; they have no idea what to expect. Whenever there is a new situation—special visitors, a trip to the dentist, dinner at a restaurant, an outing, vacation or any new event—problems are likely unless children are prepared.

We can be alert to these problems if we think about what it's like for a child or an adult to be plunged into a new situation without preparation.

To get a feel for what children experience, imagine that you were suddenly taken on a trip to an unknown place—say Eastern Lapland—without knowing where you were going, having no information about the country or the culture. The customs, climate and food are suddenly different; it's all a surprise and a weird puzzle to you. With no idea of what to expect, you might feel somewhat uncomfortable, or even apprehensive and disoriented. That's how it can feel to a child in a new situation: a visit to the doctor, an event like the Fourth of July or when special company comes to the house for dinner.

Think what a difference it would make on that trip to Lapland, if you were prepared: if you knew where you were going and what it would be like there. We can provide that kind of preparation and comfort for our children.

> *My first child hated going to the doctor. He said it was a "scary place" where strange people poked you or even hurt you. He also felt bored, sitting in the waiting room. I didn't want Pam to feel the same way, so I read her books about visiting the doctor and the dentist. Whenever a visit was coming up, we talked about what would happen and used her "doctor kit" to play "doctor visit." (Pam liked it best when she was the doctor.) We talked about how long we would have to wait; she decided what she would bring to occupy the time. And she was perfectly comfortable being there.*

Preparing Children for New Situations

In new situations we often expect children to act differently, as when special company visits, for example. Explaining our expectations ahead of time—in a clear and concrete way—can make a great difference. As we saw when we explored assertion, it's also helpful to explain the reason for our requests: "Grandma is very old; she gets upset by loud noise. I'd like you to use a quiet, indoor voice when you're near her. If that's too hard, you're welcome to play outdoors."

> *When my son, Derek, asked to have friends visit or stay over, we always talked beforehand about what was expected.*

He knew that everyone was to help prepare meals, each one choosing what he wanted to do, like grating cheese, making the garlic bread or setting the table. He agreed to have his friends play quietly in the morning until I woke up. To be sure, there were some infractions, but surprisingly few. Derek knew that if things went well this time, I'd probably say yes in the future.

We're more likely to have smooth sailing when children know what we expect ahead of time. Here's how another family solved a problem by preparing a child:

I always dreaded taking Timmy shopping when one of his friends had a birthday; there would be endless pleading and arguing when Timmy saw those irresistible toys. "Please! Why can't I have that? That's not fair!"

Finally I got smart: we made a plan <u>before</u> we went. Timmy was reluctant, but he agreed that this would be a time to buy for a friend—not for himself. When he expressed disappointment, I used my listening skills. I found that even if he didn't like it, Timmy could accept the situation if he was prepared beforehand.

As we talk with our children about what will happen at a new event and what's expected, we can try to *anticipate their needs* in that situation. If there will be waiting time, for example, what books or playthings could we bring along? Ask the child to collaborate in planning.

I like to meet friends at a coffee shop and "hang out" for a while without hurrying, but Michael is a restless child. I thought I'd have to wait until he was seven before he'd put up with that. One day when Michael was menacing every customer in sight, I noticed some kids quietly occupied at a nearby table. I walked by to see what they were doing; both kids were busy drawing futuristic cars. Their mother noticed me looking and was very friendly. Then one of the kids spoke up: "We have extra colored pencils; does your little boy want to borrow them?" Michael was busy for an extra twenty-five minutes that day; since then,

*I wouldn't think of going any place where we might have to
wait, without talking with Michael about what to bring along
for him.*

How to Plan for New Situations

The main idea is to make it a habit to *think ahead* whenever a less
familiar experience is coming up: a long car drive, a camping trip, guests
from out of town, a visit to a new place or a special event. The same
mindset we adopt when packing for a plane trip will serve us well: we
envision what will happen there—the climate, the activities we'll be
engaged in and the people we'll meet—then we choose our wardrobe
accordingly. That's the kind of thinking we need when our children will
face new situations:

Visualize

Imagine what will happen; walk through the event in your mind;
envision the physical setting and the sequence of events in detail.

Anticipate

Imagine how your children might respond to the new situation:

- How will they feel?
- What do they need to know?
- What might they need or want?
- What do I expect from them?

Dialogue

Talk with your children or teens. Let them know what will happen
and what you expect from them.

Your assertive skills will help you provide clear information about the
environment and what behavior you expect. If you encounter discomfort
or disagreement, reflection will help you deal with it. Your listening skills
will help you stay open to your children's concerns, questions and ideas.

Once again, the key is to think ahead; plan for a favorable outcome—then follow through.

Exercise: Plan for a New Situation

Think about an upcoming event and apply your planning skills. Make some notes as you take each step.

Visualize:
- the setting in detail
- each part of the event

Anticipate:
- how the children might feel
- what they might need or want
- what they need to know
- what you expect from them

Prepare to dialogue:
- what you will say
- what you will ask

Write a tentative plan:
- what you will bring
- what you will do at the event to help it go smoothly

When Children Face Difficult Situations

As children grow older, they face new situations that can be uncomfortable, upsetting or even dangerous: the first day at a new school, the death of a relative or pet, pressure to take drugs or have sex and any number of other challenging situations. Even being asked on a date, as exciting as that might be, can be quite stressful when a young person feels unprepared.

Think about your own childhood; do you remember the first time you got your period—or when you had your first wet dream? How did you feel? Were you taken by surprise? Would it have helped if you had known what to expect?

When I ask parents in class to think about difficult experiences in their own early years, many say something like, "I was anxious and disturbed by certain new situations because I was not prepared. If someone had helped me know what to expect, I would have been able to handle it better; I wouldn't have felt so alone."

It's true we can't shelter our children from all the anxiety of grappling with new and uncomfortable situations. Even if we could, it would be unwise to do so. Only by facing difficulties and overcoming them can children mature and grow as human beings. But often we *can* be helpful by sharing our experience—letting them know what's just ahead on the road we've already traveled. Then they need not feel shocked, bewildered and alone with a new and disturbing situation. We can give them vital information and be a source of support.

It's best to lay the groundwork early. Long before the need arises, we can let our children know we're open and available to talk about any subject, no matter how embarrassing or difficult. They'll judge our openness by our attitudes. Do we avoid discussing certain subjects? Are we quick to impose our opinion? Are we critical of their thinking?

Creating an open atmosphere is an enormous gift to the family; it encourages our children and teens to bring their most perplexing and disturbing questions to us. And it makes them more open to our response. Then they need not rely on peers or the streets for information that may be wrong or misleading. They will learn that they can confide in us and we will not belittle their concerns or judge them. We can earn their trust, so a healthy, supportive relationship can grow.

> *"Mom, I have a question about sex," Derek said to me one day when he was fourteen. He started to describe some intimate feelings ... then suddenly stopped. He shook his head as if surprised at what he was doing and said out loud, "Why am I telling you this?" Before I could reply, he answered his own question: "Cuz I want to know the truth. My friends will talk to me, but I never know how much of it is just B.S."*

Creating an open, accessible atmosphere over the years has still another value: when we welcome honest discussion of the most difficult issues, children gain a deeper insight into our core beliefs and values. Understanding how we think may even encourage them (may heaven help us) to *adopt* our values.

But Most Parents Don't

The plain truth is that many parents—probably most—do not prepare their children or teens for new and difficult situations. Not that they wouldn't like to; parents want to help their children all they can. Yet certain things get in the way. And if we don't understand why that happens, we might be hampered by the same barriers.

When parents fail to prepare children for new situations, it's usually because they:

- are unaware of the need
- believe they're "too busy"
- are uncomfortable discussing the topic unprepared, embarrassed or afraid
- fear that discussing a topic gives children permission

If any of these fit for you—and they do for most of us—think about whether you'd like to change and grow in this area. Failing to prepare children or teens deprives them of information and guidance they may need in order to make decisions about crucial issues—decisions that could threaten their well-being. Silence also closes the door on an opportunity to share our values and build a closer relationship.

It's worth the effort to look at each of the barriers above to make sure none prevents us from taking action.

What Parents Can Do If They ...

Are Unaware of the Need

Listen carefully when your child talks; hints might be dropped that show anxiety or discomfort. Stay in close contact with the parents of your child's friends; they might have helpful information. And most important: think about situations your child might soon experience. Does your son or daughter know what to expect? Imagine yourself in that position; how would you feel? Anticipate such experiences regularly.

Are "Too Busy"

Remind yourself what matters most in your life. How important is being a good parent?

Are Uncomfortable Discussing the Topic

See *Creating an Open Atmosphere,* below.

Fear that Discussing the Topic Gives Children Permission

Think of the ostrich. We might find comfort by hiding our heads in the sand—but the problem doesn't go away. Children and teens will get misleading information and ideas elsewhere; they will be tempted and pressured to make bad decisions. If we avoid the issue, it won't go away; we'll simply be "out of the loop." Candid discussion is an opportunity to learn what's happening and to provide information and guidance that can lead to wise decisions.

Creating an Open Atmosphere

When you were growing up, did you feel free to talk with your parents about death? Could you talk with them about masturbation? Divorce? Homosexuality? Were there any topics that you just "knew" not to talk about at home? How did you know?

Every family has a set of unwritten rules that each member somehow learns, though they're never discussed. "In this family, certain topics are not to be mentioned." That's one typical, unspoken rule. How do children learn the rules? These are some of the ways they sense them:

- The topic doesn't exist in our house; Mom and Dad never talk about it at all.
- Mom or Dad act embarrassed, uneasy or upset when the topic comes up.

- If you bring up a taboo topic, you might be seen as being offensive—out of line.
- Parents change the topic immediately if you bring it up.

A mother of a teenager shared this story:

I recoiled in shock; I had bent down to hug eleven-year-old Tammy as she came home from an overnight—and smelled the unmistakable odor of cigarettes! I felt angry and betrayed. I couldn't wait until we were alone so that I could vent my rage.

As I thought about what I would say, I realized it might be wise to calm down a little; I did the relaxation exercise to help me think more clearly. I wanted to let Tammy know that I disapproved in no uncertain terms; yet I wanted her to feel free to talk with me when situations like this came up.

I sat down on her bed and said, "I really want you to listen to what I have to say for a few minutes—and then I want to listen to you as well. Are you willing?" "What's it about?" she said. "I expect you will tell me the truth about this; you've been very honest in the past and I respect that. You know what a good sense of smell I have; there was a strong odor of cigarettes when you came home just now. I shouldn't be too surprised; I tried smoking when I was in middle school. It's pretty typical to experiment with forbidden things at your age. But I also want you to know that I feel very concerned. Smoking can become a habit very quickly, and it can take years to stop. I think you know what it can do to your health; it's a serious matter. I hope you won't feel you have to keep secrets from me; I want us to be able to talk frankly. And now I really want to listen to you."

Tammy was defensive at first; I needed all the listening skills I could muster. But I modeled an attitude of respect for both of us—and kept on listening. In the end she let me in on the pressure she felt from her best friend and the other girls at the sleepover. We talked about peer pressure and what a challenge it is; we talked about her strong need to be accepted. Out of that discussion we were able to make some agreements. And I set some firm limits. Without compromising my strong feelings and values, I gained a better understanding of my daughter's world. We built some trust; in the future I believe she might be more willing to talk with me about difficult issues like drugs and sex. If I had simply yelled and punished her, I would have accomplished much less. Now I believe the door is open and that means a lot in the years ahead.

Our goal is to create a positive message: "Feel free to ask questions and talk about sensitive or embarrassing topics. Anything can be discussed in this house." We want to create an atmosphere that encourages open discussion. Here are some useful steps:

- Question the wisdom of maintaining "taboo" subjects. Allow topics that you once considered unsettling or embarrassing to be part of normal family conversation or private discussions.

- Be aware of your own reactions: avoid being judgmental when your children or teens ask questions or talk about sensitive topics. Curiosity is a positive sign of growth; so is exploring ideas. If your children have truly done something wrong, that's different. But if we tend to be offended, or *suspect* they've done wrong, simply because they're talking about a sensitive topic, they'll feel it and keep their questions and concerns hidden from us.

- Be honest. If you don't know, say so. At *appropriate ages* share your own experiences as a youth: how you felt about them and what you learned—even if you're not proud of what you did. Children listen and respect you if you're honest. They can handle it if you're not perfect; it helps them accept themselves.

- Resolve to overcome your own discomfort or embarrassment in discussing sensitive topics with your children. I know that's easier said than done. It's been a struggle for me at times to gain the courage to talk about sensitive topics with my children. But once you begin, you're likely to find it becomes easier. The section below provides some suggestions.

Overcoming Your Own Discomfort

As always, awareness is the first step. Be aware that your own discomfort may be stopping you from creating an open atmosphere around certain subjects. Then resolve to overcome that discomfort. Begin by looking at your own experience to understand why you're uncomfortable: perhaps these topics were taboo as you grew up, or you've had painful experiences or feel ashamed or inadequate because of lack of experience. Those insights can help you gain a useful perspective. Here are some steps you can take:

Use the Three-Step Process

To help in dealing with your uneasy feelings, practice steps one and two of the Three-Step Process. In step one (Chapter Three), learn all you can about a subpersonality that may be afraid or get in the way. Draw a picture of that part of you and ask the questions: "How does it look and act?" "How does it feel?" "How does it think?" "What does it need?" Step two will help you relax and remind you that you are more than that part—you have the ability to make other choices.

Here's how one father dealt with an uncomfortable issue:

> *I was giving the kids more allowance than I knew was appropriate; I had a very hard time setting limits in that area. There was no way the family could have a good talk; I was just too uncomfortable with the issue. I didn't even want to think about it, but the parents in class gave me a loving push and some courage.*
>
> *I made a subpersonality drawing and discovered Deprived Danny—a part of me that felt I didn't get the things I deserved as a child. My parents had plenty of money but always told us we didn't have enough; all my friends had things I wanted.*

Without realizing it, I was trying to make sure my children didn't feel deprived. In the process, they were getting too much! That gave me a new perspective. I realized that was just one part of me and it didn't have to run the show; at work I was more than competent with money. With a different frame of mind, I was able to open the subject and discuss it with relative comfort. Now we can deal with that issue instead of pretending it doesn't exist.

The same approach can help you to become more comfortable—to open the door for the family to talk about difficult but crucial issues, no matter how challenging.

Become Informed

Before you open a discussion or prepare your child for a new situation, ask yourself, "Do I have the factual information I need?" If not, can you find a way to get it? Sources of information and guidance can include:

- searching the Internet, a library, or a bookstore
- talking with friends and family
- consulting your pediatrician, a drug counselor, sex educator, etc.

Before talking about the issue with your child, you might want to rehearse the discussion in your mind. Since your child or teen might protest or become uncomfortable, be prepared to use reflection. If there are strong feelings around the issue, you might need to use conscious listening.

There was no doubt about it: the time had come to talk with my fourteen-year-old daughter about sex. I knew that I should have started years earlier, but the whole subject frightened me. I thought, "If we talk about it openly she might think I condone sex for teens." It sounds crazy now, but that was my attitude. Still, a discussion was needed and I felt embarrassed and unprepared. I had no experience until I was married. And the world of teens has changed a lot!

It took courage just to talk with friends, but that was useful; they had very different experiences and that gave me ideas and helped me get ready. Still, I wanted to know more about what was going on right now in the teenage world—what they thought and how they felt. I went on the internet. It was like being back in college, researching a paper. At times it was fun; I felt proud of myself.

When we finally talked, my daughter surprised me completely; we went on for more than an hour! I think she had wanted to air some feelings, but felt ambivalent. It meant a lot to her that I took the lead. And I learned quite a bit about how she thinks and feels. It was so hard to get started—but now it seems crazy not to talk!

Seek Support

If you have tried to overcome your own discomfort and still feel ill at ease, you might want to consider consulting with a counselor or religious leader. You'll be with a trained, experienced person who can guide and support you. Their understanding may help you to overcome your own discomfort and feel better prepared to create an open atmosphere when you talk with your children.

Difficult Situations: Summing It Up

Earlier in this chapter, we saw what it takes to help children prepare for new situations. To prepare them for more difficult situations, use the same principles:

Anticipate

What difficult situations are your children or teens likely to face soon?

Visualize

What will they experience and feel? What will they need to know?

Are you comfortable with the topic? If not, address your discomfort beforehand. (But don't put it off too long! Find a way to deal with your feelings.)

Dialogue

Create a safe, accepting atmosphere. Share your own experiences and values. Be informed; provide appropriate information.

Remember to create comfort by using reflection and your listening skills when needed. Always keep the door open for future discussion.

Live in a way that creates this ideal family rule: "We can talk frankly and respectfully about everything."

Exercise: Preparing for New or Difficult Situations

Benefits:

This exercise will strengthen your skill in preparing your child or teen. Use it now to fully internalize what you've learned. You also can use it whenever a new or difficult situation arises.

Directions:

Choose a new or difficult situation that your child or teen might face in the future.

- Find a comfortable sitting position with legs crossed or evenly placed on the floor, spine erect, eyes closed.
- Take a few moments to relax your body; enjoy the calm and quiet that surrounds you.

In your mind, move through each stage of becoming prepared.

Visualize: Imagine the situation your child will face in as much detail as possible.
- See the physical environment: the specific setting, the people, material objects or equipment.
- Walk through the sequence of events in your mind's eye. Take your time, so you recognize the many details and steps that are involved.

Anticipate: Think about how your children might respond to the new situation.
- How will they feel?
- What information should they have?
- What things might they need or want?
- What do you expect from them?

Dialogue: Talk with your children.
- Provide information.
- Answer their questions.
- Make assertions.
- Involve them in the solutions.

Take whatever time you need to complete this experience.

In A Nutshell

Planning can help to remove a surprising amount of friction from family life. With fewer problems and conflicts, there is more room for laughter and closeness. It's one of the easiest and most useful skills of the centered self.

Many problems can be prevented simply by changing the environment:

- Remove objects.
- Remove or reschedule activities.
- Add structure.
- Add fun.

Daily routines can run more smoothly if we believe it's possible and make a plan that answers the question, "Who does what—and when?"

When a child or teen faces a new or difficult situation, preparation is key. Visualize what will happen, anticipate the child's response and then dialogue.

If the new situation is potentially traumatic or difficult, take time to prepare yourself. Create an open climate over the years that says, "I'm available; we can talk about these things."

At its core, planning is a mindset that often considers, "Let's stop and look at what happened today—and what might happen tomorrow. What can we do to make things work better?"

CHAPTER 14

You Don't Have to Be Perfect:

How Families Make It Work

*Dare to do the things and reach for the
goals in your life that have meaning for you.*

—Lillian Gordy Carter
President Carter's mother

THIS IS MY FAVORITE chapter. I didn't write it. Parents did. In these pages, you'll find a collection of true stories from parents who are putting what we've learned into practice—not in theory, but in everyday, messy, real life. These stories will help answer the questions we all care about:

How can I give my children the best possible start in life?
How can I create the joyful, loving family I really want?

Once You Know the Road

As you read these stories, you'll notice that parents often stumble before finding their way; *we don't have to be perfect!* These parents seldom name the three steps or move through them in a formal way. That's because they now have a "feel" for where they're going, just as we find our way home without checking the name of each street. The Three-Step Process is like a road map; the first few times we use it, we follow it closely. But once we know the way, we navigate intuitively. That's what these parents did, finding their own unique ways to make the shift.

Besides, human relationships are seldom simple and clear; we get stalled at times, or feel as if we're moving backward. Yet, if we hold the attitude that we want to work out problems with mutual respect, we're more than halfway there. At some point it's likely we'll gain the calm and insight to make the shift. And when we're centered, we'll find the skills that are needed.

Stories for Each Relationship Issue

The stories are grouped by theme; each is about a parent solving a problem that reflects one of the *five relationship issues*. But real life is fluid, spilling over boundaries. Many stories could fit under other issues as well.

I hope you'll find these stories as useful and inspiring as I do. Children really do want to become their best; they really do respond when we help them to grow toward that goal. These stories are living proof.

The Issue of Authority

Who Knows What's Best?

Whose information is accurate? Who is most informed?
Who is the expert?

The lower-self characters and what they say ...

Know-It-All   Know-Nothing

I know. You don't.   *You know. I don't.*

The **LISTENER** says ...

We respect each other's knowledge.

In these stories, we find parents modeling respect for their children's knowledge, as well as their own.

Of course they don't always begin that way; sometimes they doubt what their children know or fail to value the experience they've gained. Yet in the end, these parents show genuine interest in their children's knowledge—and openly share their own.

The morning was pandemonium. "Did you comb your hair? "I can't find my sweater!" Where's your lunch money?" We'd just moved into a different neighborhood and the kids were going to a new school. "Do you have your note?" We were running late; I grabbed my briefcase and the map showing the new bus route and we hurried to the car.

We raced to the bus stop—in time to see a cloud of gray exhaust as the bus pulled away. I told myself to stay calm, thinking, "I'll just drive ahead to the next stop." We raced ahead of the bus several blocks; I slammed on the brakes and told the kids to grab their stuff and pile out of the car. They insisted that this wasn't the right place. I was sure it was; I was proud of myself for studying the map two days before and being well organized. Afraid I'd be late for work, I felt angry with them for dawdling; I was in no mood to listen. My head was busy with angry thoughts: "They hadn't seen the material I had so efficiently filed away; they were just little kids who couldn't even get themselves out of the house on time!" The kids pleaded to no avail; they could see I was just getting more upset.

It took a while before I became aware of that tight, angry sensation in my chest; I realized I was in a state that led to trouble. I thought of techniques we learned in class—and managed (barely) to take a moment out. I cooled down enough to get a little perspective—and apologized to the kids for the anger; I asked them to explain what they knew. They pointed me to the corner two blocks ahead and said they were sure that was the right place. Finally, I was able to set aside my ego and listen. To my chagrin, they were right. We met the bus (where they said we would) and were able to start our day with some mutual appreciation. Instead of anger and frustration, we shared a laugh over our near mishap and my momentary blindness.

Seth had tears on his cheeks. I was hardly awake, when there he was with those doleful eyes, wearing his long tee shirt and socks. He had a tight grip on "Meanie," his "pet monster." I took Seth on my lap and held him, which is not easy, because he's a tall, strapping eight-year-old! "Want to tell me about it?" I said. "Today I have to take my test," he explained. I realized that this was his term exam in math. If he passed it, he wouldn't have any more weekly math checks; it meant a new, higher status for him at school. Seth had had scary feelings about division for a long time. "Oh, today is the day you have the test you've been talking about." His head nodded slightly. Long silence. "I just wish someone would give me the answers!" I rocked him some more. "You'd really like someone to give you the answers." And I thought to myself, why can't I reflect back better than this? It's too early in the morning. My mind went off on a tangent, thinking about ways I could secretly "fix" this for Seth: call the teacher; tell her my boy was actually crying this morning! Have her do something!

"I wish someone would just tell me what 4 divided by 3 is!" I grabbed a pencil and paper. "No, no! You're going to give me a lesson!" He started to cry in frustration. I realized that Seth didn't want me to take over; he just wanted me to be there as he struggled. "No, Seth, I'm just trying to figure out for myself what 4 divided by 3 is. Let me see ..." I did some writing. "It looks like 1.33 or 1 1/3." Seth stared at the paper. "We never have answers like that." I wrote down 15 divided by 3. "Does she give you problems like this?" He nodded. "The answer is 5," he said. Silence again. I could see the wheels turning in his head. Then, Seth said, "Oh, I remember. She doesn't give us low numbers at the beginning!

She gives us high numbers like 15!" Big smile. He wiped his eyes; more smiles, more hugs. I was glad that I held back more than usual.

My culture, upbringing and family have all influenced me to be about as nonassertive as you can get. In our house, children were to be seen—period! As a parent, when I'm acting from the lower self, there's no doubt that I'm passive!

It's always a struggle for me to break out of that way of being invisible. I think of the time when my two-year-old son had problems with day care. We had just moved him from a small family playgroup to a large preschool and he had trouble adjusting. Mornings were awful; Billy kicked and screamed at the mere mention of the word "school." I spent a lot of time agonizing over the guilt I felt, leaving him there.

Then he got sick for a while, and we had to begin the transition period all over again. But during that time I began to think a lot about what I wanted and what I truly felt was best for Billy. I realized that I was feeling guilty not only because I was leaving him in the morning, but also because I was being nonassertive with the director of the school. When I was around her, I acted like a combination of the Know-Nothing, the Sheep and the People Pleaser: "I don't know anything, so whatever you say must be right; I'll do whatever you want."

I watched myself repeating those old, passive ways of coping and felt disappointed. I knew I had to do something different. I started practicing the relaxation exercise and the bridge addition.

As a result I began to keep a list of things I wanted to discuss with the director. For example, I wanted to know the scheduling of activities for Billy's day, where he sleeps, who changes his diaper and what their behavior management policies are. I scheduled a time when the director and I could talk undisturbed. I said honestly what was on my mind and the director answered my questions directly. We reached a comfortable understanding of what would be best for Billy.

I can tell you that my son is not the only one who's maturing. I'm definitely growing too!

My husband and I had just separated. Our twelve-year-old was mad at me because I told him to clear the living room and to put his stuff in his room. In an angry voice my son threatened, "You always complain; I can't stand it. I'm going to go to Dad's house." Suddenly I felt insecure. Going through a separation after eighteen years of marriage is no easy task. I felt utterly vulnerable. And I worried, "Can I be a good mom if I'm not with the kids all the time?" Jason's threat didn't help. Still, I knew this was an important test; I had to set the boundaries right now. Trying to remember the work we did with assertive limit-setting, I said in a firm, but calm voice, "Dad and I have talked about this. I'm in charge when you're at this house; he's in charge at his. Whether you're happy or mad at us, there will be no changing houses. We're both very clear about this." I could see Jason's body relax in front of my eyes. The conversation ended and I knew that he got what he needed. He wasn't going to be able to take advantage of us. And it was clear that he felt good about that.

The Issue of Needs

Whose Needs Are Met?

Do I meet my child's needs or my own?

The lower-self characters and what they say …

Very Important Person   Martyr

My needs come first.   *Your needs come first.*

The HUMANIST says …

We respect each other's needs.

In this second group of stories, we find parents who have learned to meet their children's needs, while honoring their own.

They're not perfect, of course; who is? They may be tempted to make unnecessary sacrifices, or to put their our own needs above their children's. But once parents learn to distinguish between wants and needs—essentials and nonessentials—they find a healthy balance more consistently.

For the first time in my life, I went out entirely on my own and bought a new car. I felt really proud that I managed to get the car of my dreams (however humble). I worked hard to keep it looking new.

I exhorted the kids (ages 9, 11 and 13) to eat no food in the car, keep their fingers off the windows, feet off the seats, etc. One hectic morning on the way to school, I gritted my teeth and asked them for the trillionth time to stop playing with the ashtrays and seat belts. Suddenly, I heard "uh oh!" from the back seat and turned in a fury to see that the lid on the armrest had broken off its hinge. A wide-eyed and terrified kid blinked up at me while I deteriorated into a heap of self-pity. I felt like shouting, "Can't I have anything nice? Do you have to destroy everything I try to do for myself?" At that moment I wanted them all to feel deeply guilty over what they had "done to me."

Fortunately, I was able to catch myself before the words came blistering out. Instead of yelling, I took several deep breaths; in those few moments, I was able to see a different perspective. I saw that my poor son was already horrified that his playful act had caused this damage, and that his guilt level was sky-high without my help! I also realized that the fault was partly mine, for having unrealistic expectations. If you've got kids, it's not realistic to expect your car to stay in pristine condition.

I realized too, that I had issued a lot of orders, "Don't do this," "Don't do that," but I hadn't really planned—sat down with the kids and explained what the car meant to me. I hadn't prepared them. And when I did set limits, I hadn't stuck to them.

That moment of "catching myself" made a big difference. Instead of having an angry argument, we set a time for a discussion about what happened, how everybody felt about it and how we could avoid such things in the future. The repair of the armrest turned out to be a simple chore. The real challenge for me is learning to stop on the spot and reach inward, instead of erupting like a volcano. I have hope. With practice, it's becoming easier.

My wife and I had been fighting a lot about the kids; there was an uncomfortable distance between us. I feel awful when we're not close; I'm embarrassed to say that it even affects my work. I'm not a great talker, so I decided to write her a letter and explain how I felt. I worked very hard on the letter, making certain I used "clean" assertive statements. I was proud of it. I hoped that she would understand how much effort I'd put into this letter and that it would open the door to a meaningful discussion.

But was I shocked! She read the letter carefully, thanked me for it and asked if she could keep it. That's it! Nothing more.

At first, I thought, "Well what's the use; that's a dead-end road." I began to feel resentful. Then I calmed myself and realized she had no idea what expectations I had. I wanted her to initiate a discussion so we could clear things up—but I never said that. Finally I got it: if I were going to get my needs met, I'd have to be assertive and say what I wanted. Learning to be assertive isn't easy for me, but I'm making progress. At least I didn't slip back into Pouty Poor Me.

Weekday mornings I'd rush around, trying to get everyone ready on time. We were always on the edge of being late; I'd feel really anxious (and probably made everyone else feel that way too).

I thought about how I could shift—and decided to get up an hour earlier. Now I use that time to do things that make me feel good: exercise, have some coffee and some quiet moments. When it's time for Cathy to get ready, I'm a lot more relaxed. We have time to talk through what her day will be like: everything that will happen from after breakfast until it's time for me to pick her up.

Cathy likes hearing all the details; it helps her to be calmer about events in her day as they unfold. It wasn't hard to make the change; the key was to realize that mornings didn't have to be madness.

The Issue of Perception

Whose Point of View Is Right?

Who do we believe and trust?
Whose reality do we accept?

The lower-self characters and what they say …

Guru   Mute

I'm right. You're wrong.   *You're right. I'm wrong.*

The OBSERVER says …

**We respect each other's thoughts, feelings
and point of view.**

In this third group of stories, we meet parents who are able to respect their children's perceptions and their own.

That isn't always easy, of course; they may begin by claiming superiority or by refusing to express their own point of view. But ultimately they're able to take in another person's perception—and also share their own.

> *For a long time, Jeremy had been asking to stay over at his cousin's house. They always had fun together; he loved to romp with the dogs and was allowed to play "fighting" video games there, though they're banned at home. When my husband asked me to join him on a weekend business trip, I thought that would be a good time for Jeremy's visit.*
>
> *But Jeremy is always very nervous when we're away. Five days before we were to leave, I reminded him that we would be gone for two nights. I was certain he had been told this before, but he was sure that wasn't so. He became upset. He'd never been away from us for two nights before. He began to question his ability to handle the sleepover.*
>
> *My immediate reaction was to comfort him. "I'm sure you'll be just fine." As soon as I said those words, I knew I was on the wrong track. Without even acknowledging his point of view, I was rushing in to make it all better. His reaction was to become less sure of himself. Then he began to panic.*
>
> *Finally, something penetrated from the last eight weeks of class and I began to listen to his feelings. "It sounds as if you're really scared about going to your cousin's." "Yes," he said, "I'm worried about you being away two nights." I reflected, "It sounds like two nights away from us may be too long." We talked for a while, and finally I said, "Maybe this isn't the best time for Daddy and me to be away." I had my own concerns as well and felt comfortable saying, "I'm okay to change my plan and stay home with you." And then to my amazement Jeremy did an about face. "I want to go. I want to be brave, so that I can feel proud of myself. I'm really okay now." He was right; the weekend worked out beautifully for all of us.*

Here's a letter from a parent who is a graduate of our class; she recently separated from her husband:

> *You've always said that conscious listening allows us to discover our children's world, and learn who they really are. Here's what happened for me: Alisa and I were chatting at dinner one night when she said, "When Dad picks up the carpool, he doesn't talk to the other kids. He only talks to me." I acknowledged what she said: "He only talks to you?" "Yeah, and I get embarrassed that he doesn't talk to my friends. He doesn't even know most of them!" With her head down, she mumbled the word "embarrassed" as if she felt terrible saying it. I remained accepting—and I'm really proud of that; in the past, I might have put in a dig or said something critical about her father. Instead, I put my "stuff" aside and focused on Alisa. "You feel embarrassed when he ignores the other children?" "Yeah, <u>you</u> talk to all the kids. I like that, but he only talks to the ones he knows." Only when I really listened did I sense how much feeling there was behind the word embarrassed. There is so much to learn about what these young ones see and how they put it all together. Alisa is infinitely fascinating to me; when I can stay calm and centered I learn so much more about my daughter and how she's changing day by day.*

> *My husband recently got laid off and now I'm the sole provider. I woke up that first morning in a panic, worried about money. I gathered some courage and took a hard look at our finances. The problem was worse than I expected! Then this afternoon, Cecilia came home from school and told me she was invited to another birthday party. I tried to say the right things, that I'm glad for her; I could see she was so excited. But I really hurt inside. All I could think of was that we'd have to buy another gift—another unexpected expense.*

In the past I would have panicked even more. But I caught a glimpse of what I was doing; part of me realized I was out of control. It wasn't easy, but I managed to stop and take some time to chill down. I remembered that this was an old subpersonality, Panicky Pat. Her frightened energy gets me nuts and I just run around in circles. But I also knew that a subpersonality has a legitimate need. I did have to face the problem: we did have to make more money. But I needed to be centered; then I could use that energy to light a fire—to work with my husband to find more creative ways to increase our income. The financial problem was still there, but my attitude shift made it feel very different. I had a new perspective, and I had the will and motivation to take action.

I had a talk with Cecilia about our limited funds; I asked if she had any thoughts about a gift for her friend. After a while, she asked shyly, "Could we give her some flowers? She loves to come to our house to see our garden." "Sure," I said. "And do you think she'd like some bulbs of her own to plant?" I'm always surprised how kids come through when you give them a chance.

The Issue of Control

Who Should Decide?

Who's in charge?
Who makes the final decision?

The lower-self characters and what they say ...

Dictator   Sheep

I decide. You follow.   *You decide. I follow.*

The PRAGMATIST says ...

We respect each other's desire for autonomy.

In these stories, we see parents supporting their children's independence, while maintaining their own.

It takes time to find the middle ground—neither making all the decisions, nor following children blindly. In the end, these parents find ways to respect a universal human desire: to be in charge of our own lives.

I told my children (ages six and ten) that I wanted them to go to Sunday school to get religious training. They were both adamant: "We don't want to go." I tried to explain, "Daddy and I want you to know the religion that means so much to us. You'll be proud to learn the history of our people." But nothing seemed to budge them one bit. I felt so frustrated.

Then I realized that religious training for our kids is a real must for me. It's part of the dream for the family I want. Since we practice what we preach, I realized I had every right to insist our children gain this knowledge, too. I recognized they're too young to make that judgment. But we wouldn't overcome their resistance if we didn't listen carefully to what they had to say.

Later that week, my husband and I sat down with the kids and made a clear assertion: "Religious training is part of what this family does, just like helping with chores and eating meals together. We want you to enjoy this experience; tell us what seemed so unappealing, so that we can understand and find a way to help you."

Immediately, the kids complained, "We don't have enough time. We already have too much to do: homework, piano, soccer ... We don't want to have to get up early Sunday morning." I acknowledged their very full schedules and their wish to enjoy a lazy Sunday morning. Then I promised the kids I'd do some research.

After many calls, I found a religious class that met on Friday afternoons. The school had a good reputation and I felt even more comforted when I met the teachers. After the kids checked it out, they agreed to go. My daughter enjoys the classes more than she expected. My son wouldn't claim this to be his favorite activity—but he knows that it is a part of his week and a part of our family values. And he accepts that.

A perennial issue in our house was the way my teenage son kept his room. He's one of those people who saves endless "stuff" and claims he knows where every item is. He was quite content to keep his room in a state of apparent chaos. I've always felt strongly that a neat and clean house is a symbol—that it's essential for a healthy, happy family. We were on a collision course.

My emotional tendency was to say, "It's my house, young man, and as long as ..." but we all know that would have only drawn battle lines. Instead of me nagging endlessly and he finding ways around it, I thought, "Okay, why not try something new?" I realized that I really didn't understand why Peter wanted it that way; I wasn't even sure of all the reasons for my own intense feelings on the matter.

We sat down and talked it through. I said that for me, a messy room is very upsetting—a sign of a house out of control, an attitude that grew out of my childhood. Peter claimed, "My bedroom is the one single place where I have control. I put my things where I want them; that makes me feel comfortable." We each gained a better understanding of the other's feelings, and that took away the "charge" on the issue. In the end, we found a compromise: Peter would keep his room safe (no leftover food or dirty dishes) and straighten it up if there was an objective reason (like a house guest). Otherwise, I agreed that his room would be his own private haven. To be sure, we've had to talk again from time to time, to clarify our understanding. But it's getting easier. And we've been successful each time in finding mutually agreeable solutions.

On school nights I spend half the evening cajoling my nine-year-old into doing her homework. It isn't a pleasant scene; it feels like our relationship is about me pushing and her resisting, like trying to get a mule to move. Finally, I realized that it's not my job to get her homework done; all that nagging just makes her resentful and dependent on me.

Now I'm trying to cut the umbilical cord (though it isn't easy for me to change). I let her be in charge of homework. If it isn't done on time, she can't watch TV. I realize also that

I've taken the wrong tack with chores. She does nothing! I just haven't had the strength to fight about anything else.

But recently I made a start. I told her she had to help set the table. I took out the napkins, silverware and dishes and asked her to put them in place around the table. For about ten days all went great. I did my part and she did hers. But yesterday she refused. "No, I don't want to do it anymore," she announced. At first I thought, "What can I do? I'm tired of nagging and pushing. Setting the table doesn't take any time, really; I'll do it myself." That kind of thinking sounded all too familiar. I realized that it's wrong to give up and let her off the hook; that's not what's best for her—or for me.

The next day I told her we needed to sit down and talk. "Doing chores around the house is not a choice; we live together and we need to help according to our capability. If there's a certain chore you really don't like, I'm more than happy to brainstorm with you about other tasks." She was silent. Her body appeared to relax. As she set the table, she talked enthusiastically about the start of soccer. I knew I'd done the right thing. And I knew it was the old me that was taking out the napkins, silverware and dishes. Surely, she could do that herself as well. I promised myself to get out of habits that keep her dependent—to allow her to become responsible and autonomous.

"I'll do it soon," I told myself, "but not today; I need a break—and then I'll take the next step."

The Issue of Expectations

How Do We Deal with Expectations?

How do we respond when our expectations are met—
and when they're not? How do we behave when our
children place expectations on us?

The lower-self characters and what they say ...

Royal Highness   People Pleaser

I show my approval only   *I do what you expect,*
if you meet my expectations.   *even if I don't want to.*

The REALIST says ...

We respect each other's expectations
and create family agreements.

In this final group of stories, we find parents able to show respect
even when their expectations are not met. As usual, there's a learning

curve. Sometimes they show respect only when they're pleased; other times they show it even though they don't feel it. Yet in the end, these parents are able to model respect under all circumstances.

It shouldn't be any surprise, I know, but the teen years have been rough and stormy for my daughter and me. Lately it's calmed down a bit. We've found ways to work through our ups and downs; our old battles are more like small skirmishes now.

One of my big lessons has been in learning how quickly a teenager's emotions can "recycle." For example: we have a rough confrontation, and then work it out. But my heart is still "smarting" from the anger. Five minutes later, Alicia comes out of her room and asks that I do her a favor—like drive her to a friend's house. She seems perfectly nonchalant, as if nothing happened between us.

At first, I thought she just didn't care about my feelings. "She ought to approach me with a more apologetic attitude," I thought.

It was only later, with the help of the parenting class that I came to believe in her basic good intentions. I realized that in her mind, once we've cleared up a problem, it's really over. No reason not to approach me for kid-to-mom type requests. I'm a little slower to make the transition—but that doesn't mean she's being disrespectful. What I've changed is my attitude. Before, I expected the worst from her, so that's what I saw. Now I expect much better—and that's what I often discover."

I wasn't surprised when the school called: Tommy had had lots of problems with fighting. "Your son has been suspended again. We're driving him home now." But the call had come at 10 in the morning. By 11 I was worried; by noon I was angry. "Bad enough he gets suspended," I thought. "Now he's refusing to come home." I had several hours to fume—and then think about what had happened in the past few months. I'm newly sober and had lost my temper many times; Tommy was afraid I'd hit him again. No wonder he was scared to come home. By 1 o'clock I'd called the police; they went searching, as I did, and found nothing.

It was 3:15 when Tommy came walking down the sidewalk, pretending he was coming from school; he didn't know the school had called and told me he was suspended. Police and neighbors stood watching. "Tommy!" I shouted. I could see him freeze and hesitate, deciding whether to run. "I was so worried," I said, tears streaming down my face. "Thank heaven you're safe." Tommy seemed astonished; he'd been caught red-handed and was sure I'd be livid. "I was scared," I said, hugging him hard. I saw tears in his eyes too. He mumbled quietly, "I'm sorry."

I thought about it later. That might have been another awful confrontation. But I let my real feelings show at that moment, instead of jumping to my usual anger. I allowed myself to be open and real; that paved the way for Tommy to do the same. For once, we were able to talk.

School mornings were hell: tantrums, yelling, slamming things down and a house full of chaos. Danny was diagnosed ADHD (Attention Deficit Hyperactive Disorder) and ODD (Oppositional Defiant Disorder) five years ago. Much of the time, he's the sweetest kid you'll ever meet; but he has a very short fuse. School mornings left me exhausted and limp; I was at the end of my rope.

I tried different approaches to the morning routine, including behavior management techniques, directing his every move and dressing him myself. By the time he was out the door my own anger was ready to spill over. I thought, "Maybe I'll just have him quit school; then neither of us will have to go through this terrible ordeal." Of course, that wasn't exactly a practical solution; my son had to get an education.

Then I thought, "I know how awful I feel; Danny must feel miserable too. It must feel awful to be erupting with so much rage from his lower self." My husband and I resolved to talk with him.

We started by inviting and encouraging Danny to talk—and then we really listened. That was helpful; we learned how <u>much</u> anxiety he had about school (which accounted for some of the behavior). Danny's perception was that his teacher thought he was "dumb." His self-esteem was under attack. The teacher tried to motivate (so Danny felt) through fear and intimidation. Feeling thoroughly rejected, Danny resisted stubbornly. But our talk seemed to have some effect. Not long after, Danny came and asked me to "straighten the teacher out." He wasn't yet taking responsibility, but we viewed his request as an initial step toward making things better. My husband and I met with his teacher and she clarified what her expectations were.

Then we had another talk with Danny, about the difference between the lower self and centered self. I thought the concept might help him realize that he <u>does</u> have the ability to manage his behavior. He drew pictures and got the idea right away. He also made it clear that his lower-self behavior is as unpleasant for him as it is for us.

Mornings are going a little better now. He still needs me to give feedback on his behavior, but he's got a better sense of his centered self. He told me last night, "I like the part that comes from the middle."

He's learning to recognize who's on stage and that he has a choice; this helps him manage himself. He feels better about who he is. And I feel good having concepts and skills that can help him.

Some Final Thoughts

I hope these stories have as much meaning for you as they do for me; they touch my heart and lift my spirit. Ideally, they also will inspire you to continue using your skills. Keep in mind these two words—*practice and commitment*—that's what made it work for these parents.

Each day our children grow; new challenges are inevitable. At times of stress and change, we can easily lose the way. Remember, you've got a trusty "road map"—the Three-Step Process, along with the Help Chart on page 151. Let them guide you whenever you feel the need. And if you'd like a reminder of all the essentials you've learned in this book, just see the next page.

Hold on to your courage and faith; you're on a path of growth, to bring out the best in your child—and discover the best within yourself. As we said at the outset, no journey in life can be more worthwhile or more rewarding.

The Three-Step Process
A Summary

Preventing Problems

STEP ONE: *Recognize the Lower Self*

Become aware:
> This step helps you recognize the lower self, the real troublemaker in the parent/child relationship.

STEP TWO: *Cross the Bridge to the Centered Self*

Stay calm:
> By practicing the *relaxation exercise,* you can transform tension into the tranquil energy of love and wisdom.

Make the shift:
> The *bridge exercise* reminds you that you are more than the lower self: "I am the centered self. I choose how I act, feel and think."

STEP THREE: *Express the Centered Self*

Think mutual respect:
> By identifying with the centered-self characters you gain a deeper understanding of mutual respect.

Visualization:
> Imagine your ideal family, then use your skills to make the vision real.

Assertion:
> In a variety of situations, these skills help you to say—with respect—what you want, think and feel.

Reflection:

> By acknowledging your children's upset or discomfort, you help them calm down, creating an environment for further communication.

Recognition of ineffective attitudes and communication:

> Being aware of the attitudes of inequality—and the communication styles of *Mighty Parent* and *mini parent*—helps you steer clear of the lower self more often.

Planning skills:

> You can prevent problems before they happen by changing the environment and by preparing your children for new or difficult situations.

Family agreements:

> By implementing democratic agreements, you clarify everyone's expectations and help prevent problems.

Natural consequences:

> When you allow your children to experience the consequences of their behavior, you help them learn essential life lessons.

Solving Problems

STEP THREE: *Express the Centered Self*

Express concerns:

> By showing respect even when your children disappoint or upset you, you create an environment that encourages them to take responsibility for their behavior.

Conscious listening:

> When your children struggle with their own problems, acting as a *facilitator* empowers them to find their own solutions.

Words to Express Feelings

Abandoned
Afraid
Agitated
Alone
Ambitious
Amused
Angry
Anxious
Apathetic
Appreciative
Apprehensive
Astounded
Attracted
Bad
Belittled
Betrayed
Bewildered
Bored
Bothered
Brave
Bugged
Burdened
Calm
Capable
Cheerful
Cold
Comfortable
Compassionate
Competent
Concerned
Confident
Confused
Content
Cool
Cowardly
Crushed

Curious
Defensive
Deflated
Degraded
Delighted
Dependent
Depressed
Deprived
Disappointed
Disarmed
Discouraged
Disgusted
Disrespected
Distracted
Distressed
Disturbed
Doubtful
Down
Distressed
Doubtful
Dreadful
Dull
Dumb
Eager
Ecstatic
Efficient
Elated
Embarrassed
Empathetic
Empowered
Empty
Encouraged
Energetic
Enraged
Enthusiastic
Envious

Exasperated
Excited
Exhausted
Exhilarated
Fascinated
Floored
Flustered
Foolish
Frantic
Frightened
Frustrated
Furious
Glad
Good
Grateful
Guilty
Happy
Hateful
Heartbroken
Helpful
Helpless
Honored
Hopeful
Horrified
Hostile
Humble
Humiliated
Hurried
Hurt
Ignored
Impatient
Important
Impressed
Impulsive
Inadequate
Incompetent

Indifferent
Inexperienced
Infantile
Infuriated
Inhibited
Insecure
Inspired
Interested
Isolated
Jealous
Joyous
Lazy
Left out
Less than
Let down
Little
Lonely
Lost
Lovable
Loved
Loving
Low
Lucky
Meek
Melancholy
Miserable
Modest
Moved
Naive
Needed
Nervous
Optimistic
Overjoyed
Overwhelmed
Pained
Panicky
Paralyzed
Peaceful
Peeved
Perplexed
Perturbed

Pessimistic
Pitied
Plagued
Prepared
Protective
Proud
Provoked
Puzzled
Queer
Rattled
Rejected
Relaxed
Relieved
Remorseful
Resentful
Restless
Revengeful
Reverent
Ridiculous
Riled
Ruffled
Sad
Satisfied
Scared
Seething
Self-conscious
Selfish
Sensitive
Sentimental
Serene
Serious
Shocked
Shook
Sick
Silly
Slow
Small
Smart
Solemn
Sore
Sorrowful

Sorry
Startled
Stuck
Stumped
Stunned
Stupid
Sympathetic
Tense
Thrilled
Ticked off
Tired
Tolerant
Unappreciated
Uncomfortable
Uneasy
Unhappy
Unimportant
Unloved
Unmoved
Unprepared
Unprotected
Unsure
Untrustworthy
Unworthy
Uplifted
Upset
Uptight
Used
Useful
Useless
Vain
Victorious
Vindictive
Warm
Weary
Weird
Wild
Wonderful
Worried
Worthless
Worthwhile

Bibliography and Suggested Reading

Stages of Development

Clark, Jean Illsey and Dawson, Connie. (1998) *Growing Up Again: Parenting Ourselves, Parenting Our Children.* Center City MN: Hazelton Foundation.

Gesell, Arnold and Ilg, Frances (2008) *Infant and Child in the Culture of Today: The Guidance of Development in Home and Nursery School.* Lanham MD: Rowman & Littlefield.

Gesell, Arnold (1977) *The Child from Five to Ten.* New York: Harper and Row.

Lickona, Thomas. (1994) *Raising Good Children: From Birth through the Teenage Years.* New York: Bantam Books.

Murkoff, Heidi and Rader, Laura. (2001) *What to Expect at Preschool.* NY: HarperFestival.

Pearce, Joseph Chilton. (1992). *Magical Child.* New York: Plume.

Sessions Stepp, Laura. (2000) *Our Last Best Shot: Guiding Our Children through Early Adolescence.* New York: Riverhead Books.

Helping Children Learn

Armstrong, Thomas. (1999) *7 Kinds of Smart: Identifying and Developing Your Multiple Intelligences.* New York: New American Library.

Luvmour, Sambhaya and Sambhava. Josette (1993) *Natural Learning Rhythms: How and When Children Learn.* CA: Celestial Arts.

Whitmore, Diana. (1986) *Psychosynthesis in Education: A Guide to the Joy of Learning.* Rochester Vermont: Destiny Books.

Parenting

Covey, Stephen. (1997). *The 7 Habits of Highly Effective Families.* New York: Franklin Covey Company.

Clinton, Hillary Rodham. (1996) *It Takes a Village.* New York: Simon & Schuster.

Damon, William. (1995) *Greater Expectations: Overcoming the Culture of Indulgence in Our Homes and Schools.* New York: Free Press Paperbacks.

Elium, Don and Elium, Jeanne. (1996) *Raising a Son: Parents and the Making of a Healthy Man.* Berkeley CA: Celestial Arts.

Elium, Don and Elium, Jeanne. (1996) *Raising a Daughter: Parents and the Awakening of a Healthy Woman.* Berkeley CA: Celestial Arts.

Faber, Adele and Mazlish, Elaine. (1998) *Siblings Without Rivalry: How to Help Your Children Live Together So You Can Live Too.* NY: Quill.

Firman, Julie and Firman, Dorothy. (1989) *Daughters and Mothers: Healing the Relationship.* Amherst MA: Synthesis Center.

Fugitt, Eva D. (1983) *He Hit Me Back First!: Development of the Will in Children for Making Choices.* Rolling Hills CA: Jalmar Press.

Gordon, Thomas. (1970) *Parent Effectiveness Training: The Proven Program for Raising Responsible Children.* New York: Three Rivers Press.

Ferrucci, Piero. (2001) *What Our Children Teach Us: Lessons in Joy, Love, and Awareness.* New York: Warner Books, Inc.

Parenting and Divorce

Krementz, Jill. (1996) *How It Feels when Parents Divorce.* New York: Alfred A. Knopf.

Lansky, Vicki. (2003) *Divorce Book for Parents: Helping Your Children Cope with Divorce and Its Aftermath.* Minnetonka MN: Book Peddlers.

Learning More about Psychosynthesis, Humanistic and Transpersonal Psychology

Assagioli, Roberto. (2000) *Psychosynthesis.* Amherst MA: Synthesis Center.

Assagioli, Roberto. (1974) *The Act of Will.* New York: Penguin.

Brown, Molly Young. (2004) *The Unfolding Self: The Practice of Psychosynthesis.* New York: Allworth Press.

Ferrucci, Piero. (1982) *What We May Be.* Los Angeles: Tarcher.

Maslow, Abraham. (1999) *Toward a Psychology of Being.* NJ: John Wiley.

Parfitt, Will. (1990) *Psychosynthesis: The Elements and Beyond.* Dorset Great Britain: Element Books Limited.

Rowan, John. (2001) *Subpersonalities: The People Inside Us.* Philadelphia PA: Brunner-Routledge.

Small, Jacquelyn. (1982) *Transformers: The Therapists of the Future.* Marina del Rey CA: DeVorss & Company.

Walsh, Roger. (1999) *Essential Spirituality: The 7 Central Practices to Awaken Heart and Mind.* New York: John Wiley & Sons, Inc.

Index

About the Author

ILENE VAL-ESSEN, PH.D. is an innovator in the field of parent education. She has influenced thousands of families and professionals who work with children and teens. Dr. Val-Essen is a featured speaker at international and national conferences and leads workshops in the U.S. and abroad. She counsels families, teens, children, and couples in her practice as a psychotherapist.

Dr. Val-Essen developed the *Quality Parenting* program, which helps parents create a family environment based on mutual respect. In the U.S., Great Britain, Sweden, Japan and The Netherlands, Dr. Val-Essen has trained instructors—psychotherapists, social workers, teachers and parent educators—to teach her programs. The *Quality Parenting* program has been translated into Spanish, Dutch and Swedish, and is currently being translated into Japanese.

Based on the *Quality Parenting* program, with its Basic and Advanced Class, Dr. Val-Essen created *What About the Children?* a program for divorced or separated parents. At UCLA, Education Extension, she teaches *Quality Parenting / Quality Teaching: Encouraging Mutual Respect.*

As a presenter and teacher, she is known for her passion, humor, clarity and interactive style.

Dr. Val-Essen has served on the Board of Directors for Psychosynthesis International and on the steering committee for the North American Association for the Advancement of Psychosynthesis. Dr. Val-Essen is a founder and past president of the Parent Instructor's Network, Los Angeles, and has served as California Coordinator for the National Parenting Instructors Association. She is a member of the National Association for the Education of Young Children, the Association for Humanistic Psychology, the Association for Transpersonal Psychology, and the American and California Associations for Marriage and Family Therapy.

As a mother and stepmother, psychotherapist and parenting consultant, Dr. Val-Essen has an intimate understanding of children and parents. What began as a need in her own family evolved into a lifetime of dedication to help parents, therapists and educators *bring out the best* in children and teens—and discover the best within themselves.

Contact Information

The content of this book is based on the *Quality Parenting* program. To learn more about professional training, consultation, speaking engagements and classes, please contact us.

WEB SITE: www.BringOutTheBest.com

E-MAIL: Ilene@BringOutTheBest.com

PHONE: Toll free: (866) LUV-KIDS or (866) 588-5437
                  Local: (310) 839-1571

FAX: (310) 839-1614

MAIL: *Quality Parenting*
           4909 Saint Louis Court
           Culver City, CA 90230-4317
           USA